AS FILM STUDIES

The Essential Introduction

'It covers all the main topics thoroughly and the material selected and introductions are pitched at exactly the right level – challenging but accessible'

Steve Bennison, *Bridgwater College*

AS Film Studies: The Essential Introduction gives students the confidence to tackle every part of the WJEC AS level Film Studies course. The authors, who have wide-ranging experience as teachers, examiners and authors, introduce students step by step to the skills involved in the study of film. The second edition follows the new WJEC syllabus for 2008 teaching onwards and has a companion website at www.routledge.com/textbooks/9780415454339 with additional chapters and resources for students and teachers. Individual chapters address the following key areas, amongst others:

- British stars – Ewan McGregor
- Genre – horror
- British production – Working Title
- US film – Westerns
- Spectatorship
- The practical application of learning

Specifically designed to be user friendly, the second edition of *AS Film Studies: The Essential Introduction* has a new text design to make the book easy to follow, includes more than 100 colour photographs and is jam-packed with features such as:

- Case studies relevant to the 2008 specification
- Activities on films like *Little Miss Sunshine*, *Pirates of the Caribbean* and *The Descent*
- Example exam questions
- Suggestions for further reading and website resources

Matched to the new WJEC specification, *AS Film Studies: The Essential Introduction* covers everything students need to study as part of the course.

Sarah Casey Benyahia is a teacher of Film and Media Studies. She is the author of *Teaching Contemporary British Cinema* (2005) and co-author of *A2 Film Studies: The Essential Introduction* (2006).

Freddie Gaffney is Chief Moderator for Film Studies with the WJEC. He is also a screenwriter, filmmaker and Senior Lecturer in Location and Studio Production at Ravensbourne College of Design and Communication.

John White is an A-level examiner for Film Studies with the WJEC and a teacher of Film, English and Media at Parkside Community College and Anglia Ruskin University in Cambridge. He is a co-author of *A2 Film Studies: The Essential Introduction* (2006).

The *Essentials* Series

This series of textbooks, resource books and revision guides covers everything you could need to know about taking exams in Media, Communication or Film Studies. Working together the series offers everything you need to move from AS level through to an undergraduate degree. Written by experts in their subjects, the series is clearly presented to aid understanding with the textbooks updated regularly to keep examples current.

Series Editor: Peter Wall

AS Communication and Culture: The Essential Introduction, Third Edition
Peter Bennett and Jerry Slater

Communication Studies: The Essential Resource
Andrew Beck, Peter Bennett and Peter Wall

AS Film Studies: The Essential Introduction, Second Edition
Sarah Casey Benyahia, Freddie Gaffney and John White

A2 Film Studies: The Essential Introduction, Second Edition
Sarah Casey Benyahia, Freddie Gaffney and John White

Film Studies: The Essential Resource
Peter Bennett, Andrew Hickman and Peter Wall

AS Media Studies: The Essential Introduction for AQA, Third Edition
Philip Rayner and Peter Wall

A2 Media Studies: The Essential Introduction for AQA, Second Edition
Peter Bennett, Jerry Slater and Peter Wall

AS Media Studies: The Essential Revision Guide for AQA
Jo Barker and Peter Wall

A2 Media Studies: The Essential Revision Guide for AQA
Jo Barker and Peter Wall

Media Studies: The Essential Resource
Philip Rayner, Peter Wall and Stephen Kruger

AS FILM STUDIES
The Essential Introduction

Second edition

**Sarah Casey Benyahia,
Freddie Gaffney and John White**

Routledge
Taylor & Francis Group

LONDON AND NEW YORK

First published in 2006

This edition published 2008
by Routledge
2 Park Square, Milton Park, Abingdon Oxon, OX14 4RN
Simultaneously published in the USA and Canada
by Routledge
270 Madison Ave, New York, NY 10016

Routledge is an imprint of the Taylor & Francis Group, an informa business

© 2006, 2008 Sarah Casey Benyahia, Freddie Gaffney and John White

Typeset in Novarese and Bell Gothic by Keystroke, 28 High Street, Tettenhall,
Wolverhampton
Printed and bound in Great Britain by Bell & Bain Ltd, Glasgow

British Library Cataloguing in Publication Data
A catalogue record for this book is available from the British Library

Library of Congress Cataloging-in-Publication Data
Benyahia, Sarah Casey.
    AS film studies : the essential introduction/Sarah Casey Benyahia,
Freddie Gaffney and John White. — 2nd ed.
      p. cm. — (The essentials series)
    Includes bibliographical references and index.
    1. Motion picture. I. Gaffney, Freddie, 1964– II. White, John, 1956–
III. Title.
    PN1994.B4335 2008
    791.43—dc22   2007048273

ISBN10: 0–415–45433–6
ISBN13: 978–0–415–45433–9

CONTENTS

FIGURE ACKNOWLEDGEMENTS

INTRODUCTION

What is Film Studies? What does it mean to study films? This introductory chapter:

■ puts forward the idea that studying films will involve you in something over and above simply enjoying going to the cinema – what that 'something' is should begin to become clearer as you work your way through this book

■ suggests studying films will involve you in taking a more analytical approach to your whole experience of cinema

■ highlights how important it is for you to be prepared to entertain new ideas about something that is perhaps already an important part of your life

■ offers an initial introduction to some of the activities you will need to be prepared to undertake if you are studying films

■ suggests the sort of questions you might need to consider asking yourselves about films

■ introduces a range of different writing skills required of Film Studies students

INFORMATION BOX

This chapter will be directly relevant to the module FM1 – Exploring Film Form in that it starts to introduce possible ways of approaching films. In particular it is directly relevant to what the examiners describe as

continued

encouraging candidates 'to develop an awareness of their active role as spectators', which is essentially about how each of us watches and makes sense of films. More importantly though this section should act as a general introduction to the whole idea of Film Studies allowing you to gain an overview of the subject and the sorts of things that are going to be asked of you before you begin work on the more specific syllabus requirements.

Going to the cinema

Going to the cinema has been a pleasurable pastime enjoyed throughout the world for around 100 years. With a fast expanding DVD market it seems people are increasingly enjoying watching films at home (see Chapter 9 of the UK Film Council's Statistical Yearbook 2005/6 at www.ukfilmcouncil.org.uk/information/statistics/yearbook), but even so, the spectacle offered by the cinema experience continues to be appreciated as something distinctively different.

ACTIVITY

1   How often do you go to the cinema? If possible, discuss this in groups. What seems to be the average? Who goes the most and how often is this?
2   Now, a perhaps more difficult question. Why do you go to the cinema? Try to decide on a list that covers as many reasons as possible for you personally. If you can, discuss your ideas with others. Are there similarities or differences in the reasons given?
3   If you are in a class with others, in small groups try to decide on a collective list that covers as many reasons as possible.

> **We all enjoy watching films, whether in the cinema or on TV. Cinema attendance, after many years of decline, is increasing each year and a new generation of film-goers is appreciating the pleasures of the 'big screen', a pleasure which even a 30-inch TV set cannot provide.**

(Nelmes 2003: 1)

Figure I.1 The cinema a l'aire lliure a montjuïc in Barcelona offers quite a spectacle and a distinctly different experience to watching in a darkened auditorium or at home

Note the double use of the word 'pleasure(s)' here, emphasizing the key factor determining why we watch film and also why we choose to try to study it in more depth.

Can't we just enjoy films?

Among some people who attend the cinema and/or watch DVDs on a regular basis there is a certain resistance to the idea of 'studying films'. For people taking this approach watching films at the cinema is seen as an especially intense form of entertainment that offers the chance of escapist fantasies that will only be undermined or devalued in some way by analysis. After-the-event discussion of the emotional experience offered by one film compared to another is encouraged and indeed is an important part of the whole experience as far as these fans are concerned. The physical attributes (whether of strength or beauty or some other feature) of one star are readily compared with similar attributes in other stars. The thrills provided in one film are marked against the thrills provided in another. Discussion and debate over the relative merits of one star over another, or one film over another, are endlessly recycled. However, engagement in an academic way with film is seen as detrimental to the experience itself.

Hopefully, as a film student you will continue to enjoy these sorts of discussions with your friends since it will form an important foundation to your studies, but you will also be prepared to try out new methods of approach that will often involve being more analytical in your viewing.

ACTIVITY

- On average how often do you watch films at home: once a week, twice a week, or more?
- Do you watch on your own generally, or with others? And, if with others, is this family or friends?
- Do you usually view films you have recorded from TV, bought DVDs, rental DVDs, pay-to-view movies, or film channel movies?
- Do you discuss the films you have watched with other people? If so, try to compile a list of the sorts of things you talk about (e.g. stars, storylines, special effects).

1   Write a short 250-word review of a film you saw recently for a film magazine or newspaper of your choice. Name the magazine and try to write in an appropriate style. Write a further 50–100 words describing who you were seeing as your target audience and how you were trying to write the piece.
2   If you are able to, in groups exchange reviews and read those written by other people.
3   Decide on the best piece in each group to be read out to the whole class. List the features of the chosen article that as a group you believe made it the best.
4   After the chosen articles have been read try to compare the lists of key factors for these articles that each group has arrived at. Has each group used the same sorts of criteria or are there significant differences?

No problem

There is no problem with adopting an attitude towards films that sees them as pure entertainment or escapist fantasy since pleasure is clearly an important part of the whole experience of cinema. Indeed, this is a part of the experience we will be seeking to emphasize and explore in some depth.

> **PLEASURE:** films clearly give us pleasure in a range of ways, otherwise we would not watch them; yet studying academic subjects is somehow often seen to be at odds with the idea of pleasure. However, since pleasure is the thing that beyond all else stimulates our initial interest in films we should not dismiss it out of hand. In fact, the idea of exactly how films provide us with pleasure will be a key approach to film for us.

The way in which films give pleasure is most apparent when we consider not just audiences in general but our own personal response to films, and yet this is often neglected by those of us who wish to study film. Perhaps this is because the concept of pleasure does not seem to sit well in relation to the idea of study. Or perhaps this neglect of the pleasure principle is to do with a difficulty in deciding how to study such a seemingly vague notion.

However we view all of this, the concept is clearly important not only in relation to narrative structure but also to the way in which human beings seem to be able to respond to the sheer aesthetic joy of colour, movement, light, shape and size, and in particular changing colour, movement, light, shape and size.

The best way to think about the ways in which films create pleasure for an audience is to analyse our own enjoyment of films. Pleasure could be provided by (among other things) an exciting or romantic narrative, the escapism of identifying with characters who are unlike us, or by the visual pleasure provided by flashing images on to a big screen. Film Studies academics have spent a long time trying to explain the different pleasures experienced by film spectators, particularly the enjoyment of aspects of film which do not immediately seem pleasurable, such as watching horror films.

Figure I.2 Film as pleasure – stars are often dressed (or undressed) to appeal to the audience. Daniel Craig in *Casino Royale* (2006)

ACTIVITY

At this early stage in your studies, how would you describe the pleasures film gives you? Try to list the variety of possible pleasures and compare your list with others.

Film Studies as a subject

Using films as pure escapist entertainment is one possible approach, but as Film Studies students we are going to be concerned with considering a much greater range of ways of understanding and experiencing film. This will involve recognizing the complexity of our interaction with film and acknowledging that there is no simple way of approaching film. Hopefully you are now beginning to gain some idea as to what Film Studies is and, perhaps, some inkling of what studying film is going to involve.

ACTIVITY

Before you read the rest of this section, put the heading 'Film Studies' at the top of a sheet of paper and take a few minutes to list all the things you would expect to be doing while studying film. Remember to take into account the sorts of things you have been asked to do so far. If possible compare your list with others.

You may have heard other people joke that Film Studies is just about sitting around and watching films. Happily, it has to be admitted, there is a certain element of truth to this since it is clearly impossible to study a film without first watching it closely, just as it is impossible to critically analyse a novel without first reading it carefully. However, there is rather more to Film Studies than this description suggests.

Questions we might ask ourselves

Early in our investigation of possible ways of approaching films it would be useful to ask ourselves exactly what activities we should expect to undertake in order to explore films in a way that will offer more than immediate, easy entertainment.

So, what does it mean to study a film? Dictionary definitions of 'study' often involve the idea of 'devoting time and thought'. So we could suggest studying film would involve spending time thinking about it; but how would we do this and what would we think about? What exactly are we supposed to be contemplating as we are watching a film at the cinema or a DVD or video at home?

Initial uncertainties might raise questions such as:

- Are there particular ways of thinking about film that we should be adopting?
- What should we be looking for as we watch these films?
- How will we know if we have found anything worth commenting upon?

And then, if we do find something we think is interesting, how should we comment?

- Is there a particular sort of language, or range of critical terms, that we should be using?
- Or is this really nothing more than jargon and should jargon be avoided?

And, perhaps most interestingly, what is meant when people talk about 'reading' films?

- In what sense is the activity of watching films akin to reading?

'Reading' films

Reading is often defined as interpreting symbols in relation to intended meanings. So, in the straightforward everyday sense of 'reading', the symbols 'c', 'a' and 't' can be combined in that sequence to suggest a certain type of animal that exists in our common, shared experience of the everyday world. The concept of 'reading' implies a shared language that is common to the writer and the reader and that enables messages to be transferred, or communicated. It also implies a shared world in some sense and a shared understanding of that world. Thinking about this we might wonder:

- What symbols might we need to interpret when 'reading' films?
- How will we know the intended meanings?
- Do we naturally go through this process as we watch films, or is this a special activity we are going to have to learn in the same way that we learnt to read books in our early years?
- Is it true to say that films depend upon the existence of a shared language common to both the makers of films and their audiences?

READING: this is a fundamental term for our whole approach to Film Studies. 'Reading' immediately suggests a depth of investigation and an intensity of focus that 'watching films' simply does not convey.

ACTIVITY

How would you define this shared language that is common to both filmmakers and the audiences for their films? In writing we obviously have words, sentences and paragraphs but what do we have in film that might in some way correspond to these elements? If possible discuss your thoughts with others.

(Do not worry if your thoughts are rather vague and uncertain at the moment: the key thing is simply to start to think about the idea of film as a language that we might be said to be reading as we watch.)

What are films?

For the moment we will go no further in trying to answer these questions to do with the concept of 'reading', but let us bear them in mind as we try to set out from a slightly different starting point. Let us begin by asking ourselves the apparently straightforward question, what are films? To start with we might suggest that they are stories recorded on film by a camera to be shown in cinemas via projectors (although even this is becoming increasingly problematic, since both the form implied by 'film' and the outlets available for 'film' are becoming increasingly diverse as new technologies multiply).

Stories

We could argue that stories, cameras and cinemas are likely to be some of the key elements in our investigation. In which case we would need to question the nature of stories:

- What subject areas do the stories typically cover?
- Are there particular subject areas in which film has shown special interest over the years?
- How are the stories constructed? Are there typical elements, often or always to be found?

ACTIVITY

1 Go through each of these questions and answer them quickly in note form.
2 Discuss your ideas in small groups if possible and report back to the whole class. Try to add other people's ideas to your initial notes as the discussions develop.

Cameras

Let us look now at the issue of cameras.

- What are these cameras like and how are they used?
- Has the technology of cameras changed over time and how has this affected films and the filmmaking process?
- What is the relationship between the director, the camera and the actors in the making of films?
- What is the relationship between cameras, the real world and the fictional world of stories?

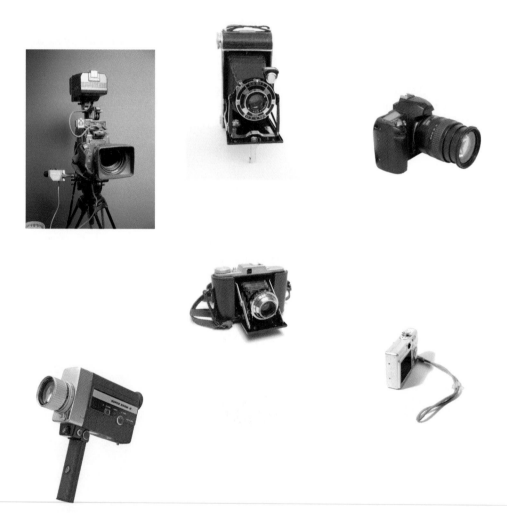

Figure I.3 Cameras, cameras, cameras

ACTIVITY

1 Go through each of these questions and answer them quickly in note form.
2 Discuss your ideas in small groups if possible and report back to the whole class. Again, add to your own notes as the discussions develop.

(Once more, do not worry at this stage if you are rather vague and uncertain about how to answer some of these questions; the key thing is simply that you should begin to think carefully about the nature of films.)

Cinemas, or 'the viewing experience'

Let us now consider more closely the whole notion of cinemas: the strange idea of entering a darkened auditorium with a group of strangers to sit and watch projected images on a large screen. (Although, to emphasize the point once again, we need to be aware that this viewing experience seems to be changing with people increasingly turning to DVDs.)

Figure I.4 Films may be viewed in conditions very different to those we imagine – a darkened auditorium vs. a light living room

- What are cinemas exactly and what are the key elements to a cinema? To what extent have these always been the same?
- Who goes to cinemas and why do people go to them? Has the type of people who go to cinemas changed over time? Are the sorts of people who go to the cinema different from country to country and from place to place within a country?
- What is the experience of being in the cinema like and how has this changed over time?
- How is the film and the experience of watching it altered when we watch at home? Is the experience (and therefore the film) changed when we watch at home with others? And what if the 'others' are parents or alternatively friends of our own age? Does that alter the experience?

ACTIVITY

1 Go through each of these questions and answer them quickly in note form.
2 Discuss your ideas in small groups if possible and report back to the whole class. Add to your own notes.

INFORMATION BOX

Try to keep your notes for film studies together in one place and organized in such a way that you can find specific topic areas as and when required. Above all, try to find a few minutes after each session to go back over the notes you have made and the ideas that have come up; this will remind you of the key ideas and will help to ensure you have really taken them on board. So much to do with studying is really simply about organization; and above all, about *organizing your time* effectively.

Questions, questions, questions

As we have been asking these questions about film in relation to stories, cameras and cinemas more questions might quite naturally have come to mind.

- Aren't films shown on television, video, DVD, i-pod, mobiles and the Internet now as well as in cinemas?
- And aren't they shown not just on terrestrial television but via satellite, cable and pay-per-view?
- And so, how would watching films via these different media change or affect the experience?
- And, are films all stories? What about filmed documentaries; are they part of our study?
- And, where is the boundary between a fictional story and a factual documentary? And what are docudramas?

In some ways this is moving into the realm of philosophical questions because we are going to be forced to ask: what is fact and fiction, what does it mean for something to be true to life and, indeed, what is truth and how do we recognize it? Soon the questions will begin to come thick and fast.

- Why are films made? There must be a whole host of reasons, but what are they?
- Who makes them? We always hear about the stars and the directors, but who else is involved?
- How are films made and what exactly does the process involve?
- To what extent is it a creative process? To what extent is it an industrial process? To what extent is it a commercial process?
- Why do we talk about different types of film (e.g. sci-fi, horror, film noir, thriller, melodrama, western)?
- What about these cameras: who operates them and who decides what to shoot and when?
- And then how do they decide the order in which to put the shots together, what bits of film to use and what not to use?
- What is the role of actors? They seem to be accorded quite a degree of importance. What exactly is a star? How do you move from being an actor to being a star?
- For that matter, what exactly is a director? What does he do? Or, what does she do? I wonder if there have been many women directors? How many female directors do you know?
- And, who runs the production companies that make films and the chains of cinemas that show films? These must be powerful people: how much control do they have over which films are made (and which are not)?
- And, what about the marketing and the advertising, who is responsible for that? We are constantly being subjected to it but who decides the level of publicity and advertising?

> **INDUSTRIAL PROCESS:** an industrial process is one that is involved in the manufacture of goods that are being made for sale.
>
> **COMMERCIAL PROCESS:** a commercial process is one that is focused upon achieving a financial return, in other words making a profit.

You should notice how both of these terms emphasize the idea of films as being at the heart of a series of processes. These processes may be followed through for individual films and this will give us a greater understanding of the exact nature of films and their place within our society.

The more we consider the nature of films, the more it sounds as if there is a whole massive industry of multinational proportions behind what definitely seems to amount to a huge commercial enterprise.

- How does it operate both within individual countries and globally?
- Has it always been as big as it would seem to be today?
- Is it set to get bigger still or is it in decline in the face of new technologies?

INFORMATION BOX – QUESTIONS

If there is one key to understanding the approach taken throughout this book this is it. As a Film Studies student (indeed as a student of any sort) you must be continually asking yourself questions and seeking answers. It sounds easy and only too obvious but adopting a questioning attitude demands real effort, commitment and, above all, thought. If you can get this questioning and thinking approach right then everything else will fall into place.

History, social context and politics

We are beginning to get somewhere. We have a whole series of questions, the answers to which would seem to form some part of finding out about film and the way it operates within the present context, and the way it has operated within a historical context. We also have the feeling that the more questions we ask the more we find, with all of them taking us further into the subject and each seeming to demand some part of our attention. In fact, we begin to get a sense of the wide-ranging nature of the studies we are about to undertake.

- Already we begin to realize that films do not exist outside of a society and certain social relations.
- Already we begin to see that since we are dealing with an industry we are going to have to at least be aware of business and economic considerations.
- Already we begin to see films as products of particular societies at particular moments in their historical development.

But at the same time we are wondering about the contributions of directors and actors, and perhaps cameramen (or cinematographers, if we know the word). Clearly close investigation of individual films is going to be necessary, but at the same time it is already looking as if we are not going to be able to 'read' films in isolation but rather that we are going to have to see them to some extent at least within social, historical, cultural and perhaps even political contexts.

Hollywood and alternative cinemas

Most of the films we will be looking at in this book would probably be seen as representing the dominant Hollywood mainstream, while others might be seen as constituting art-house or alternative offerings. Most of the films we deal with will be American or British but we will also be considering one or two films from other countries. So, we are going to need to be aware from the beginning of our studies that there have been different film movements in history and that there are different national cinemas around the world, and also that each of these film movements and national cinemas may be seen in some sense to be operating against the backdrop of a dominant Western cinema known as Hollywood. Sometimes there will be a strong sense of alternative cinemas being anti-Hollywood, but at other times the most powerful impulse will seem to be towards cross-fertilization between different cinemas (or approaches to filmmaking) and the Hollywood 'norm' or 'standard'.

CONCLUSION

Studying film requires us:

- to 'read' individual films carefully and thoughtfully;
- to recognize that films are made and viewed in particular ways that can be studied;
- to be aware of the need to adopt a questioning attitude.

References and Further Reading

Dyer, R. (1998) 'Introduction to Film Studies' in J. Hill and P. Church-Gibson (eds), *The Oxford Guide to Film Studies*, Oxford University Press, Oxford

Monaco, J. (2000) 'Preface to 2nd edition' in *How to Read a Film: Movies, Media, Multimedia* (3rd edn), Oxford University Press, New York and Oxford

Nelmes, J. (2003) 'Introduction' in *An Introduction to Film Studies* (3rd edn), Routledge, London

Phillips, P. (2000) *Understanding Film Texts: Meaning and Experience*, BFI, London (ch. 1)

part 1

EXPLORING FILM
FORM (FM1)

FILM FORM
SPECTATORSHIP
CREATIVE PROJECT

1 FILM FORM

What is film construction? What does it mean to say a film has been 'put together'? The following three chapters:

- outline the four key areas of film 'language' denoted as *mise-en-scène*, cinematography, editing and sound
- consider ways of analysing film construction techniques

Although each chapter will have a slightly different focus in relation to the demands of AS Film Studies, taken as a whole this part of the book should work as direct preparation for the WJEC coursework module FM1 – Exploring Film Form.

INFORMATION BOX

i

This chapter will be directly relevant to your study of film form in FM1 – Exploring Film Form for the WJEC's AS level in Film Studies, providing vital underpinning knowledge for both parts of the AS coursework; that is, both the 1500-word analysis of a film sequence and the creation of a two-minute short film. They will also help to put in place vital underpinning foundations for all that you will be asked to do in FM2 – British and American Film.

Important 'health warning'!

There are numerous possible activities on offer in the following three chapters. It is not expected that you will have time to complete all of them. It is suggested that you pick and choose according to your own interests, and more pragmatically according to the resources available to you.

Films mentioned

As you are working your way through the following three chapters you will find it useful to have watched two or three of these films:

- *Casino Royale* (Campbell, 2006)
- *Little Miss Sunshine* (Dayton and Faris, 2006)
- *Pirates of the Caribbean: Dead Man's Chest* (Verbinski, 2006)
- *Seven* (Fincher, 1995)

You will also find it helpful to have access to scenes, clips and single shots from at least some of the following films:

- *Lock, Stock and Two Smoking Barrels* (Ritchie, 1998)
- *Lord of the Rings: The Fellowship of the Ring* (Jackson, 2001)
- *Whale Rider* (Caro, 2002)
- *A Hard Day's Night* (Lester, 1964)
- *Mildred Pierce* (Curtiz, 1945),
- *The Crying Game* (Jordan, 1992)
- *East is East* (O'Donnell, 1999)
- *Psycho* (Hitchcock, 1960)
- *On the Waterfront* (Kazan, 1954)
- *La Haine* (Kassovitz, 1995)
- *Raging Bull* (Scorsese, 1980)
- *Schindler's List* (Spielberg, 1993)
- *The Searchers* (Ford, 1956)
- *My Beautiful Laundrette* (Frears, 1985)
- *Visions of Light* (Glassman, McCarthy and Samuels, 1992)
- *Reservoir Dogs* (Tarantino, 1991)
- *Bloody Sunday* (Greengrass, 2002)
- *The Blair Witch Project* (Myrick/Sanchez, 1999)
- *Donnie Darko* (Kelly, 2001)
- *Jackie Brown* (Tarantino, 1997)
- *Russian Ark* (Sokurov, 2002)
- *M* (Lang, 1931)
- *The Killing Fields* (Joffé, 1984)
- *Secrets and Lies* (Leigh, 1996)
- *Orphans* (Mullan, 1999)

Note

Having said all of this there is also plenty of room for you to use films of your own choice and to adapt activities accordingly wherever necessary.

What does it mean to say films are 'put together'?

What people mean when they use this phrase is that each of the films we see in the cinema is built by using a few basic elements of film construction. As a filmmaker you always need a setting or a location in which to film and a cast of actors who will be dressed in certain ways and be expected to use certain props while delivering certain (usually) predetermined lines. You will also need a camera or cameras to film the action, and then some means of chopping up the resulting footage you have taken and putting it back together again in the order you decide suits the story you are trying to tell. Settings, actors, costumes, props, a script and the derived footage to be edited: out of these basic elements you will 'put together' your film. Out of convention but also in order to evoke certain responses from your audience you might also add a music soundtrack.

Any successful approach to the study of film will depend upon coming to terms with the idea that films are constructs that have been 'put together' by filmmakers from a series of common component parts that we can identify and name. To create a film, filmmakers work with each of these individual parts; and so in studying any film we can take it apart in an effort to see how and (most importantly) why the various elements might have been used in the particular way they have.

Mise-en-scène: setting

Mise-en-scène is a French term that refers to a series of elements of film construction that may be seen within the frame of the individual shot; perhaps the most obvious and all encompassing of these is setting.

ACTIVITY

■ Consider the opening to any film you have seen recently. What was the setting and why do you think it had been chosen? Was it appropriate to the film and if so, in what ways?

If, as in the opening to *Lock, Stock and Two Smoking Barrels* (Ritchie, 1998) (see FM2, Section B, British Film Topics: British Film, Social and Political Study – Living with Crime), we find ourselves in an urban landscape of markets, small shops and lock-ups that is full of East End 'wide-boys' we know where we are in film terms and begin to have an idea of what to expect. If, as in the opening to *Lord of the Rings: The Fellowship of the Ring* (Jackson, 2001), we find ourselves in a fantastical other world of grey volcanic mountains, expansive plains and vast 'war games-style' armies we know we ought to prepare ourselves for a different experience.

Figure 1.1 *Lock, Stock and Two Smoking Barrels* (1998) and *Lord of the Rings: The Fellowship of the Ring* (2001)

The settings given to us during the openings to some films may leave us with more questions and not place us within a particular world with quite the same certainty. *Whale Rider* (Caro, 2002), for instance, cuts between two very distinct settings within the first few minutes: there is the relatively straightforward naturalism of the hospital maternity ward, but there is also the fantasy-style, other worldly, underwater space. Nevertheless, these settings have been carefully and appropriately chosen to set us up for what we should expect from the film.

ACTIVITY

- Consider the opening to *Casino Royale* (Campbell, 2006). What settings were used during the first three-minute sequence before the opening credits? Why had they been chosen? As a group of settings were they appropriate to the film and, if so, in what ways?
- You should begin by describing the settings employed in as much detail as possible, listing the settings and the key features of each with the help of other people if possible.
- The descriptions you eventually arrive at should give you clues as to how you could see these settings as appropriate to the film as a whole and perhaps especially to the character of Bond as portrayed in this particular movie in the long-established series.

MISE-EN-SCÈNE: this is a term that is borrowed from the theatre and really refers to staging, or 'putting on stage'. It sometimes helps to think of the elements you can see in the staging of a play: a particular location will be suggested on the stage, characters will be dressed in particular ways, particular objects will be carried by characters or prominently placed on the stage, and the actors will be directed to move or perform in particular ways. These theatrical elements are the subsection parts of the cinematic term; and this effectively reminds us of the way in which the theatre is a key element of film's cultural and artistic origins.

Lighting (including the use of areas of darkness or shadow) will also be part of any theatre performance and is often also classified as part of a film's *mise-en-scène*, since its effects can clearly be seen 'within the frame'. However, this aspect of film construction also links into cinematography (or the use of the camera). (Even those of us who have only taken holiday snaps will know the extent to which the correct lighting determines the success or failure of any photographic efforts.)

In addition, this way in which lighting in effect straddles both *mise-en-scène* and cinematography helps to alert us to something very useful: the demarcations we are dealing with here are essentially no more than a convenient device to help us to gain an overall understanding of the range of techniques available to film-makers for the creation of meaning. We need to be alert to the creative ways in which these aspects of film construction overlap and, in particular, to the ways in which they can interrelate with each other in order to amplify meaning.

In a somewhat similar way, sound effects (to say nothing of the words themselves) will also be an important part of the total effect created on the audience in a theatre, but here with respect to film we are dealing with these elements under the heading of 'sound'.

Mise-en-scène: performance and movement

As with setting, the performance and movement of the actors (also part of *mise-en-scène*) can operate in similar ways to suggest possibilities for how we might understand given characters and relationships between characters. Characters sitting with their backs to each other present a certain sense of relationship, while characters moving towards each other and embracing clearly present a different sense of relationship. This much is obvious, but within the performance and movement between any two characters there is, of course, a limitless range of possible permutations.

ACTIVITY

Consider again the opening to *Casino Royale*. How do the performances of characters here contribute towards our understanding of the scene? Which facial expressions adopted by the actor playing the corrupt British agent seem to you to be important in conveying meaning to the audience? More importantly, what do we learn about Bond from his performance and movement during these opening three minutes? Consider, for example, his acting immediately before and after apparently drowning the man in the hand basin in the toilets.

PERFORMANCE AND MOVEMENT: this refers to the acting that is taking place but the phrase also helps to define a little more clearly what it is we should be looking for: there is a performance going on and

> essentially it revolves around movement. These movements can range from the miniscule to the expansive, and can involve the whole body or the smallest parts of the body. Everything is included, from slow movements of the eye to sudden running and jumping, and each may be 'read' in some way (or several possible ways) as creating certain possible or potential meanings, or understandings of character and/or emotion.

However spontaneous any movement may appear to be, it has in all likelihood been tightly choreographed and is carefully calculated to create a particular impression on the spectator. You often hear of actors who improvise while the director allows the camera to roll in order to capture some inspirational acting moment, but the reason you hear about these occasions is because they are the exception to the rule. In reality actors talk about the ability to 'hit the mark' – to move across the acting space and arrive at a set point at exactly the moment previously agreed with the director (and camera operator). The 'mark' is literally that, a piece of tape on the ground/set floor that in choreographing the scene it has been agreed the actor should 'hit' at a precise moment in the script.

Body language

We need to be alert to the subtleties of such interactions, bearing in mind that each movement and gesture will have been decided upon in order to convey some meaning. Interactive movements involving two or more characters will have been carefully choreographed with attention to the details of body language that is designed to communicate a sense of character and/or character relationships to us, the audience. Once again, as with all aspects of film construction, choices will have been made for particular reasons by those involved in the creative process and we need to ask ourselves why those particular choices might have been made. Often the reason becomes clear upon simple reflection. When in *A Hard Day's Night* (Lester, 1964) (see FM2, Section B, British Film Topics: British Film and Culture – Swinging Britain (1963–1973)) the Beatles find their way out through a fire escape and free themselves from the various entrapping room spaces in which they have previously found themselves, the resulting change in their movements is clear; they cavort wildly through the open, outside space, running, jumping and extending limbs in all directions. (And, in case we should miss the point being made through performance, Lester uses fast motion to bring further attention to the sudden change.) The idea behind the exaggerated change of movement is obvious: they have found a momentary escape from a confined existence; but it can be easily missed if we neglect the active thinking interaction with the screen images that is vital for Film Studies.

Figure 1.2 *A Hard Day's Night* (1964)

The range of body codes

Actors are able to generate audience response to their performance in a whole range of subtle ways. A range of ten body codes have been identified:

- direct bodily contact;
- the proximity of one character to another (or proxemics);
- the orientation of one to another (i.e. the extent to which characters stand with their bodies turned towards or away from each other);
- general appearance of individuals (e.g. tall and thin, or short and fat);
- head movements (e.g. nodding or shaking of the head);
- facial expressions;
- gestures (or kinesics);
- body posture;
- eye movement or contact;
- aspects of speech, such as pitch, stress, tone, volume, accent, speech errors (all of which are termed paralinguistic codes).

(adapted from Argyle in Hinde 1972 and Fiske 1982)

You do not need to memorize these ten body codes, nor do you need to use any of the jargon associated with this list such as proxemics and kinesics. It is useful, however, to have a series of areas such as eye movement, body posture, facial expressions and so on to look out for as you are watching the performance of any particular actor. You will no doubt be used to discussing the performance of actors in films with friends and may be pleased to know that film studies will in part require you to undertake more of the same sort of discussions, although from a slightly more carefully analytical perspective.

Performance and movement in *Seven*

It is only when you look closely at actual examples of screen acting that you begin to realize the ways in which all these elements can be employed. There are, of course, countless examples that would serve to display a range of these elements of performance; but to take one example consider *Seven* (Fincher, 1995) (see FM2, Section C, US Film – Comparative Study). In this film there is a scene in which Morgan Freeman and Brad Pitt (playing two detectives who do not get on well) are together in the confined space of an office that Pitt's character is about to take over from Freeman's older character who is leaving the force. While they are cramped together in what is a small space, made all the more uncomfortable by the fact that they do not really like each other (note the use of setting for a specific reason again), they receive a phone call from Pitt's wife.

ACTIVITY

- If possible, watch this scene several times; as you do so, consider:

  - the different ways in which the actors' bodies are orientated in relation to each other
  - the body postures adopted by both
  - the facial expressions used by the actors
  - any changes in speech patterns they employ
  - the timing required for the delivery of the lines

- Note your thoughts on each of these points before discussing your ideas with a few other people.

By way of contrast, in the same film you could consider the lines delivered in the grey, box-like space of the police interview room by the man from the brothel who has just been forced to commit the 'lust' murder. This is delivered in close-up but notice how the body posture remains important (and how the use of clothing in the shape of the white towel works to frame our attention on his face). Each movement of the facial muscles is intimately linked to movements of the eyes and to the carefully timed rising and falling voice pattern used to deliver the lines themselves.

To further illustrate the point being made above, watch the scene in *Seven* in which, in the face of opposition from Freeman's character, Pitt as Mills asks the police chief to be allowed to take over the whole case himself. Both his language and his gestures are brash and expansive but this air of confidence is reinforced by the use of low-angle camera shots. Then, by contrast, when next morning Mills is given his own case involving the murder of a district attorney we are given an image of someone who is nervous and uncertain of his abilities. This is shown through Pitt's performance, especially the way in which he folds his arm across the top of his head to reveal an almost childlike vulnerability. But notice that this gesture is highlighted for us by the use of a close-up and our interpretation is further aided by the use of point of view sound as Pitt's character enters the building that is used to give a sense of the isolation and pressure he is feeling. It is Pitt's performance that gives us an understanding of his character as someone who displays confidence but is in reality much more fragile and vulnerable, but it is his performance in conjunction with the use of camerawork, sound and editing (the juxtaposition of these two contrasting scenes) that is really at work here.

Figure 1.3 Brad Pitt in *Seven* (1995)

ACTIVITY

1   Find two examples of your own that seem to you to show effective acting: one of a single character on her or his own in front of the camera and the second of two actors working together.

continued

2   Bring your examples to show to other members of the class. Screen your clips for a small group and talk them through your chosen performances, pointing out how various effects are being achieved and trying to refer to elements of the ten body codes. (Make sure you also try to consider ways in which the camera and the editing process may be said to be working with the actors to achieve particular effects.)

3   Working in the same groups choose one example from those that were screened showing two actors working together and attempt to re-create this scene with two members of the group taking on the required roles.

4   If possible, use a camera to record the scene using the same shots as in the original, edit your film and then play the scene back to compare your version with the original. (In order to do this you may need to storyboard the scene in an effort to get it as close to the original as possible. You should find that the planning that is inevitably involved in the storyboarding process will save time in the long run and enable you to be more accurate in what you are trying to achieve. You may even like to have one group storyboarding and another trying to complete the task without going through this stage in order to enable you to compare and discuss the results.)

Mise-en-scène: costume and props

Allied to the performance and movement of the actors, and still within the overall area of *mise-en-scène*, are considerations by the filmmakers regarding costume to be worn and props to be placed within a setting or used by a particular character. So, for instance, again taking *Seven* as an example, notice the way in which the two detectives Mills and Somerset are dressed differently right from the start of this film. What do the differences in costume tell us about the two men? (You may also be interested in the way in which in the same film the 'baddie', John Doe (Kevin Spacey), is sometimes shown as being dressed in a similar way to Somerset; that is, in a dark hat and long cloak-like coat. Why has this been done? Does it suggest something about these two characters, and if so, what?)

In order to consider the differences between Mills and Somerset, you could look at the scenes in which we are shown the two cops dressing to get ready to go to work. If you do this, notice that it is not simply a question of the types of costume or props being employed but also the nature of the way in which the two actors perform the actions of putting on particular pieces of clothing or laying out particular items to be used. When we are shown Somerset getting dressed by methodically laying out items of clothing and picking up a series of, again carefully

Figure 1.4 *Seven* (1995)

laid out, objects to put in his pockets we immediately know something of his personality and character.

So, in trying to consider props we again notice that our convenient demarcations between elements of film construction does not really hold up when we begin to analyse any given film clip. It is the relationship between objects in the scenes discussed above and the performances of the actors (highlighted and brought to our attention by editing and camerawork) that creates meaning.

ACTIVITY

Watch the opening two minutes from *Pirates of the Caribbean: Dead Man's Chest* (Verbinski, 2006).

How are props and costume used in this sequence to convey information to the audience? Teacups set out in the rain, a wet sheet of music blowing away, a bouquet of predominantly white flowers held by a woman dressed in a particular way and with no immediate shot of her face, black silhouetted soldiers in boats with, bizarrely, the outline of a man on

continued

Figure 1.5 *Pirates of the Caribbean: Dead Man's Chest* (2006)

horseback seemingly on the water, a specific flag with a particular logo, black rowing boats seen from the shore, soldiers coming ashore but now in very clearly denoted uniforms, the hooves and legs of a horse, a shot of a man on horseback in a black cloak with a black hat and black bow: why have these props and costumes displayed in this particular order been chosen for the opening to this film? At some points you might like to relate your interpretation to *Pirates of the Caribbean: The Curse of the Black Pearl* (Verbinski, 2003) but if you didn't know this earlier film what would you be able to make of these particular displays of props and costumes?

(You may also like to think about why the opening shot of the movie before the film title appears takes us from a black screen to an extremely dark image simply of an expanse of sea. Here we have a very particular location or setting but nothing happens within it, at least not at this stage. So, why has it been employed and placed here at the start of the film?

In addition, what meanings do you take from Keira Knightley's performance? What movements does she make (remembering that absence of movement can be just as important and can make little movements stand out all the more)? How is her hair used, and what would you say about the use of her eyes?)

> **COSTUME AND PROPS:** this refers to items of clothing being worn by characters or objects seen within any given setting. At its simplest, costume clearly acts as a type of uniform, linking a character to a particular group and often to a rank or position within that group. But costume can also 'announce' a character, giving an insight into what this person is supposed to be like; for instance, shy or flamboyant. At their simplest, props work to give an authentic sense of place, but may also be used in more complex ways to suggest important characteristics of particular individuals or even key themes for the whole film.

Dress code and character

It has often been pointed out that when Joan Crawford taking the title role in *Mildred Pierce* (Curtiz, 1945) (see FM2, Section C, US Film – Comparative Study) changes her clothes from stereotypical suburban housewife attire centring on an apron to power-dressing businesswoman-style suits, an important indication of her personal transformation of character is being presented to us. A similar alteration to character (although with vastly different outcomes) occurs in *The Crying Game* (Jordan, 1992) in which the IRA operative Jude (Miranda Richardson) adjusts her persona markedly from the first half of the film to the second and signals this change by a distinctive change of dress; as with the central

Figure 1.6 *The Crying Game* (1992)

character in *Mildred Pierce* she re-emerges in the film in a suit and with a distinct change of hairstyle. In other words, costume has always been important in helping to create meaning for the viewer. In *East is East* (O'Donnell, 1999) (see FM2, Section B, British Film Topics: British Film and Genre – Comedy) our awareness of Nazir's change of lifestyle and assertion of his (homo)sexuality is reinforced for us by his new-found dress sense when he moves to Manchester. Whenever a character appears in a film their dress will have been carefully chosen to 'announce' their character.

INFORMATION BOX i

In fact, the example involving the film *Mildred Pierce* given above has been used far too often according to some film examiners and usually with little real understanding of the film. So, important point: make sure you try to come up with your own examples for as many of the general ideas being given here as possible.

Take away with you the general points that are being made in any film textbooks and then make sure you try to apply the ideas to films you know. In this way you will gain a much better understanding of the concept itself and have at your disposal an example that is fresh and exciting instead of stale and overused.

Props and character

As regards props, consider the way in which books are used in relation to Mills and Somerset. Where Somerset studies the original texts in the calm academic environment of a library in order to try to understand the killer, Mills tries to read student guides to the texts but finds even these hard work. Or, consider the way in which, when he cannot sleep, Somerset throws a flick-knife at a dartboard: What does that suggest about his character? It certainly seems to add some sort of complication to our understanding of him as the orderly, emotionally controlled, academically minded cop.

In a similar way, as Norman Bates leads Marion Crane into his parlour behind the reception area of the Bates Motel in *Psycho* (Hitchcock, 1960) (see FM2, Section C, US Film – Comparative Study) we cannot avoid noticing the stuffed birds. There is the predatory owl in mid-swoop and then the ominously sharp-beaked shadow of a crow, a harbinger of death. Nor should we miss in this scene the paintings of classical nudes on the walls: the female body displayed in all its naked vulnerability before the essentially male gaze. For the purposes of Film Studies we have to be intensely aware of all of this in an analytical fashion that is going to enable us to decide exactly how meaning is being created for us as members of the audience.

Figure 1.7
Psycho (1960)

Props as symbols

In this way props or costume items can take on considerable significance for the whole film; they can in effect become symbols for some key idea or concept. In *On the Waterfront* (Kazan, 1954) when the first person willing to speak out against the corruption in the docks is murdered, his jacket is symbolically passed on to the next person willing to do the same and ultimately to our hero, Terry (Marlon Brando). In effect, what is seen within the film as the mantle of truth and justice is being passed from one to another. In *East is East*, Sanjid's parka coat, standing perhaps for an attempt by the character to shield himself from the pain of the world around him, has the hood accidentally but highly symbolically ripped off towards the end of the film. In *La Haine* (Kassovitz, 1995) the key prop of the gun is symbolically handed over to Hubert by Vinz towards the end of the film in acknowledgement of the fact that he has learnt something important both about himself and about the reality of gunplay. Once again, the prop takes on a role and significance within the film over and above its mere presence as a material object. If you look back to Miranda Richardson in *The Crying Game* you will notice that it is not just her clothes that are important in our chosen shot but her assured use of the gun, adding to the image of determined (if not deadly, femme fatale-style) female power. And if you look at the whole film you will notice that the prop of 'the gun' returns throughout as an object that not only raises issues of power and carries bloody connotations but also as an object with phallic associations.

ACTIVITY

- Watch the first half an hour of *Casino Royale* – to the point where Bond emerges from the sea in his swimming trunks. Note each change of clothes used for Daniel Craig's character to this point in the film.
- Why has each costume been chosen for the character? How and why are the costumes chosen appropriate to each scene? What, if anything, do the changes of clothes tell us about the character?
- If possible, discuss your ideas with other people, and take careful note of any ideas they might have had that you hadn't thought of.

ACTIVITY

1 Find two examples from a film or films of your choice that seem to you to show effective use of costume and/or props.
2 Bring your examples to show to other members of the class. Screen your clips for a small group and talk them through your chosen scenes, pointing out how you feel the clothes and/or props that are used have been chosen to convey certain information to the audience. (Make sure you also try to consider ways in which the camera and the editing process may also be said to be contributing to focusing our attention on your chosen aspects of costume and/or props.)

ACTIVITY

Watch the library scene from *Seven* or a scene from a film of your own choice (or, if you like, the parlour scene from *Psycho*) and write an analysis of the ways in which props are used to assist in the creation of certain potential meanings for us as spectators (500 words).

Cinematography: colour

One of the key points to recognize as a Film Studies student is the way in which as spectators of film our reading (or interpretation) of one strand of film construction, such as performance and movement, or costume and props, can be influenced or reinforced by the filmmaker's use of further elements of visual language. The cinematographer's choice (made in conjunction with others) of lighting and colour, for example, can clearly affect the 'look' of the film as a whole but can also influence our understanding of individual scenes.

For a film that is often spoken about in terms of the flamboyant, colourful performance of Johnny Depp as Jack Sparrow, *Pirates of the Caribbean: Dead Man's Chest* is actually a very dark film with continual use of murky greens and cold blues and greys. By way of contrast, a film like *Little Miss Sunshine* (Dayton and Faris, 2006) employs an entirely different, more naturalistic, use of colour and

Figure 1.8 *Little Miss Sunshine* (2006)

lighting. Is this simply a matter of one film being a fantasy and the other attempting a much stronger relationship to the real world, or does this 'look' of the film contribute much more to determining our response?

COLOUR: this may be used in highly artificial ways for particular expressive purposes: the cold blue tint and contrasting red lipstick employed for the scene with the changed Jude in *The Crying Game* (where one thing suggested is the danger of a femme fatale) or the cold, lifeless, washed-out greys achieved in the interview scene in *Seven*.

In the more general 'look' of a whole film, vibrant, enhanced colours can be used to suggest the excitement of a Hollywood world of action and adventure, or simple natural colours can be employed in an effort to recreate a realistic image of the real world.

Black and white

The choice of black and white over colour may often be driven by economics (quite simply, it's cheaper) but it can also be a more creative decision: consider the use of black and white in *Raging Bull* (Scorsese, 1980) which looks back to boxing in the post-war period, or *Schindler's List* (Spielberg, 1993), in which the story is set amidst the horrors of the Holocaust. In these cases the choice seems to have been made for particular creative reasons. With the size of the budget available for Bond movies, the decision to film the opening sequence of *Casino Royale* in black and white has obviously been made on the basis of wanting to achieve a certain 'look' and to create a particular effect on the audience. In this case there is a harking back to the Cold War period in which the austerity associated with countries behind the Iron Curtain was often portrayed through this type of colouration. But there is also a noir (or dark) feel that is immediately given to the film and by association to the character of Bond.

When watching *Seven* there are any number of scenes where you almost have to remind yourself that this is a colour film; greys and 'washed-out' colours almost totally predominate in order to give a sense of this bleak, murky urban landscape. In the case of *La Haine* which looks at confrontations between the police and young people in and around Paris in the mid-1990s, a very deliberate creative choice has been made to screen this film in black and white. The question we must ask ourselves is why this might have been done. How might this have been considered appropriate or 'correct' for the film? There will be a range of possible answers but the key point is that we must ask ourselves the question.

ACTIVITY

ACTIVITY

Watch the opening to *La Haine* and discuss with others why you think the filmmakers decided to make this film in black and white.

ACTIVITY

Watch the opening to *Casino Royale* (if you need to remind yourself of it) and discuss with others how you feel the use of lighting and colour in this case helps to determine audience response.

> Spielberg's brilliant decision to film Schindler's List in black and white is a key ingredient in the movie's aesthetic success ... The lack of colour allows Spielberg to be explicit without becoming tastelessly graphic.
>
> Spielberg's black and white also achieves a number of other coherent aesthetic objectives. It echoes newsreels and documentaries of the Holocaust made at the time, thus establishing historical context and a feeling of authenticity.

(Alan A. Stone, 'Spielberg's Success', Boston Review (www.bostonreview.net))

ACTIVITY

If possible, look at relevant extracts from some more of the films mentioned here and decide why you believe black and white might have been used on each occasion. As usual, it would be good to try to compare your ideas with those of others.

ACTIVITY

1   Choose a film you know that seems to use colour in an interesting way and pick an extract that seems to demonstrate an especially good example of the way in which colour works in this film. Think about how you feel colour is contributing to creating meaning and generating audience response in your film extract.
2   If possible, show your extract to others, take them through your reading of the use of colour in this clip and allow time for them to discuss your ideas.

Colour

Most obviously colour as with bright lighting simply gives pleasure to the audience. Film can literally bring light and colour into our lives. However, particular colours or tints may also be used to suggest (often through their association with the colours of the natural world) warmth or coldness, or particular seasons, or types of emotion. They may also be used symbolically, as, for example, in the use of red to suggest blood and danger, or passion and lust. One way to make this clear would be to consider the way in which colour is used in *Seven*. Look at the scenes in the brothel, the interview room and the library, decide the dominant colours in each scene and ask yourself why such colours have been chosen. Notice too how colours can be saturated (made as vivid as possible) or de-saturated (washed out to be as dull and muted as possible). Finally, it is worth noting that colours can have different associations and significations from culture to culture and that our discussion has so far been dictated by the response generally found to be culturally agreed within Western societies.

Cinematography: lighting

In terms of the lighting for a film the fundamental choice is obviously whether to use natural lighting or not (i.e. whether to film outside or in the studio), but in reality even natural lighting will usually be supplemented by lights set up by the film crew. The use of relatively bright lighting sources (high key lighting), for example, in romantic comedies, suggests a certain atmosphere or attitude to life that is distinctly different from that set up by the relatively dark lighting (low key lighting) used in film noir, or a neo-noir like *Seven*. Similarly, hard light that is created by a narrow, intense beam of light and gives sharp-edged objects and shadows sets up a distinctly different mood from the soft lighting created by a broad, more diffuse beam that gives soft-edged objects and shadows.

You will be aware of all of this from your own experience of film. Once these ideas about lighting and colour are pointed out you will be able to give your own examples quite easily. Again, Film Studies is in a sense only asking you to take what you already know and to think about it in a slightly more analytical fashion. You now have to watch for uses of lighting and colour, and ask yourself the recurring vital question of why the filmmakers have chosen to use these particular creative aspects of their trade in this way.

Possible sources of light

Lights can be placed anywhere around, above or below the object being photographed. Consider a face lit from the front (front lighting), compared with a face lit from behind (back lighting), or from the side (side lighting), or from above (overhead lighting), or from below. Each will obviously create a different image and, within the context of the particular film, suggest something about the character being lit in this way. Overhead lighting, for example, may be used to cast heavy shadows, conceal the eyes and create an image of a face that is mysterious, sinister, perhaps conveying danger (a classic example of this would be some of the shots of John Wayne's character Ethan Edwards in *The Searchers* (Ford, 1956) (see FM2, Section C, US Film – Comparative Study) with the shadow of the brim of his hat casting his eyes in deep shadow). Or, sometimes, the left or right half of a character's face may be lit while the other half remains in shadow, perhaps again suggesting a person with darker and lighter aspects to their character, or possibly a confused character who has yet to choose which way to turn. This is the case when we encounter the Daniel Day-Lewis character, Johnny, with the other members of his British National Party gang beneath the railway line in *My Beautiful Laundrette* (Frears, 1985) (see FM2, Section B, British Film Topics: British Film and Culture – Thatcher's Britain (1981–1989)).

ACTIVITY

1 Working on your own or with one or two others, find a range of shots that light faces in interesting and perhaps distinctive ways.
2 Try to decide how you think the lights must have been arranged to create the shots you have found. You may like to experiment with lighting arrangements to see if you can re-create the types of shots you have been considering. (Your equipment does not need to be sophisticated: simple torches will suffice to give some sense of the possibilities for casting shadows on the face.)
3 If you are working in groups you could try to construct a filmed re-creation of one of these shots perhaps with any dialogue included and then compare your efforts with the original. If possible, show your work (alongside the original) to an audience, explain what you were trying to achieve and ask for their response.

Figure 1.9 John Wayne in *The Searchers* (1956)

Lighting from below challenges the viewer by reversing all our usual expectations for lighting, which derive from the positioning of the sun overhead; we are used to facial shadows falling in a certain way and when this norm is disrupted we are disorientated, finding that with which we are confronted to be strange and otherworldly. This reminds us that, as with colour, lighting can be used in highly contrived, artificial ways to achieve particular purposes or in naturalistic ways in order to achieve in some sense a replication of the real world.

ACTIVITY

- If possible, discuss with other people the ways in which you believe lighting has been used for particular purposes in any films you have seen recently. Try to talk as accurately as possible about specific scenes in specific films.
- Make a note of any films that are mentioned in the discussion that you haven't seen but which sound interesting and worth a look.

LIGHTING: this refers to the various ways in which the light, whether in the studio or on location, is controlled and manipulated in order to achieve the 'look' desired for a particular shot or scene.

ACTIVITY

- Choose one film you know well that seems to you to use lighting in an interesting way and pick an extract that seems to demonstrate an especially good example of the way in which lighting works in this film.
- If possible, show your chosen extracts to others and explain in as much detail as possible how you feel lighting is contributing to creating meaning and generating audience response in your film extract.

(In order to make a good job of this you will need to practise your delivery. You are not aiming to give an in-depth talk but you should still attempt to be as professional as possible.)

Conventional lighting norms

Most often in the filming of a commercial movie a combination of lighting positions will be used around the main subject. This will conventionally involve a key light (usually on an arc 45 degrees either side of the camera), a fill light (giving softer lighting from the opposite side of the camera to the key light) and a back light (making the subject stand out from the background). But these are only general positions; more lights may be added or taken away, the angle at which any light is positioned in relation to either camera or subject can (obviously) be varied, and there is a choice of hard or soft lighting that is available for each lighting position. All of this begins to make it clear why the work of cinematographers has often been referred to as 'painting with light'. (This is a key phrase in the highly recommended film *Visions of Light* (Glassman, McCarthy and Samuels, 1992) which looks back at key cinematographers in Hollywood.)

INFORMATION BOX

As with every other aspect of film construction so far discussed, we again notice not only how extensive the range of choices available to filmmakers is but also how critical these choices are to the creation of a particular meaning, or range of potential meanings, for the spectator.

ACTIVITY

1 Watch the scene in *Seven* where the detectives, Mills and Somerset, go down into the brothel to investigate the 'lust' murder. If possible, discuss in detail with others the ways in which light and colour have been used in this sequence.
2 Write a short piece (400–500 words) explaining the meanings you see as being created for the audience and the responses likely to be generated by the use of light and colour in this short sequence.

ACTIVITY

1 If you have time, watch *Visions of Light*, stopping, rewinding and watching again any effects of cinematography you find particularly interesting.

2 List interesting films (with dates), along with the cinematographers and directors who worked on them. Make a note alongside of the features of these films that made you see them as interesting in some way.
3 If possible, discuss the choices of interesting films you have made with other people who have looked at *Visions of Light*. When these other people watched the film did they identify the same clips, or different ones, as being especially interesting? Were you able to express clearly the reasons for each of your choices?

(The word 'interesting' has been used several times above. It is a vague word and usually you should expect to try to use language in as precise a way as possible. Try never to describe a film as simply 'good', or 'enjoyable', or even 'interesting', but instead always attempt to suggest why you found it to be any of these things. As always, 'why' is our key word: by referring to details of film construction you should try to identify exactly what it is about any film that makes it 'interesting' (or 'good' or 'enjoyable'). The usefulness of such a vague word as 'interesting' here is that it leaves it open for you to come up with your own ideas.)

Cinematography: camerawork

All of the elements of construction considered thus far can influence the way in which we 'read' the visuals being presented to us; but, in addition, the filmmaker also has within her control the manipulation of our physical point of view through camerawork. Filmmakers can put us into positions that make us feel comfortable or uncomfortable, dominant or vulnerable, simply by deciding on the positioning and movement of the camera.

If you have seen the well-known scene in *Reservoir Dogs* (Tarantino, 1991) in which the police officer has his ear sliced off you may have noticed the way in which the camera as it were 'looks away' at the actual moment of the cutting almost as if the whole thing is too uncomfortable or painful to watch. If you have seen the interrogation scene in *La Haine* in which two police officers racially abuse and beat two of the central characters, you may have noticed how, in contrast to *Reservoir Dogs*, a static camera is used, refusing us any respite from viewing what is going on. In this film the filmmakers deny us the potential relief of looking away and yet by refusing this possibility they in fact only highlight how much we would like to turn our head away. The point is that choices that are made about the use of the camera are often made in order to create particular effects on the audience.

> **CAMERAWORK:** this clearly and quite simply refers to the work done with the camera in the making of a film.

Although the general term 'camerwork' is quite easy to understand, the possibilities open to the cinematographer are anything but simple. Fundamentally, the camera may be positioned at any distance from the subject being filmed and at any angle to that subject. It can be turned left or right to follow a subject within a horizontal plane, or tilted up or down to follow the same subject in a vertical plane. It can also be moved at any speed towards, away from or around the subject, and this movement can be as smooth or as shaky as the filmmakers decide. In addition, lenses may be used to give the appearance of movement towards or away from the subject at any speed, or to make the image of the subject either sharper or more indistinct, or even to alter the appearance of the subject in the style of a fairground 'hall of mirrors'.

The only limitation on the fluidity and mobility of the camerawork in any film is the availability of the necessary technology to enable the desired effect to be achieved; and, in general terms, camera and lens technology has developed throughout film history in such a way as to permit increasingly complex camerawork. So, for instance, new lightweight cameras (and sound-recording gear) in the 1950s made it easier to take the equipment out on location.

However, what you will find if you get the chance to watch some clips from old silent movies is that even from very early in film history, cinematographers were devising imaginative ways of getting moving shots with these rather large, heavy wooden cameras. So, yes, available technology must to some extent impose limitations upon what can be achieved, but it is often the creativity with which available technology is used that is of most interest.

(Please note: this is not to say that simple camerawork is not possible, nor to suggest that simple camerawork cannot be at least as effective as complex permutations of distances, angles, movements and lens usage. Recall the example from *La Haine* given above which highlighted the carefully chosen use of a static camera.)

Distance and angle of shot

By varying the distance between the camera and the subject the cinematographer can employ anything from an extreme long shot (ELS) (often used to establish the setting and then also known as an establishing shot), to an extreme close-up (ECU) closing in on just part of the face. In between there are possibilities for a long shot (LS) giving a full-length character shot, a medium shot (MS) giving half a standing character, and a close-up (CU) giving a head-and-shoulders shot (and obviously all sorts of further slight variations within this range of possibilities).

By varying the angle of shot the cinematographer can place the spectator in the position of looking down on or looking up at a character; alternatively, we can be positioned at eye level with a character in shot. If the editing suggests the camera is taking up the point of view of a particular character (a point of view shot, or POV), then again the angle may be used to create a particular impression of the character's situation. So, a low-angle POV shot might suggest that a character was being overpowered by whatever was towering over her.

Choices within the camera set-up

All of the above discussion of distance and angle of shot is complicated by choices open to the filmmaker regarding the technical set-up within the camera itself. These are decisions to do with type of lens, size of aperture (the opening on the camera that allows light in) and type of film (or film stock). By varying the combinations of possibilities here the filmmaker is able to determine depth of field; how far into the distance objects within the shot will remain in focus, how much of the space behind or to the sides of the main subject is shown, and how deep the shot will seem to be or how much sense of 'going on into the distance' the shot will have.

Different types of film are more, or less, sensitive to light. Slow film stock requires more light than fast film stock. So, if you are filming somewhere where you can employ an intense lighting set-up (often on set, of course) you are more likely to use a slow film stock since it allows you to achieve a more finely detailed final image. Fast film needs less light and so is often used in situations where it is not easy to enhance the natural lighting. It gives what might be called a more documentary look to the final image.

In terms of the lens to be used, the filmmaker essentially has a choice between a wide-angle lens, a normal lens or a telephoto lens. In order to shoot something approximating to the same shot, say, a male or female subject in a field, but using different lenses it is necessary to move the camera in relation to the object being studied; from the standard position you choose to adopt with a normal lens you move closer with a wide-angled lens and much further away with a telephoto lens. A normal lens gives an image that approximates to what the human eye is used to seeing when standing looking at a character in a field. If, however, we move closer to the subject and employ a wide-angle lens then there is something approximating to the original shot but with the areas to either side of the character and in particular the depth of space behind the character given more emphasis; essentially more of the space around the character is taken in, perhaps giving an enhanced sense of vulnerability or isolation. Moving away from the subject and using a telephoto lens would make the background appear much closer to the subject. Again perhaps this would give some sense of isolation and vulnerability, but possibly with the sense of a more immediate threat with the background seeming to encompass or engulf the subject.

If instead of moving the camera towards or away from the subject to allow for the different lenses you were to leave the camera in the same position at a set distance from the subject the telephoto lens would give an intense, essentially 'close-up', image of the subject with everything around the subject cropped away, whereas the wide-angle lens would reduce the relative size of the subject within the frame and take in much more of the space to the sides and behind the subject. It would also, incidentally, take in more of the space between the subject and the camera.

These ideas are not easy to absorb when reading about them but become much clearer when you begin looking through a camera viewfinder for yourself. From the point of view of analysing films the key point here is that you need to become more aware of what is going on within the frame as it has been composed by the filmmaker. It is not just a question of what the subject, or character, is doing within the shot that is important but how he or she has been placed within the frame. Is the space to the sides, behind or in front of the character being emphasized, and if so, why? Are objects behind the main subject in focus or out of focus, and if so, why? On each occasion the filmmakers will have made a decision to film in this way and your job is to ask yourself why this choice has been made.

A further possibility is offered by an extreme wide-angled lens, or fisheye lens, which produces distortion to the image.

Once again, however, the key point is that this will have been used by the filmmakers to suggest certain meanings or to generate certain responses and this is the area to which we need to be as alert as possible.

ACTIVITY

- Find a shot or series of shots from a film that you believe have used the space behind and/or to the sides and/or in front of the main subject in a particular way to create meaning for the audience.
- Show the shot(s) to other people as part of a film extract and discuss possible meanings and responses with your audience.
- Try to work out what you believe may have been the particular combination of choices relating to use of the camera that went into the making of this shot, or these shot(s).
- You will need to choose the extract carefully to introduce enough of the sequence from which the shot(s) come to allow your audience to understand a little of the context and you might also need to introduce the film carefully for those who don't know it already.

Establishing shots

Usually you will find that each scene in a fictional narrative film uses an establishing shot; that is, a shot that gives the setting in which the scene is to take place and

Figure 1.10 Example of a picture taken with a fisheye lens

enables the viewer to establish the spatial relationships between characters involved in the scene. However, although this is what might be known as the Hollywood standard and was certainly the expected norm throughout the period of Classical Hollywood, the practice of using an establishing shot has not always been followed by filmmakers. By omitting an establishing shot the viewer is put in the position of struggling to make sense of the relationship between the characters shown. We are effectively disorientated and this will be part of what the filmmakers are attempting to achieve; as well as perhaps defying the expected filmic norm and thereby challenging any presumption that there are certain correct (and therefore certain incorrect) ways of making films.

ACTIVITY

1   Choose a sequence from a film that you know that seems to use camerawork in a significant way.
2   In small groups show your chosen sequences to each other and explain in as much detail as possible how you feel camerawork is being used to contribute to creating meaning and generating audience response in your chosen extracts.

(In doing this you should expect to refer to distances and angles of shot, and you may like to use diagrams (perhaps as handouts or on an overhead projector) to illustrate your points. As an alternative, you may like to use members of the group to take roles within your chosen film clip, enabling you to move among them in order to demonstrate your understanding of how the camera has been positioned and used to film the sequence.)

ACTIVITY

Working with one or two other people devise a short sequence of shots within a recognizable narrative that employs as many permutations and differences in distance and angle as possible. Storyboard the sequence of shots and then film it and show it to an audience, if you have the time.

Camera movement

The variations in terms of permutations of distance from subject and angle of shot are obviously endless; but in addition, the cinematographer can also move the camera while taking the shot. This could involve panning to left or right to take in more of a scene or bring into view additional objects, or tilting up or down to create a similar effect. But it could also involve moving the whole camera along on a track (a tracking shot), or simply on wheels (a dolly shot), or even on a crane (a crane shot). And by using the lens on the camera the cinematographer can create further adjustments to the type of shot we see. She could zoom in to give more detail or out to take in more of the setting; or adjust the lens to bring some objects more sharply into focus while leaving others blurred; or employ deep focus to have objects from foreground to background all in acceptable focus. If you return again to the shot of Miranda Richardson as Jude in *The Crying Game* you will notice that she is made very much the centre of our attention by the way in which the background is blurred and deliberately out of focus. All sorts of combinations are obviously possible, so, for example, the camera could pan while tracking forward and rising up on a crane. Finally, shots could also be handheld and therefore deliberately somewhat shaky.

If you watch *Bloody Sunday* (Greengrass, 2002) one of the first things that will strike you will probably be the distinctive use that is being made of the camera. We are familiar with shaky handheld camera effects from films such as *The Blair Witch Project* (Myrick/Sanchez, 1999) and tend to associate it with low budget movies. But what both of these films demonstrate is that these sorts of uses of the camera can be employed to create very particular atmospheres and involve the audience in the experience in very striking ways.

Figure 1.11
*The Blair
Witch Project*
(1999)

In both of these cases, you will probably be immediately aware that something different from what you are used to is being done with the camera. This highlights the fact that because we tend to be familiar with mainstream Hollywood films we do have certain expectations about how the camera will be used. Changes from the norm, or the 'Hollywood standard', will be potentially challenging to us.

The extent of the range of camera possibilities

The important point, of course, is that if the cinematographer and director as a team are 'on top of their game' then each permutation of possibilities will be carefully chosen in an effort to achieve a particular desired effect whether in the creation of meaning or the generation of audience response. Consider the elaborate camera movement forming the opening to *Donnie Darko* (Kelly, 2001) in which the camera seems to track past half-lit undergrowth before moving towards the central character lying in the road and circling him. There is then a cut to what at first looks as if it may be a point of view shot panning across the early morning skyline before the character stands and emerges suddenly into the foreground of the shot, half turns towards the camera and seems to smile, almost laugh to himself. Why has this opening camera movement been chosen, how does it work to introduce the film and the central character, and in what ways is it appropriate for the film and the character? How does it contribute towards ensuring that the opening engages our attention? Or, what about the opening to *Jackie Brown* (Tarantino, 1997)? What sorts of camera movement are being used here? If you get a chance to look at this you will see the way in which the opening tracking shot has been complicated by having the central character standing on a moving walkway somewhat confusing our sense of movement. You will also see how a low camera angle has been used in places to perhaps give a sense of a strong individual. Consider all of this for yourself and ask the same three questions as for *Donnie Darko* above:

- Why has this opening camera movement been chosen, and how does it work to introduce the film and the central character?
- In what ways is it appropriate for the film and the character?
- How does it contribute towards ensuring that the opening engages our attention?

There is much more that could be said about camerawork and many more terms that could be used, but the essential point to recognize is the range of possibilities that are open to the director/cinematographer. And also of course that every choice of position, movement or lens will be made with the aim of creating some sort of impression on the spectator and generating some meaning. Film exists only in relation to those who are watching it. (This is a key point, perhaps *the* key point: do think about it carefully.)

Be reassured that knowing all of the technical terms here is not what Film Studies is really essentially all about. The important thing is to respond thoughtfully to the way in which the camera is being used to create potential meanings for you as a reader. Try to work out what the filmmakers are attempting to get you to feel and think about; these are the important things. Asking yourself why this or that technique has been used; this is the crux of the matter. Knowing the technical terms simply allows you to describe in a succinct, shorthand fashion the effect within the film that you are attempting to focus upon.

ACTIVITY

1   If possible, watch the opening to *Donnie Darko*, *Jackie Brown* and one other film of your choice.
2   Try to find time to discuss these scenes with other people, noting any particular aspects of camerawork you find interesting. Do not be afraid to play and replay these scenes as many times as necessary in order to try to see exactly how the camera is being used.

(You need to attempt to detach yourself from the narrative so that you are mentally in the position of watching over the shoulder of the cinematographer as the scene is being filmed.)

The skill mentioned above of being able to detach yourself from the film and imagine you are on location with the crew as they are filming is immensely useful for Film Studies. Essentially it involves the attempt to try to imagine just how the shots you are being given as a viewer of the film have been achieved.

ACTIVITY

■   Watch *Little Miss Sunshine* from the moment the father, Richard, says there is a phone message for Olive to the long shot of the camper van travelling through an arid semi-desert landscape (15 minutes 40 seconds to 21 minutes 40 seconds).
■   Working with others if possible, analyse the camerawork employed in this extract.
■   Try to identify particular uses of close-ups, two-shots, tracking shots, panning shots and handheld camera movements. Are there any shots in which the characters seem to be rather small within the frame almost swamped by the setting, shots in which the camera seems to

continued

be further away from the characters than would be strictly necessary so that more of the surroundings are taken in? Are there distinct phases within the extract where one sort of camerawork or another dominates? How does depth of field vary from shot to shot?

■ In each case make sure you not only identify the nature of the camerawork being employed but also discuss thoroughly why each choice has been made.

Case study
LITTLE MISS SUNSHINE (2006)

Little Miss Sunshine is a wonderful example of the preoccupation of Hollywood with the family and family relationships. There is often an over-riding concern with dysfunctional families and/or dysfunctional individuals within mainstream American film. Repeatedly the drive behind the narrative is to restore functionality, either by eradicating those seen to be dysfunctional or by restoring them (and thereby their immediate family) to acceptable functionality.

Figure 1.12 *Little Miss Sunshine* (2006)

You may like to consider why this is the case: What does it suggest about American society? Is it comforting for members of society to see these problems resolved on the screen? Is it reassuring to experience films dealing with problems that cannot be addressed effectively within society? Do these films direct attention towards resolving these issues within society at large, or do they detract from any sense of a 'real' and wider difficulty existing outside of the cinema?

Often 'problems' are seen as being safely contained and enclosed within the family (or within the individual) as if they are not a reflection of the wider society. This particular film, however, does also perhaps suggest some wider sense of dysfunction within American society through its examination of the nature of children's beauty pageants: this strange parading before the adult gaze of young (vulnerable) girls within a supposed context of innocence while also encouraging them to aspire towards a display of female sexuality.

(This is a difficult issue that is pushing you as a student to see film within a wider social (and ultimately political) context. Gradually over the two years of this course you should begin to fit films into these wider contexts but don't worry if at the moment this is not something you've ever thought about before. If you can take on board the idea that films do not simply exist as entertainments that we go to see at the cinema but can also be seen as related to the society that produces them, you will have understood the main point and will be moving in the right direction.)

ACTIVITY

- Watch *Casino Royale* from the moment when Bond's helicopter lands to the close-up of Bond telling M (Judi Dench) that she knew he wouldn't let the case drop (52 minutes 0 seconds to 55 minutes 30 seconds).
- Working with others if possible, analyse the camerawork employed in this extract.
- Try to identify particular uses of close-ups, two-shots, tracking shots, panning shots and zooms. Consider the use of particular angles for shots and whether the camera is static or moving. How does depth of field vary from shot to shot?
- Make sure you not only identify the nature of the camerawork being employed at each moment but also find time to discuss thoroughly why each choice has been made.

Editing

After the film has been shot in the camera it still has to be edited, and what you will have found while discussing camerawork is that it is actually almost impossible to talk about either of these two elements of film construction in isolation. Editing gives narrative shape and coherence to the array of shot sequences recorded by the camera(s). This part of the process involves hours of film that may have been taken being cut to what is as a matter of convention deemed to be an appropriate exhibition length: sometimes 90 minutes, usually around 120 minutes, and occasionally 150–180 minutes. As with much else connected with narrative film, these lengths seem to owe most to the traditional time spans allocated for theatre drama, and apart from that there seems little reason for the choice of the lengths of films shown at cinemas.

Shots, scenes and sequences

A shot is an uninterrupted number of frames during which no cutting takes place. Within this combination of frames the camera may be static, or pan or tilt, or track or dolly, or move on a crane, or combine any arrangement of these movements in any one of an infinite array of possibilities (limited only by the imagination and ingenuity of the filmmakers). As long as there is no break in the film that either suddenly moves us to an entirely new location, or instantly changes the position of the camera within the same location without our being aware of the movement that has taken the camera to this new vantage point, then we remain within the same shot.

A scene is a section of film that attempts to give the illusion of uninterrupted action taking place within one continuous space or place during one continuous moment in time. This can often be highly edited so that we can, for example, shift backwards and forwards between a series of viewpoints of different characters as an exchange between the group members takes place in any given location. The camera in fact 'jumps' between positions in order to give the viewer the story of what is happening between these characters within this space during this particular moment in time. We accept the editing cuts, or 'jumps', from one position to another because of our familiarity with this as one of the conventions attaching to film narrative story-telling. Or perhaps we accept them because of the powerful forward momentum of storytelling that sweeps us up and carries us forward in our desire and curiosity to know what happens next. There is also the fact that skilled editors cover the 'jumps' in various ways so that they are not as immediately obvious as might otherwise be the case. So, for example, if two people are talking we have a shot reverse-shot pattern in which we see one person talking from over the shoulder of the listener and then jump to a view from over the shoulder of the original speaker in order to see the reply to the initial piece of dialogue. The convention here has become accepted over a long period and so is seen as unobtrusive, but also we actually desire the shift as a viewer in order to find out what the second speaker has to say. The editing is carried out at the moment we desire the move in order to not only hear but also see the reply, and so it is experienced by us as in some way 'natural' despite the fact that it is in fact highly contrived.

You may like to think about the whole notion of what is considered 'natural' and what is not. Is anything that human beings do 'natural'? If so, to what actions or sorts of actions would you apply this term? Are most things that we call 'natural' actually learnt or socially ingrained behaviours? Are women 'naturally' mothers? Are men 'naturally' aggressive and women 'naturally' passive?

A sequence is a series of related scenes that for some clear and logical reason hold together as a coherent whole. Taken together the scenes in a sequence may be considered as a well-defined, integrated 'unit' from the overall narrative. Therefore, if you are going to describe a particular section of a film as being a sequence, you should have a clear reason for doing so that shows the consecutive combination of scenes under consideration as functioning in some sense as an integrated whole within the overall narrative structure.

ACTIVITY

- Watch the opening seven minutes 30 seconds of Fritz Lang's *M* (1931).
- Work in groups to storyboard this sequence of scenes showing clearly each shot that is used. You should end up with about 25 individual shots. Within this there will be at least two that contain elaborate camera movements – one near the beginning as the camera moves up and away from the children to the woman on the walkway above, and another when Elsie is bouncing her ball and moves to the poster where she meets the murderer.
- How many scenes are there? Notice how this is complicated by the section where we switch backwards and forwards between Elsie's mother at home and Elsie on her way home from school.
- The application of the concept of 'sequence' is rather arbitrary and ultimately down to individual judgement. However, how would you describe the integral 'coherence' that this series of scenes might be said to have that would enable us to describe it as a sequence?

(This is also an excellent piece of film to analyse in four groups with each group taking one from either *mise-en-scène*, cinematography, editing or sound, in order to identify key points about film construction. *M* is not the sort of film you are expected to deal with in the first year of A level where the focus is on American and British film, but if you have the time it is good to challenge yourself occasionally. It is also the sort of exercise you might consider coming back to right at the end of the AS year in order to begin to move towards the A2 year.)

To use a long take, or a montage of shots

For some theorists (as mentioned previously) the long take involving filming a lengthy sequence of events without cuts has been seen to be the essence of filmmaking allowing the spectator to follow a whole scene as a privileged 'presence'. (This idea was taken to its logical extreme in a film called *Russian Ark* (Sokurov, 2002) which was one highly choreographed long take without editing.) For others who have come up with theories about the best way to make films, cutting a variety of shots together in a montage that challenges the spectator to make meaning from perceived connections between the shots has been seen as the key to filmmaking. At its extreme, under this approach each shot is fleeting and depends for meaning on the equally fleeting shots that precede and follow it. In practice, most filmmakers have not gone to extremes with their use of either cinematography or editing but have instead recognized that both are useful tools of their trade and can be employed effectively in combination with each other.

Continuity editing

For Hollywood, continuity editing has been seen to be the key approach to this area of film construction. Here the effort is to make the editing as unobtrusive as possible, to prevent the audience from becoming aware of the cuts. The attempt is to make shots appear to 'flow' from one to the other. One trick is to ensure that all shots show the subjects from one side. This is what is known as the 180-degree rule whereby if you have two people standing next to each other there is considered to be an imaginary line running from one to the other over which the camera is not allowed to venture. If the camera moves across this line the effect will be for the two characters to appear to suddenly jump from one side of the shot to the other.

- Try this for yourselves. Organize a set-up with two people talking to each other, film them from one side and then move behind them and look through the viewfinder.
- Return to *M* and watch how Lang handles this movement across the imaginary 180-degree line when the washerwoman is talking to the mother early in the sequence. Does it feel like a 'jump'? Did you notice it as such on a first viewing?

Editors can also 'cut on action'. This involves making the cut at a point where a character is performing a certain action and then filming the completion of the same action from a different position. The action that is taking place provides a strand of continuity for the viewer who is absorbed in the action taking place and therefore barely registers the edit that has occurred. It is also possible to use 'eyeline matches' to 'cover' a cut, or make it go as unnoticed as possible. In this technique a character looks at something off-screen and there is then a cut to show, from roughly that same character's position within the imagined space, whatever she has been looking at.

You will notice how crucial the viewer is to the editing process and to maintaining the sense of continuity under discussion. The editor constructs the scene with great care from a series of carefully put together shots, but it is the viewer who must maintain within their mind an imagined space (including off-screen space) within which certain characters are 'held in place' in relation to each other as they perform certain actions.

Editing tools and 'tricks'

Editors can use straight cuts so that we are instantaneously transported from one shot to another. Or they can use 'fades' where the shot fades out to a blank screen (and fades in to the next shot from a blank screen), or 'dissolves' where through superimposition one shot dissolves into another; or a range of other less used transitions. They can aim to maintain continuity through using cause and effect, ensuring each shot has a 'cause' in the previous shot and an 'effect' in the following shot. Or they can construct a discontinuous sequence that disorientates the spectator and makes them 'work' to make sense of the series of images with which they are confronted. At all times the juxtaposition of shots will be vital to the creation of meaning, with one shot in some way 'commenting on' or adjusting the potential meaning of the previous shot.

Case study
THE KILLING FIELDS (1984)

[Director: Roland Joffé. Screenwriter: Bruce Robinson. Editor: Jim Clark. Cinematographer: Chris Menges. Music: Mike Oldfield. Cast: Sam Waterston (Sydney Schanberg), Dr Haing Ngor (Dith Pran), and John Malkovich (Al Rockoff).]

Camerawork and editing

There is an interesting scene in this film around the point where Pol Pot's rebel communist forces are entering the outskirts of Phnom Pen. The journalist, Sydney Schanberg, whose story we are following, finds himself in a Coca-Cola warehouse and the 'camera-eye' (from a privileged viewer's position) becomes involved in trying to make sense of the situation. Initially it calmly surveys the scene taking in the irony of the expulsion of American influence from this country occurring in the midst of so much bottled essence

Figure 1.13 *The Killing Fields* (1984)

of American Dream. As soon as the first explosion takes place, however, perhaps significantly shattering the fragile glass bottles, the camerawork becomes increasingly frantic and the editing from shot to shot much quicker. Thus the sudden confusion of the situation is reinforced and the spectator finds herself having to work at an increased pace to take in all the images being thrown in front of her. Images of Coca-Cola dispenser machines and lorries (first of all relatively intact even if broken but later being blown up) continually intrude, inter-cut with shots of child soldiers, lost or abandoned toddlers screaming, and cattle in their death throes. East and West are continually juxtaposed, the West in the shape of high-tech weapons and Coca-Cola, and the East in the shape of a low-tech Cambodian bullock cart way of life. Coca-Cola is the symbol, perhaps, of Western capitalism, the American way of life, multinational globalization of trade, and American imperialism. We note the American soldier's introduction of himself as 'Made in the USA' as well as the way he enters at speed, in a jeep, sounding the horn. However, more powerfully than anything else because of the editing the spectator notices the presence of children in this extract: this is an indictment of war, and of what war does to ordinary people and to children, and the innocence of children. These children have guns instead of toys: see the carefully composed shot of the child-soldier firing above a dead child and the final shot of the child crying with his hands over his ears. Through the juxtaposition of a series of shots additional meaning is produced (although the exact nature of that meaning is highly dependent upon the work being done in terms of interpretation by the viewer).

(Although this look at *The Killing Fields* has been subtitled 'camerawork and editing' you will have noticed that the reality is that we cannot divorce these elements of film construction from *mise-en-scène* (setting, performance and movement, costume and props) and we certainly cannot divorce all of this from the way in which film continually works to create meaning for us.)

In order to achieve special effects, editors can superimpose one image on top of another. They can hold the superimposition for long enough to give the viewer a clear sense of one image being on top of another or they can move it through more quickly so that we barely register the overlaying process that has occurred. If the technique is used there is clearly some sort of relationship between the two images that is being suggested. The commentary of one shot on another that is achieved through the juxtaposition of shots is in a sense intensified by this process of superimposition. Famously, at the end of *Psycho* (1960), the face of the central character, Norman Bates, is superimposed over the skull of his dead mother that viewers have seen previously.

Editing and time

It is via editing that film is able to transport the spectator through space and time, allowing a flashback to a previous temporal and spatial dimension (and even flash forward to the future) to take place or permitting movement (cross-cutting) between parallel actions taking place contemporaneously. In *La Haine* the film-makers need to show the boredom of everyday life for young unemployed people living in the working-class satellite towns around Paris: a single static shot of our three central characters sitting equidistant from each other in a bleak, waste area is held for some time and then a flash-forward edit is used to a shot of the same three characters in the same space but occupying slightly different positions within the frame. Because they have moved slightly we experience the cut as a 'jump', a jump forward in time. It is the combination of holding the initial shot for longer than we might normally expect and then using a distinctive editing cut that ensures the required meaning is conveyed clearly and effectively to the viewer.

Figure 1.14 *La Haine* (1995)

'Jump cuts' where, in contrast to continuity editing, attention is deliberately drawn to the cut that has taken place, are often used by filmmakers to confuse or disorientate the viewer. If, for example, the viewer is being placed within a chaotic situation in which people are rushing in all directions, then a sense of the resulting confusion can be given through a form of editing that confuses the viewer's sense of a coherent imagined space. There are various ways this can be achieved: the 180-degree line could be broken, the camera could suddenly shift to take in the action from a totally different angle than the previous shot, or the camera could appear to be in the same position but suddenly the background could change. In each case clearly the type of 'jump', or 'jolt', that is being experienced would be different but in each case the effort would be to draw attention to the cut rather than the more usual process of attempting to make the cut pass unnoticed.

Editing pace

Clearly if a film cuts rapidly from one shot to another and maintains this pace of editing for a sustained period then the experience for the viewer is very different from that gained when sitting before a film in which for the same period there are few (or no) edits. The classic example is obviously the chase scene in which editing invariably speeds up in order to enhance, and even replicate, the sense of frenetic activity taking place. By way of contrast we would usually expect a romantic love scene to be handled in an entirely different way centring on a much slower pace of editing. As with all other elements of film construction the technique can be used to achieve a multitude of meanings for and responses from the audience. In critically analysing a film sequence the first job is to recognize the pace of editing being used and then as always to ask ourselves why this approach has been chosen. It would be possible to edit a love scene using a fast pace of cutting, for example, although then we might hesitate from labelling it a 'romantic' love scene and might feel that an entirely different response was being generated, perhaps a comic effect.

ACTIVITY

- Experiment with the pace of editing. In groups film a short scene you have created yourself as a storyboard, or that you have copied from a well-known movie. Film and edit it in such a way that you have two versions, one in which there are just one or two long takes and the other in which you chop and change between a whole array of different shots. At its simplest you might have an exchange of dialogue between two people sitting next to each other in the same frame and then film the same exchange using shot, reverse-shot technique. If you wish you could take a section from the exchange between Cynthia and Hortense in *Secrets and Lies* (Leigh, 1996) in which the two characters sit next to each other and then try to replicate the same exchange as shot, reverse-shot.
- Show the two versions of your film not simply to the group who have been involved in the filmmaking but to a wider audience if possible, and discuss the ways in which people respond to the two versions.

A montage is a quick succession of shots that attempts to convey a lot of information in a short span of screen time. Often in Classical Hollywood films the attempt will be to suggest the passage of a lengthy period of time; so, famously in *Citizen Kane* (Welles, 1941) the increasing physical and psychological distance between Kane and his first wife over a period of time is shown within a two-minute montage of shots of them around the breakfast table. But, by way of direct contrast, in the equally famous Odessa Steps sequence in *Battleship Potemkin* (Eisenstein, 1925) the information conveyed through a montage of shots relates to something that has taken place in a very short space of time rather than an extended period. Here it is the effort to express the intensity of the mayhem experienced as ordinary people are attacked and shot by advancing soldiers that has dictated Eisenstein's decision to use a technique of rapid cutting.

ACTIVITY

- Return to the extract from *Little Miss Sunshine* discussed under cinematography (15 minutes 40 seconds to 21 minutes 40 seconds). After rewatching this section of the film, if possible discuss with others the nature of the editing employed.
- How does the pace of the editing vary? Is this piece of film careful to use continuity editing? Try to give examples of this. Are there any sections within the extract where a longer take has been employed? Are there any uses of a shot reverse-shot technique? (There is one example of this technique that is slightly complicated by the continual addition of a further shot type within the sequence.)
- Make sure you discuss as fully as possible why you believe each editing choice has been made.

(Because the elements of film construction operate within a sequence as an integrated whole you may well find that you have already discussed some of these issues if you undertook the previous activity relating to this extract. Even so, you should still attempt to clarify your thoughts but this time with a specific focus upon editing.)

ACTIVITY

- Return to the extract from *Casino Royale* discussed under cinematography (52 minutes 0 seconds to 55 minutes 30 seconds). After rewatching this section of the film, if possible discuss with others the nature of the editing employed.
- Does the pace of the editing vary? Is this piece of film careful to use continuity editing? Try to give examples of ways in which strict continuity rules might be broken here. Are there any sections within the extract where a longer take has been employed? Are there any uses of a shot reverse-shot technique?
- Make sure you discuss as fully as possible why you believe each editing choice has been made.

Sound

What we have considered so far in this chapter are those elements of film construction that deal with the visual aspects of filmmaking, but there is of course a further obvious dimension to film, that of sound. This may be said to operate on three levels: via dialogue or vocals, sound effects, and musical accompaniment.

Each of these three aspects of sound can be recorded during the shooting of a film or added afterwards. The use of direct sound recorded on location may be employed in an attempt to create a particular sense of realism, in which case passing unanticipated sounds that occur as filming is taking place (perhaps a police or ambulance siren) may be retained on the final soundtrack. The alternative to direct sound and that favoured by mainstream cinema is the use of archived recordings of sound effects or music that can be added afterwards in the studio, or the use of sound effects and music specially created and recorded for the film.

Recording vocals in the studio means the audience are given a highly privileged position in which they are able to hear clearly everything that is being said. Depending on the particular scene and the amount of turmoil that is taking place within it, this enhancement of the vocals can amount to a highly artificial experience. However, as with continuity editing, since we are brought up with these film conventions (and since we are being carried forward by the intensity of our desire to follow the story) we accept what is in reality a highly contrived clarity of sound.

ACTIVITY

- Find a scene in a film you know where a range of types of sound seem to you to be used particularly effectively.
- In small groups screen your chosen scenes and explain why you think the filmmakers have chosen to use sound in these ways at this point in their film. In particular, try to explain how you think the particular uses of sound found in your film extract contribute to meaning and enhance audience response.

The uses to which sound can be put range from merely conveying a sense of realism to helping to suggest quite subtle aspects of character or theme. In a sequence from *Seven* mentioned earlier, the younger detective, Mills, is allocated his own murder case to work on after displaying great confidence in the police chief's office (low-angle camera shots, for example, adding to a sense of his personal assurance in this scene). However, when he arrives at the scene of the murder and walks in we follow him, and the sound we are given is what may be described as 'point of view' sound, the indistinct, half-audible voices of those around him. It is this distinctive use of sound (added to several other aspects of film construction such as performance and editing) that gives the viewer the idea that Mills is in fact not as confident as his 'performance' in the police chief's office might have suggested.

ACTIVITY

- View *Casino Royale* from the moment Bond and Vesper Lynd enter the hotel reception area to pick up a package to the point at which Bond hides the bodies of his attackers under the stairs (1 hour 14 minutes 35 seconds to 1 hour 18 minutes 33 seconds). But pay special attention to the variety of ways in which sound is employed in this extract.
- List as many different sound effects (SFX) as you can identify. Does each example of SFX sound authentic? If not, what seems to have been done to the sound and did you recognize it as unrealistic on a first viewing?
- List the different uses of vocals in the extract. Note in particular where volume, pitch, tone or emphasis have been used in a particular way.

- Are there any moments at which a musical soundtrack is not employed? Try to identify moments at which there seems to be some significant change to the music and try to explain how and why this change has occurred.
- As usual, for each sound that is identified you need to ask yourself why the filmmaker has made this choice of sound, remembering that there may often be several types of sound functioning together in order to achieve a particular end.

INFORMATION BOX – SILENT CINEMA

i

The period stretching from the start of cinema in the mid-1890s to about 1930 has come to be known as silent cinema; although in fact it was no such thing, with live musical accompaniment being the order of the day from early on. In creative terms this music (provided by anything from a single piano to a small orchestra) added meaning by, for example, enhancing dramatic or romantic moments; while in practical terms it drowned out any accompanying mechanical noises from the projector.

Dialogue

Clearly dialogue (which may include a narrator's voiceover) is today an important part of film and vital to our perception and understanding of the narrative. It makes a critical contribution to the way in which we gauge who the characters are, what they are like, what they have done, what they are going to do and what their relationship might be to others in the film. But dialogue is also often critical in alerting us to any wider ideas or themes that might be dealt with by the film. So, in the extract considered above from *The Killing Fields*, although it was minimal, dialogue contributed to our awareness of the importance for the film-makers of the theme of American imperialism and globalization of trade, with the American officer using the very distinctive phrase 'made in the USA' to describe himself. In *La Haine* the word 'killer' comes back time and again, particularly as a way of describing the punch-line to a story, and in the light of the film's ending this usage takes on a special resonance.

Sound effects

In addition to dialogue there are also sound effects. These may be used simply to enhance a realistic sense of place, as in the use of traffic noise for a city street setting. However, they may move beyond this and work to engage heightened audience response and expectation, as in the sound of the kitchen knife being drawn from its holder in the opening to *Scream* (Craven, 1996).

Or, to return to our traffic noise, look at *Seven* to see how the noise of the city as this oppressive, intrusive presence is always there in the background. In *La Haine* you will find that the sound of the Metro train running on its tracks which might be seen simply to add to a sense of realism is in fact also used at the start of the final sequence to echo what is perhaps the key recurring sound effect in the film: that of a clock ticking. In the opening to *M* the sound of the girl bouncing her ball performs the same function of echoing a clock ticking.

Sound effects can also come from off-screen, creating a very particular response from the audience in which they have to imagine something they cannot see on screen. Clearly this use of sound can have special purposes within a genre such as horror. In addition, dialogue can also originate from off-screen space. Here an audience can be given a visual image but hear a voice from elsewhere, commenting on the visual as it were. You might like to look back to the opening to *M* again to see how Lang handles this possibility.

Sounds from the everyday world such as thunder and lightning may be used to convey the sorts of connotations normally associated with these noises (in the case of thunder and lightning this would obviously be something like sudden fear). However, it should be noted that sound effects are often considerably enhanced and not at all what you would hear in the natural world with all sorts of imaginative activities being used by Foley artists (the people who create sounds in the studio) to produce a range of sounds designed to generate particular responses from the audience.

Figure 1.15 Drew Barrymore in *Scream* (1996)

Background music

There is also the possibility of using background music that does not arise realistically out of the imagined world on screen to give a sense of mood or atmosphere. If you ever hear people suggesting that film is a naturalistic medium you could alert them to this use of music in film. (Where are the violins, is it just me who is not hearing them?) In addition to having the flexibility to 'describe' emotions, moods, characters, relationships and place, music can direct the viewer's attention to a particular aspect of the action or suggest a particular time period.

It is important to remember that silence, the absence of sound, can be used just as effectively (and sometimes more effectively) to create audience engagement. Again, as with all other elements of film construction, if there is a period of silence on the soundtrack it is likely to have been chosen and placed there very deliberately in order to achieve a particular effect.

One of the difficulties with discussing the use of music within film (or discussing music in general) is that it is often difficult to find words that adequately explain the response generated by the sound. Language seems to be inadequate to give a full sense of the effects of a passage of music. Nevertheless, the effort often needs to be made and the best way to do this is sometimes to start by brainstorming a series of associated and linked words that might help your description. So, if you associate fear with a particular piece of music used in a film you might brainstorm words like 'dread', 'apprehension', 'dismay', 'horror', 'panic' and 'anxiety', and you might then find that some of these words help you to express more clearly how the music makes you feel as you watch the film.

ACTIVITY

■ Find a scene in a film you know where silence seems to be used particularly effectively.
■ In small groups screen your chosen scenes and explain why you think the filmmakers have chosen to use silence at this point in their film, and how you think it contributes to meaning and enhances audience response.

ACTIVITY

■ View *Pirates of the Caribbean: Dead Man's Chest* from the moment when we hear the first rendition of 'Fifteen Men on a Dead Man's Chest' to the point at which we cut away to a long shot of Jack's ship sailing away beneath storm-filled skies (4 minutes 10 seconds to 9 minutes 30 seconds). Pay special attention to the variety of ways in which sound is employed in this extract.
■ List as many different sound effects as you can identify. Does each example of SFX sound authentic?
■ List the different uses of vocals in the extract. Note in particular where volume, pitch, tone or emphasis has been used in a particular way.
■ Are there any moments at which a musical soundtrack is not employed? Try to identify moments at which there seems to be some significant change to the music and try to explain how and why this change has occurred.
■ How does sound work to bring us into this sequence from the scene that has gone before and to take us out to the next scene?
■ As usual, for each sound that is identified you need to ask yourself why the filmmaker has made this choice of sound, remembering that there may often be several forms of sound functioning together in order to achieve a particular end.

Sound editing

As with the visual shots there will be moments when one sound is replaced by another, when in effect we cut from one sound to another. With sound this is further complicated by the layered effect that is often achieved. So, for instance, there may be several sound effects being used at the same moment. As with visuals rather than straight cuts it is possible to have one sound fading out as its replacement fades in; in effect, a dissolve is achieved.

Usually, as the visuals for one scene end so too will the sound, and then a new set of sounds will begin with the new scene. However, sound can sometimes be carried over from one scene into the next; so, if there is a scene in a street with appropriate noises, that sound may continue in a more muffled way into a following scene that moves the action indoors. Or, if the characters are preparing to move outside, a sound from the next scene such as the wind howling may begin when they are still inside. The key point to note is that as with the editing of visuals the editing of sound offers a range of suggestive possibilities and an infinite number of possible permutations.

Film Form: overview

Filmmakers use a vast array of strategies for communicating ideas and/or emotions. These revolve around the use of various settings, the presentation of character, the application of a range of camera techniques, the editing of shots into particular scenes and sequences, and the use of sound. Each of these strategies is used to influence our perception of events as shown and deliberately suggest ways of making sense of any film. Awareness of the techniques being used and careful consideration of the effects that might be achieved by the application of these techniques is perhaps the fundamental skill required by anyone wishing to study film, since it enables us to either accept or reject the suggested meanings that seem to be on offer.

ACTIVITY

1   Watch the whole of any film mentioned earlier in this chapter; then, with a group of others if possible, choose one sequence of no more than seven minutes to analyse in detail.
2   Spend time as a group discussing how your chosen sequence works in terms of its use of *mise-en-scène*, cinematography, editing and sound.
3   Individually write a commentary (1,000–1,200 words) discussing the ways in which one or two of these areas of film construction work

to create meaning and generate audience response in your chosen sequence. Give your piece of writing a title in the form of a question:

How do *mise-en-scène* and/or cinematography and/or sound and/or editing work to create meaning and generate audience response in the (*name or timing of scene*) scene in (*name of film*)?

Case study
ORPHANS (1999)

(Director: Peter Mullan. Producer: Frances Higson. Scriptwriter: Peter Mullan. Cast: Michael (Douglas Henshall); Thomas (Gary Lewis); John (Stephen Cole); Sheila (Rosemarie Stevenson); Tanga (Frank Gallagher).)

Figure 1.16
Orphans (1999)

The opening sequence to this film offers an interesting contrast in camera movement and carefully directed understated performances from the actors.

In the initial shot we are shown a series of objects before a hand comes in from the right to pick up a pair of scissors. In film terminology this is an example of props being used for particular effects. What is our reaction to each of these items and how does starting like this make the spectator feel? Is the response different on a first viewing compared with subsequent viewings, and if so how? There are a lot of items here. Make sure you identify each of them and consider their significance.

It is only after this series of shots that there is a cut to a shot of the room in which these objects are to be found and we gain some impression of the four main characters. The spatial context within which the scene is about to be played out is established. How do we view these characters in relation to the previous panning shot of the objects? In other words, how does this cut work? What response does it gain from the audience? Again, does our understanding change or develop on subsequent viewings, and if so in what way(s)? How do we initially respond to each of the main characters and what is it about them that makes us respond in this way? Notice at this point the role that casting might be said to play in the process of creating meaning and how important dress, appearance, body language and the smallest of movements can be in creating understanding.

How does camera movement contribute to creating meaning at this stage? How would you describe the camera movement and how does it make the audience feel? What is the effect on the audience of the central prop in the room and how is the camera movement appropriate for a scene involving this sort of prop? How do we feel as the scissors are passed around? How does each character use the scissors and what does this tell us about them? At each point notice the responses of the other actors as well as the particular character with the scissors. In what order are the scissors passed around and why?

When the haircutting is over how do we respond to Sheila's request to kiss her mother and the way in which Michael and John lift Sheila? How do we feel as an audience at this point? (Remember that we could feel several emotions at any one point in a film and that it is even possible that these emotions could be contradictory.) How are the ways in which each of the characters performs the kissing individualized? What about the things each character has to say during this time around the coffin? How are the lines both in terms of content and delivery appropriate for each character? What other sounds apart from the characters talking are used in this scene, and why?

When we move to the next shots of the box, how do we feel as an audience, and why do we feel this? Then, when we cut to the four siblings again, how are they arranged in relation to each other and in what ways might this be significant? How would you describe the camera movement at this point and in what way could it be considered as appropriate and contributing meaning to the scene? How does sound now begin to work? How would you describe the following elaborate camera movement and why has it been chosen? How do the colours change at this point and why has the change been chosen by the filmmakers? How do the colours used at this point contrast with the earlier shots around the coffin? In what ways are the mother's words and the setting given to this flashback scene appropriate? What other sounds can you hear in the scene and why have they been chosen?

Using the notes you have made in response to these questions write an analysis of the ways in which film language creates meaning in the opening sequence of *Orphans* (1,000–1,500 words).

CONCLUSION

- A film is constructed from the *mise-en-scène*, cinematography, editing and sound.
- The possible combinations of these elements available to filmmakers are endless.
- In analysing film we can dissect these chosen uses to understand how meaning is created in film.

References and Further Reading

Argyle, M. (1972) 'Non-verbal communication in human social interaction' in Hinde, R. *Non-verbal Communication*, Cambridge University Press, Cambridge quoted in Fiske, J. (1982) *Introduction to Communication Studies*, Routledge, London.

Bennett, P., Hickman, A. and Wall, P. (2007) *Film Studies: The Essential Resource*, Routledge, London and New York (chs 1, 2 and 11)

Bordwell, D. and Thompson, K. (2000) *Film Art: An Introduction*, McGraw Hill, New York (chs 5, 6, 7 and 8)

Lacey, N. (2005) *Introduction to Film*, Palgrave Macmillan, Basingstoke and New York (ch. 1)

Nelmes, Jill (ed.) (2003) *An Introduction to Film Studies*, Routledge, London (ch. 4)

Phillips, W. H. (2005) *Film: An Introduction* (3rd edn), Bedford/St Martin's, Boston, MA (chs 1 to 4)

Roberts, G. and Wallis, H. (2001) *Introducing Film*, Arnold, London (chs 1, 2 and 3).

Useful Websites

www.bfi.org.uk
www.filmeducation.org
www.imdb.com/Glossary

2 SPECTATORSHIP

In this chapter we will consider how we should approach a film we have not seen before. We deal with:

- essential questions to ask yourself when studying a new film
- the importance of adopting a pro-active, questioning attitude
- possible model approaches to interrogating films

INFORMATION BOX *i*

In terms of preparing for the WJEC's AS in Film Studies, this chapter should help you to draw together ideas for a sensibly organized approach to the viewing of films. This chapter will outline the underpinning approach necessary to the work you will be doing under FM1 – Exploring Film Form and FM2 – British and American Film.

Films mentioned

If you are working your way through the whole or parts of this chapter you will find it helpful to have access to scenes, clips and single shots from at least some of the following films:

- *My Beautiful Laundrette* (Frears, 1985)
- *My Son the Fanatic* (Prasad, 1997)
- *Independence Day* (Emmerich, 1996)
- *La Haine* (Kassovitz, 1995)
- *Sin City* (Miller/Rodriguez/Tarantino, 2005)

Questions

By now you should have noticed just how much emphasis is being placed in this book on the need to adopt a continually questioning approach towards film. In order to analyse a film text it is being suggested that we need to be prepared to ask ourselves a whole range of key questions. This chapter will try to give a brief overview of what those central questions should be.

The fundamental basis to this approach is that we should always confront ourselves with the question of why the filmmakers have chosen to use certain sounds or images at particular points in their film. Remembering that there are a whole array of possible choices and combinations of choices (with regard to setting, costume, props, performance, camerawork, sound and editing) before the filmmakers, we must question why particular clearly identifiable choices have been made.

Posing questions for ourselves as we watch films is at the heart of film analysis. In order to study film effectively we need to have questions such as the following in mind throughout the viewing experience.

1 Messages and values

- What are the main subject areas of interest in this film and what are the main themes and ideas being addressed? Could it be said that there are certain key messages and values that underpin the film?
- Answering these sorts of questions demands the ability to be able to stand back from the narrative and attempt to see the film from an objective distance, but we can make it seem to be much more difficult than it actually is. For example, if the film is made within a predominantly white society but focuses on an ethnic minority, as with films such as *My Beautiful Laundrette* (Frears, 1985) or *My Son the Fanatic* (Prasad, 1997) (these films could be considered further under FM2 British Film: Identity Study – 'Being British'), then the film will inevitably be dealing with issues of race in some form or other. And, if you have a Hollywood film that is called *Thelma and Louise* (Scott, 1991), there is a good chance that in some form or other it might have something to say about the female experience in modern Western society. Or, if you have a film entitled *Independence Day* (Emmerich, 1996) (see FM2, Section C, US Film – Comparative Study), it is very likely to be addressing the American understanding of the United States as a freedom-loving democracy.
- Of course, you need to go further than this and ask in some detail exactly how men and women, or different races, cultures and creeds are represented in any particular film. Do they comply with stereotypical role models, or defy the conventional and challenge social norms in some way? Or, exactly how are ideas of democracy and freedom being represented and with what relationship to the politics of the real world?

La Haine (Kassovitz, 1995) has been attacked as a film that has a message that is anti-police: whether this is true or not would depend upon how we interpreted characters and scenes within the film and how we understood the filmmakers to be using film construction techniques to emphasize and elevate certain perspectives above others. This may also, of course, depend upon your own personal views about 'the police' and your background within any particular community. At its most obvious, if you were a policeman yourself you might read *La Haine* and its messages differently than if you were a member of a minority ethnic group feeling itself under pressure from mainstream society. *My Beautiful Laundrette*, in part, deals with homosexuality. If you're homophobic you might well respond to this film in a different way from someone who was more prepared to be accepting of sexual difference. It also features characters who are right-wing members of the National Front, and, depending on your politics, you could respond to the portrayal of these people in a whole range of ways. *The Crying Game* was heavily criticized for offering a sympathetic representation of a character that was essentially, in mainstream political terminology, an IRA terrorist.

Figure 2.1 *The Crying Game* (1992)

Fergus, the character in question, deals directly with the issue of the naming or labelling of those who are involved in such organizations when he describes himself as a 'volunteer'. In contrast with soldiers in the British Army he is not doing this as a job; he didn't enlist and then by chance find himself in Northern Ireland; he volunteered because this was a cause in which he believed. Clearly we might respond to this aspect of the film in a whole variety of ways that would largely depend upon our cultural background. If we were members of the Roman Catholic minority in Northern Ireland we might respond very differently from people from a Protestant Loyalist background. However, just because we lived and had been brought up in one very particular community would not necessarily dictate that we would respond in the same way as others from 'our' community; we might have personal views over and beyond, or even at odds with, the more general ones of 'our' community.

ACTIVITY

- *My Son the Fanatic* deals in part with a father's response to seeing his son become a Muslim fundamentalist. How would you respond to such a film? What prejudices would you bring with you to watching the film?
- Outline how you think you would respond to such a film (100–200 words). If possible, exchange your work with other people and read their responses.
- Watch the film and then return to your initial thoughts in your piece of writing and assess whether you actually responded in the way you expected.
- Discuss this experience with others, listening carefully to what they have to say in order to gauge any similarities or differences between their response and your response.

2 Genre

- Is this film typical of any particular genre (e.g. sci-fi, horror, action, comedy, musical, road movie) or sub-genre (e.g. dystopia, alien invasion, 'slasher', vampire, zombie)? In what ways is it typical and in what ways is it not typical (or atypical)?
- Could this film be said to use several genres, and if so which ones and why have they been combined in this way? Does it demonstrate the current trend towards hybrid genres?
- More importantly, how does the chosen genre relate to views and perspectives in society in general, and how does it reflect the period in which it has been

made? How does a noir film like *Sin City* (Miller/Rodriguez/Tarantino, 2005), for example, adapt its particular chosen genre and in doing so reflect contemporary society?

3 Narrative

■ How is the story being told: is a narrator used, and if so, why? Does s/he have a marginal or important role in the story itself? What effect does using a narrator or not have on the perspective given to the viewer?

■ How effective is the opening, and what makes it so? How effective is the ending, and what makes it so?

■ Are there clear moments of complication and climax within the film? Could you plot as if on a graph the rising tensions and climaxes of the story?

■ Could you usefully complete a diagram, or diagrams, representing the relationships between characters within the story?

■ Are conventional aspects of storytelling, such as the confrontation between good and evil, or the use of a journey as a narrative device, being employed?

■ Most importantly, what are the meanings being created for us by the particular narrative structure and devices being employed?

4 *Mise-en-scène*

■ What would be your evaluation of the performances of the actors? Are the characters created complex or simple to understand? Is their motivation clear? Are they rounded and complex, or flat and stereotypical?

■ What is the social status of each character and how dominant are they? Does their use of language reflect their character? What tone or attitude does each character adopt? What ideas or feelings are being expressed?

■ What can you tell about the character from the body language and delivery of lines? How long does each person speak and what does this tell us (in different circumstances it could convey different things, of course – a silent foreboding Clint Eastwood in a spaghetti western is very different from someone who is being marginalized by the force of events taking place, such as the rookie policeman forced to witness a racist attack by fellow officers in the interrogation room in *La Haine*)?

■ What is the significance of costume in particular scenes? Does it help to convey character and/or oppositions? Does it operate to mark out particular groups? Is it used simply to suggest period and place? Are the costumes wonderfully authentic but actually used to little effect in terms of conveying meaning to the audience?

■ Are there any significant uses of props? Are there any props used in such a way as to become recurring images? Do the props remind us of themes or ideas in the film, or tell us something about character?

■ How is the setting or location used? Is it used to create a sense of realism? Is it used to create mood? Is it used to create a sense of certain states of mind or feelings? Is it used to stand for, or symbolically represent, other things?

5 Cinematography

■ Are there any scenes or single shots in which you think the camerawork has been particularly effective? If so, how and why do you believe it to be successful?

■ What significance do particular shots or camera movements have in terms of creating meaning for us? (Referring to particular shots and scenes to illustrate meaning in this way will be a key skill.)

■ What is the significance of the lighting in particular scenes? Are some scenes particularly light or dark? If so, why? How is shadow being used? Is it being used in particular ways in relation to particular characters?

6 Sound

■ Do any extracts from the dialogue seem to be especially important? In what ways might these lines be seen to be significant? Why have particular words or phrases been chosen? If it is a Hollywood script the dialogue will have been honed to the bare minimum in all probability, which only means that each utterance is even more certain to have been chosen for a specific reason.

■ Are sound effects used simply to create a sense of place, or do they in some way contribute towards meaning over and above this?

■ What is the significance of the music chosen for particular scenes? How does it work to contribute to the creation of meaning? Is it diegetic or non-diegetic, and what difference does this make?

7 Editing

■ Is the pace of the editing in particular scenes giving us images that are flashing quickly before us, or images that we are able to survey in a leisurely way? Why has this style been chosen?

■ How do the shots as they are structured into sequences via editing work to create meaning? Is the manner in which one shot follows another used in such a way as to allow one to comment on the other?

■ Which images are stressed? Why? Are there repetitions of certain visual images, or parallels between individual shots or sequences?

Pro-active reading

With so much to look out for this must mean that our reading of films has to be intensely active and analytical; at no time should we sit before the screen in classic 'couch potato' mode. Naturally there is an extent to which we may simply wish to enjoy the cinema experience on first encountering any film. However, even during a first viewing we should remain alert; otherwise we potentially end up in the position apparently reached by a majority in Hitler's Germany of accepting the implied message behind watching shots of Jews intercut with shots of rats scurrying across the screen. Passivity before the media in any form allows that medium to be used not as a site of democratic discussion but as an agent of indoctrination. Josef Goebbels apparently said of *Jew Suss* (Harlen, 1940) in which the central character, an 'evil Jew', rapes Aryan women that it was: 'Highly recommended for its artistic value, and to serve the politics of the state recommended for young people.'

A practical approach

Obviously investigating a film in this way means that there are big questions raised that can never be answered in any final sense. Is *La Haine* anti-police? The presence of the police in so many controversial scenes within the film means it must be seen to raise the question of the role of the police in relation to issue of race within contemporary French society, but whether this makes it anti-police is another question.

The point to be aware of is that we will never get to the stage of even noticing the existence of these bigger issues within the film unless we devote ourselves to a detailed questioning of the text. It is in the asking of the 'why' questions (why is there that little moment in *La Haine* where Sayid and Hubert get Vinz to speak for them when they enter the expensive block of flats in central Paris?) that we stumble our way towards some awareness of the larger issues that could be at stake. (Quite simply, Sayid is of ethnic Arab descent and Hubert is black, while Vinz although a Jew is at least white. It is a minute incident that we can easily miss but, if we slow our viewing down so that we notice it, it becomes a telling comment.)

Before you can begin to answer some of the questions posed by a film like *La Haine* you may need to have watched the film several times and have taken some notes along the way. If you are studying in a formal way you will need to sit for some time with a DVD (or video) stopping and starting it, rewinding and rerunning it, and all the time adding to your notes.

Your notes should be made up of references to settings, characters, props (and perhaps their symbolic significance), the soundtrack, themes and ideas the film seems to be addressing, clues about the director's approach, ideas on the acting approaches being taken, and possibly significant extracts from the script; in other words, all of the areas detailed briefly above and a little more fully in the previous chapter. A series of viewings should allow your reading to become steadily less narrative-driven and increasingly technically and thematically analytical.

ACTIVITY

1   Choose your own film to analyse, preferably one you have at home and therefore can easily access. As you are watching this film for the first time note any interesting elements of film construction, but at the same time try to record ideas you may have about when and where this film is set.
2   After you have watched the film write 200–300 words assessing how important you think it might be to understand the historical context in order to gain a full appreciation of this film.

ACTIVITY

1   Rewatch the opening to this film several times and make detailed notes about film construction.
2   If possible, spend time discussing with others how this opening sequence works in terms of creating meanings for the audience and generating responses.

3 Write a commentary (500–600 words) discussing the ways in which meanings are created and responses generated in this sequence.

CONCLUSION

Approaching a new film requires that we:

- already know the sorts of questions that need to be asked of any film;
- apply those questions in a probing, analytical way;
- always maintain a thoughtful, proactive approach to the viewing experience.

3 CREATIVE PROJECT

In this chapter about the practical application of learning we look at:

■ how learning from other areas of the course can be applied to a piece of practical work (storyboarding, screenwriting or production)
■ how to develop ideas in a cinematic way
■ practical techniques of constructing storyboards, screenplays and filmed extracts

Studying film offers a wealth of learning about technique, styles, approaches, methods and devices which of itself is a fantastic way of understanding more about how films make meaning, and what filmmakers have to do in order to get their meanings across to audiences. A great way to make further sense of this learning is to use it to make a filmed sequence, a short film, or even a feature, and in doing so apply the learning that has been gained in other areas of the course.

The Practical Application of Learning (PAL) allows this earlier learning to be applied to a choice of practical projects in order to convey meaning to a specific, defined, audience, and in so doing to demonstrate constructional and technical ability. While it is an opportunity to apply previous learning, it is also an opportunity to develop new learning in the practical arena, and practise skills that are used in all areas of the film industry to make movies.

INFORMATION BOX – PAL: FILM FORM

A number of micro aspects may be applied directly to the construction of a practical piece of work:

- Cinematography
- Editing
- *Mise-en-scène*
- Performance
- Sound

These aspects are all directly manipulated either by technicians or by the director in order to maximize the opportunity to ensure an audience is exposed to an intended meaning. These are elements that are absolutely in the control of a filmmaker: there should be nothing in a shot, scene, sequence or film that is there accidentally, as all these ingredients should have been within the filmmakers' control. They of course play a significant part in the construction of narrative and genre:

- NARRATIVE: a structuring device, both across a whole film and across a single scene or sequence. The ordering of information within a practical piece of work is of vital significance to how a spectator will make meaning from it.

- GENRE: the use of signifying devices within a practical piece of work that are recognizable as belonging to a group of films. Use of codes and conventions will help structure a work and ensure that the spectator views it in terms of other, similar, films.

In the PAL there are three options for the creation of practical work, each in equal value to another, and each developing and demanding particular skill bases:

- *Digital or photochemical storyboard* (not drawn or computer generated): the opportunity to visualize how a film sequence would look as it moves from shot to shot. While photographic skills are not being judged here (indeed, it is possible to Photoshop an image and 'buy in' up to five images), framing is absolutely vital. Using lens-based media to produce a storyboard clearly allows the maker to gain a better understanding of how things actually look within a frame, and how they relate to other frames. The individual frames are important, but the transitions between frames and the interplay between frames are equally important.
- *Extended step outline*: the opportunity to visualize a set of linked key scenes from an imagined film, where activity is the key and where dialogue is not considered. What is important here is that the story is treated *cinematically*, in that it is clear that this is a story for the screen, using the conventions of cinematic construction. This uses a standard step-outline form and extends it by concentrating on the description of micro features in making meaning.

■ *Video production*: the opportunity to put together a short (one- to two-minute) sequence and filmically apply micro learning. If this is made by a group, then each group member must take responsibility for a particular micro component relevant to their role. It is accepted that there will be varying quality between productions (some may be shooting on a domestic VHS camera while others may be using Digi-Beta and a Steadicam rig), but it is the approach to the role and the achievement despite any limitations that are significant here.

Accompanying each of these three options are two pieces of written work that give the practical production work a context, and offer a reflection on intentions and on the finished work. The **aims and context** is the first piece of work that goes towards the project (though does not attract any marks) and sets out to give a context for the assessment of the sequence and reflective analysis. At the other end of the process, after the production work is completed, comes the **reflective analysis** where the creator analyses the application of micro aspects to the production work in making meaning.

These practical skills developed in the PAL are the building blocks of movie making, and as such are the essential tools for making meaning. Each contributes to the production line that is filmmaking – extended step-outline, storyboard, film – and all stem from the most important fundamental: the idea.

INFORMATION BOX – THE IDEA

The idea is the key starting point for any practical work and as such it is worth spending some time working through an idea to make it as good as it can get.

An idea initially develops into an outline for a story, and as such may well begin to grow characters. At this stage it is important to keep control of the idea to stop it spiralling off into unstructured developments. This can be done very easily by applying a simple set of questions:

1 **What is the situation?** This opens the story and may well be disrupted.
2 **Whose situation is it?** This defines the lead character (or *protagonist*).
3 **What is the central quest?** This relates to the main body of the story and is often defined by a lead character trying to restore what has been disrupted. This is where most conflict and drama arises in a story (and is often described simply as the *conflict*).
4 **Who stands in the way of success?** This defines another principal character, who will be in opposition to the lead character (and is often referred to as the *antagonist*).

5 **How does the quest end?** Often this will be where the antagonist is defeated, and the protagonist's situation is restored. This is often called the *resolution*.

Once the story idea is fleshed out, it is then important to check whether or not it is actually a *filmic* idea.

If it is set in one room with two characters talking to each other for ninety minutes, then it may be better placed on the stage.

If it involves considerable internal monologue (the characters' thoughts rather than their actions or conversations), then it may well make a better novel or short story.

Filmic ideas are ones that involve action – not necessarily fights and car chases, but rather activity – characters *doing* things on screen. Activity is visual, and this is most important in film stories. Activity tells an audience not only about the events, but also about the characters performing those events. A character who dashes off a perfect love letter is defined by the activity in the same way as the character who spends the scene crossing lines out, screwing up paper and throwing it to the floor, and sitting with pen in mouth looking skyward. Similarly the character of a bank robber is defined by their actions – the hooded figure that bludgeons a customer to the floor to make a point is different to the suited robber who passes a note calmly to a bank clerk and walks away with the money without the customers even realizing a robbery is taking place.

Aims and context

This piece of paperwork is extremely important not only in explaining the meanings you are trying to develop and the learning you are applying in one of the three practical activities, but also in getting your thoughts together in order to undertake the practical activity. As such it is possibly the most important (non-assessed) element that foregrounds a context for the assessment of the sequence and the reflective analysis. It is always advisable to head this with an appropriate title for the film: 'Galaxy Wars' does far more to locate a film in the mind of the reader than 'Imaginary Film', and shows that the creator has genuinely thought about the nature of the movie, and is making the effort to engage with the task.

The aims and context should not offer a synopsis of the sequence, but instead should offer a list of the micro features being focused on, and the way in which each will be applied to the storyboard, extended step outline or filmed sequence. As this is the context for the sequence selected for creation, it may be useful to offer some sense of where the chosen sequence sits in the film timeline, and so should allow the marker the opportunity to place the sequence in relation to the rest of the imagined film, and in relation to the conventions of structure.

Following a broad contextualizing summary of features, the focus switches from the overview to the specific, identifying what the intention is behind the use of the micro elements involved in its production.

For groups carrying out a video project it should be noted that each group member's aims and context should be different: it should be *their* intentions in relation to the film (not a combined group intention) and the micro elements should relate to *each* member's chosen focus and role (so, for example, the camera operator may well look at cinematography and/or *mise-en-scène*).

If the film has been identified as a genre film then it would be sensible to highlight how genre-specific micro elements will appear and shape the sequence. Similarly, if the film is adopting a particular style (e.g. documentary realism) then the sequence should reflect this in the micro elements, as these will be more identifiable in the sequence.

It is worth writing a number of drafts of the aims and context in order to craft the words to maximize the potential for success. This also serves to encourage a way of thinking about the sequence and the film as a whole that sees it not as fixed as soon as the first idea hits the page, but as fluid and developing continuously. Drafting the aims and context allows each idea to be questioned, challenged and weighed against the others in the piece, resulting in only the strongest, most focused remaining in place.

This will be presented as a cover sheet and should identify micro aspects in relation to particular points in the sequence. It is worth relating chosen aspects to specific points, as this makes it clearer for the reader to imagine how they will work, but also demonstrates that the techniques employed have been thought through and located in the sequence, and so have clear relevance. The micro aspects considered include cinematography (lighting and camera), *mise-en-scène* (location and dress), sound (both diegetic and non-diegetic), and editing (pace, duration, rhythm).

DIEGETIC SOUND: the sound that is heard in the fictional world, the sound that the characters in that world can hear. Most diegetic sound is not recorded 'on location' but is fabricated and 'dubbed' on to the film by sound designers and 'Foley artists' (people who generate sound effects such as cutting into a cabbage to mimic the sound of someone being guillotined).

NON-DIEGETIC SOUND: the sound that is outside the fictional world, and that characters in the fictional world cannot hear. This would include overlays of soundtrack music and any voiceover narration.

CONTRAPUNTAL SOUND: a great technique where the sound is not directly related to the image, but when placed together an additional meaning (or depth of meaning) is created. Thus the sound of a boxing match playing on a television in shot becomes more significant when the person watching the match walks into another room and begins beating an elderly person in there. The sound carried across from the television to the room where the beating is taking place is in counterpoint to the image of the abuse, yet serves to make a bigger statement about violence in general. It may be that a mix of contrapuntal sound and the diegetic sound of the beating may heighten this statement further.

ACTIVITY

Look at a sequence of activity from a film that is familiar to you. What actions and information is built into it? How are they conveyed? How is the sequence structured? What does this structure do in terms of storytelling?

Under the micro headings of Cinematography, Editing, *Mise-en-scène*, Performance, and Sound, list the significant features of this sequence. Do you notice that one heading has more features listed? Why do you think this is?

Write out the Aims and Context for the sequence you have looked at. Avoid retelling the story. Which particular micro aspects are important?

The extended step outline

Screenplay writing is a lengthy and complex process, with a feature film taking anything from six weeks to six months of intensive work to produce a decent first draft, and up to two years to get to a stage where the script could go into production. Importantly, it is the screen story that sets all other activities in motion, from storyboarding, through casting, through production, distribution and exhibition, to a spectator telling someone what a great (or lousy) film they saw last night.

Feature screen stories are largely broken down into 'acts' (units of action in which the story is following a particular path). The most common structures for screen stories revolve around either a three-act structure (beginning/establishing, middle/developing, end/concluding) or a five-act structure (set up, development, recognition, crisis, resolution), with each act broken up into sequences, which in turn are made up of scenes (small units of action, usually located in one place). Each scene, no matter how small, can also be further broken down into set-up, development and conclusion.

Screen stories are inhabited by three-dimensional characters who have past histories, ambitions, problems and relationships. These characters have internal aspects (e.g. beliefs, hopes, fears, dreams, opinions) that are shown through their external actions: the hardened ruthless criminal who stops to pick up and return a child's dropped teddy bear; the cop whose hand shakes when he points his gun at a suspect; the doctor who unlocks the desk draw at the end of the day, pours a large whisky, and stares at it without drinking. Internal characteristics, that are the essence of novel writing, are of no use to the screenwriter unless they can be externalized, unless they can become an action, a look, a gesture or expression which conveys this internal aspect.

While dialogue is a key feature of screenplay writing and of characterization, it is an aspect that is often over-relied on to 'tell' the story. Good screen stories do not tell the story, they 'show' the story through the actions and interactions of the characters populating them, and in doing so reveal more by relying on the audience to 'fill in the blanks'.

Scriptwriters commonly use a **step outline** as a planning tool for producing scripts. For AS Film Studies, this film industry planning and visualizing technique is being adapted: it is being 'extended' to include the micro details of the scene being outlined.

The extended step outline will thus provide students with the opportunity to develop ideas for a series of scenes – between five and eight is required, totalling 1000 words – while still developing visualizing skills. As a guideline, the average length of a scene for this extended step outline is envisaged as being between 175 and 200 words (excluding the context boxes above the scene description).

Looking at the step outline sheet below, you will see that half of the page is given over to a scene description and it stresses 'without dialogue'. The reason for this is to give you space to describe the setting and what is going on without worrying about what is being said or how it is delivered. This allows you to visualize the setting, the action and the **micro aspects** without reliance on dialogue carrying the scene (something that happens all too often), and means you will be focused on *mise-en-scène*, on sound, and on how it might be shot, or how it might be edited (although this is not directly your concern, it should be in your mind so that you can then write a scene to suggest the way it should be shot).

A typical step outline may run like this:

Scene no. 28	Page no. 3
Slugline	Interior flight deck of the space freighter 'Pole Star'. Day
Endpoint of last scene	Canton scrabbles desperately to reach the Failsafe lever as the Gyroscope powers up, lighting the hull of the ship
Characters in scene	Hunt, Fischer, Cruise, Rodriguez
Point of scene	To show that Hunt is a better flight commander than Fischer
Conflict	Hunt's desire to see Fischer fail set against the consequences for all of failure
Ending/central question	Hunt is forced to countermand Fischer to save the ship/Will they be able to escape before the oxygen fails?
Key micro elements employed	*Mise-en-scène*, sound, lighting

Scene description (without dialogue) focusing on key micro aspects (e.g. *mise-en-scène*, camera, sound, editing)

Consol lights flicker illuminating Cruise from below with coloured lights. He looks across to the shadowed, leather captain's chair where Fischer sits crouched forward. A nearby sun flares. The sunshields descend with a worn mechanical sound. Fischer leaps and crouches to see Canton, as the shields descend.

Bulkhead doors clang as Hunt and Rodriguez enter. Rodriguez, sweat-covered and dishevelled, looks to Cruise. The lights turn red. A pulsating siren begins. Hunt runs to Fischer, whose face is lit by the red from the consol. Hunt grabs his face and lifts his wildly flicking eyes to hers, but he cannot look at her and he retreats into the shadows. Hunt turns and barks instructions. A moment of hesitation. Cruise and Rodriguez look from a red-lit Hunt, to a silhouetted Fischer.

A distant rumbling explosion rocks the ship. They are thrown to the floor. The Gyroscope camera activates. Rodriguez leans over a monitor, bathed in blue light, sweating. On screen an interference-strewn image of Canton appears unmoving as the lights on the Gyroscope come close to reaching the top. Picking herself up, Hunt barks a command, and Cruise hits a button. The Gyroscope lights power down, the monitors and lights on the consol slowly die. A fading screen displays descending bars and a flashing oxygen warning. Another explosion rocks the flight deck and they are thrown into darkness.

The first thing you may notice is that there are no specific camera or editing instructions included in the extended step outline: camera and editing decisions are not made by screenwriters – they are made by directors, directors of photography and editors who interpret the 'master scene script'. A good screenwriter will be able to write action to suggest a particular shot, which a good director, DoP or editor will be able to visualize from the description. In the PAL, however, it is accepted that there may be a desire to indicate camera shots and angles, and highlighting some key shots or edits (although not advised) will not disadvantage you.

ACTIVITY

In the extended step outline extract above what camera shots do you think the writer had in mind? How would you sequence the shots for the opening scenes? How would you sequence the shots for the final section?

In a group, make up individual shot listings (LS, MS, CU) for the extended step outline extract. Sequence the shots so that they 'flow'. Consider the timing of each shot, and the duration of the sequence as a whole.

Compare sequences. Are there any individual shots that are the same (or roughly the same)? Are there any combinations of shots that are the same? Are the shot durations similar? Are the sequence durations similar?

Can you account for any similarities?

The scene number is at the beginning of a line of essential information, called the 'slugline'. The slugline begins with the designation of INT (Interior) or EXT (Exterior), the location, and whether it is day or night (sometimes this may be more specific, but realistically this is simply an indication of what lighting set-up will be needed, and this falls easily into these two categories). It is important that slugline conventions are adhered to, as these enable the production crew to do their jobs more easily.

Following the slugline comes the 'Endpoint of last scene'. This usually consists of a few lines to 'set the scene', and serves as a context for the current scene. It is here that you will see whether 'scenes' flow or not. The 'characters in scene' are simply listed, and you should remember that if they are mentioned in this box then they should be seen in the scene.

The 'point of scene' is key to the motivation of the scene and the direction it will take. Behind all scenes there is a key point that is the reason why the scene exists.

If you cannot find a point for the scene then the scene should be deleted. The point can be character driven, narrative driven, or even merely structural (getting characters from A to B).

Another essential is 'conflict'. All scenes should have some form of conflict – even if it is waiting for a kettle to boil when thirsty – as conflict drives drama, and drives scenes along. Without conflict, a scene serves no dramatic purpose and so should be excised.

The 'ending/central question' delineates the motivation at the end of the scene towards which the scene should be written. The question posed serves as motivation for a subsequent scene where the question will be answered and may be resolved.

The final box in the top section of the extended step outline is simply a list of the 'key micro elements employed' and is there to help you focus on what elements you intend to use.

The larger section is devoted to 'scene description (without dialogue)' and it is intended that this should offer a concise but visually descriptive focus on the scene's events. Dialogue is unnecessary here, and working through the step outline process usually results in screenwriters writing less dialogue than they would have normally done.

Screenwriters should always be wary of writing something that cannot be physically expressed – a thought, for example. In the extract above, Hunt forces Fischer to come face to face with her, but Fischer is unable to look her in the eye, and has to retreat into the shadows. From this the audience can infer his guilt and impotence. Other than inferring this, the only other way to tell the audience this would be for one of the crew to have a conversation with someone about it (or even for Fischer to beat himself up verbally about it – this would really be the worst kind of exposition).

EXPOSITION: the 'blatant' *telling* of a story, of facts and information that the writer sees as essential for the audience to know. In dialogue exposition usually take the form of conversations that humans rarely have ('George – you must remember George! Born in 1896 and got a VC during the Great War before being invalided out when gassed. Took a job as a telephone operator for the Post Office, where he stayed until retirement . . .', and may be seen as clumsy writing. This can be expressed just as clumsily in images also, if compressed into a short space of screen time.

How could you convey this information visually with minimal dialogue, and without falling into the trap of clumsy exposition?

The storyboard

The purpose of the storyboard is to photograph (either traditionally or digitally) each and every shot of a film with a list of key information written underneath, so that a director can see how the finished film will look before a single frame is shot. This allows them to calculate out the technical requirements of a shoot, and gives them the opportunity to revise sequences that seemed like a good approach when thinking the story through, but seem less possible or less appropriate with pictures in place.

The storyboard is made up from a set of 'standard' shot sizes each with an accompanying abbreviation, see figure 3.1 opposite.

Between these shot descriptors are a range of other shots (such as MLS and MCU) which help to describe the photographed images, and which help the production crew make sense of the requirements for a shoot. Other abbreviations and terms that are likely to be found on a storyboard include:

H/A	High angle	**Track/dolly**	Move camera on wheeled platform
L/A	Low angle	**Crab**	Sideways move
POV	Point of view	**Pull focus**	Change what is focused on
2-SHOT	Two people in shot	**Fade**	Shot fades in/out
OTS	Over the shoulder	**Dissolve**	Shot fades in/out as another fades in/out underneath

This terminology offers an industry shorthand that enables all the crew to use the same document to relate their part of the process to an overall objective. Apart

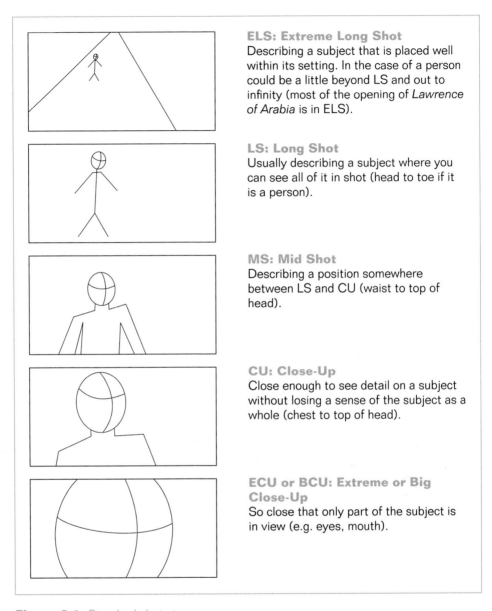

ELS: Extreme Long Shot
Describing a subject that is placed well within its setting. In the case of a person could be a little beyond LS and out to infinity (most of the opening of *Lawrence of Arabia* is in ELS).

LS: Long Shot
Usually describing a subject where you can see all of it in shot (head to toe if it is a person).

MS: Mid Shot
Describing a position somewhere between LS and CU (waist to top of head).

CU: Close-Up
Close enough to see detail on a subject without losing a sense of the subject as a whole (chest to top of head).

ECU or BCU: Extreme or Big Close-Up
So close that only part of the subject is in view (e.g. eyes, mouth).

Figure 3.1 Standard shot sizes

from a picture and the camera descriptions the storyboard should also contain other relevant information such as:

- **Shot number**: each shot in the storyboard must be numbered so that the intended sequence of shots can be followed. Although this is only a minor detail it can have serious consequences for shooting and editing if it is not adhered to.

- **Action**: a brief description of what is happening in the shot allows one frame to be used for the whole shot, even though there may be much movement within the shot. If it is radically different from the beginning of the shot to the end, or if there is camera movement that results in radically different framing, then the shot may be drawn across a number of storyboard frames (numbered a, b, c).
- **Camera**: this should not only indicate shot size and angle but should also give a clear sense of what is being framed.
- **Dialogue**: single lines may be written, but for longer speeches only the first and last few words covered by the shot are included to save space (Morgan: 'Hell no, I'd never . . . no sir, never!').
- **Sound FX**: this indicates specific sounds that will stand out against the general soundscape; ones that the makers wish to draw attention to.
- **Sound atmos**: the overall background 'atmosphere' of a fictionalized location is important in capturing the nature of the place.
- **Sound music**: this largely relates to non-diegetic music; the soundtrack that has been placed on the film to create an emotional response. It may include diegetic music if it transforms into non-diegetic sound.
- **Shot duration**: this is a vital piece of information, as it gives the storyboard rhythm and indicates that the filmmakers have considered the shot-to-shot relationships and the overall relationship of individual shots to the timing of the film as a whole. It is important not only to be able to calculate how long an action may take, but also how long it should take on screen.

ACTIVITY

- Look at a one-minute-long film extract that you are familiar with. Using the list above analyse the way the extract has been constructed.
- What do you notice about the way in which shot size and angle varies?
- What do you notice about the way each shot deals with movement within the frame?
- Generally, what framing is used for dialogue?
- How are sound FX, atmos and music related? What does the combination achieve?
- Is there a rhythm to the extract? Do you notice anything about the timings? Do they relate to the shot sizes? What does the rhythm do for the extract?

On p. 100 you will see a photographic storyboarded extract from *The Crossing*, from which it should become clear how the pictures and text support each other and how they aid the construction of meaning.

Video Production

Essentially the making of a video sequence can be divided into three distinct areas: pre-production (planning), production (shooting) and post-production (editing). Both scripting and storyboarding come into the pre-production stage, and so may be seen as primary functions that have to occur before any other pre-production stage can happen.

Pre-production

Even a short sequence can take an enormous amount of planning, and the time involved in organizing a shoot should not be underestimated. Other than scripting and storyboarding the essential tasks in pre-production are casting, location scouting, budgeting, scheduling and rehearsing. If each task is carefully managed, then it is likely that the shoot will go relatively smoothly. If one area is ignored, then it can easily impede or even prove disastrous for a shoot.

- **Casting**: the difficulties of finding any actors yet alone talented ones are well understood, but there are some things that can be done to mitigate against circumstance. First, it is important to get the right person for the right role – no point in casting a 17-year-old as the ageing father of a 15-year-old – and the right 'look' can cover many casting problems. If possible, look to performing arts groups or local amateur dramatics companies, as they will have had some acting experience, though not necessarily in the cinematic medium. Try to ensure there is real choice in casting and that it is not done merely as an exercise in first come first served.
- **Location scouting**: many productions are marred by using the wrong or inappropriate locations, and again, with some foresight and preparation this should never be a problem. Discussions with the screenwriter at an early stage can head off script decisions that are almost certain to prove a location nightmare – outside a spaceship in mid-flight; a Transylvanian castle; inside the cabin of a commercial jet liner. However, with a little effort one location can become another: a local church can become the Vatican with some Italian signage, some Latin hymns added in, and a couple of extras speaking Italian in the background. Locations that are secured should be confirmed with time and date, preferably in writing, and preferably at least a week in advance of shooting.
- **Budgeting**: this is not an essential component of this task, but it is worth remembering that in group productions money is often the source of argument, so it may be worth establishing a budget from the start, and establishing who is going to contribute what to it. If the budget starts to run away from the production, then it is important that this is brought to everyone's attention as soon as possible.

Shot no. 9

Action: There is slight movement behind the open window. Sunlight catches something inside and a reflection flashes briefly out.

Camera: L/A LS window

Dialogue: N/A

Sound FX: N/A

Sound atmos: City Square

Sound music: N/A

Shot duration: (2 seconds)

Shot no. 10

Action: The flash catches Colonel Inchalyka's eyes and he looks up to the window.

Camera: MS (side) Colonel Inchalyka on Embassy steps

Dialogue: N/A

Sound FX: N/A

Sound atmos: City Square

Sound music: N/A

Shot duration: (2 seconds)

Shot no. 11

Action: Colonel Inchalyka scans the building from where the flash came. Seeing nothing he hesitates, then shrugs it off.

Camera: H/A ECU Colonel Inchalyka's eyes scan the building's windows

Dialogue: N/A

Sound FX: N/A

Sound atmos: City Square

Sound music: N/A

Shot duration: (4 seconds)

Figure 3.2 Three photo storyboard shots

- **Scheduling**: a well-scheduled shoot is one where everyone knows when and where they are supposed to be, how long they will be there, and what they are supposed to be doing. It is wise to ensure that a schedule over-estimates the amount of time it takes to travel to a location, and the amount of time the shoot itself will take – people will thank you if they finish early, but curse you for running late. On average a production should be able to shoot between 12–18 well-crafted, considered shots per eight-hour day on location, and usually slightly less if they are in the studio or have significant lighting set-ups. It is worth spending some time preparing 'call-sheets' for cast and crew detailing daily arrangements and contact information.
- **Rehearsing**: the area least likely to be considered is possibly one of the most important. Rehearsals are not only a way of working the script through with actors, but they also ensure that members of a production team get into the rhythm of working with each other.

Production

Production is unquestionably a team effort, and it is essential that each team member has a defined role and area of responsibility, along with a specific micro aspect to focus on. A small crew is likely to have the following production roles:

- **Director**: responsible for the overall construction of the work and for ensuring that both actors and crew perform to their best. The dual role means that the primary responsibility of getting the actors to deliver a performance is matched by the need to direct the crew to ensure that this performance is captured in the best possible manner. The director is likely to choose performance as a focus area, but may also look to *mise-en-scène* in structuring the 'look' of a finished sequence.
- **Cinematographer**: or director of photography is responsible for capturing the image to film (or more likely tape), and will be focused on camera and lighting (though again may focus on *mise-en-scène*). The skill here is in manipulating camera controls and lighting techniques to create (and enhance) the director's vision.
- **Art director**: directly responsible for set dressing, set design, props and costume, and as such entirely focused on *mise-en-scène*.
- **Sound recordist**: responsible both for location sound and for providing sound intended for post-production. On set it is likely that the job will simply involve recording the purest sound possible, and being cautious of outside noise (e.g. planes flying overhead, traffic, neighbours arguing).

There are some basic shooting rules that it is wise to adhere to even if they are not fully understood at this level, in order to produce material that is usable and most importantly editable. With a minimum structure in place shooting becomes a less stressful process, and the results are dramatically improved. However, ignoring the simple rules of production leads to material that simply will not cut together, and well-planned shoots, with all the accompanying effort, being ruined.

1   Always use a tripod to support the camera, unless you have a specific reason for wanting the shaky look that handheld will give you. This can be dynamic in certain situations (e.g. chase sequences) but often it simply makes a production appear lazy or amateurish.

2   If something is wrong in shot, call 'cut' and retake the shot. If you accept a shot that has problems, then that will be the shot that creates problems for you in post-production.

3   Always adhere to the 30° rule. This states that to avoid 'jump cuts' (where the camera appears to lurch towards a subject or the subject appears to 'jump' position between shots) any shots that are intended to be joined with each other in editing should be shot from camera positions that have at least 30° between them.

4   Avoid cutting while in mid-camera movement – let the shot come to a 'rest' position, as this will benefit the editing.

5   Let the camera run for five seconds prior to calling 'Action' and after calling 'Cut'. This not only serves the editing, but it also gives some 'moments' where the actors' bodies and expressions are relaxed – these are often valuable.

6   Always adhere to the 180° rule. This rule is often complex to understand and even more complex to implement. The 'line of action' is an imaginary line – usually between two people, but it can run through one person – that the camera must stay one side of. The camera can travel anywhere on a 180° axis as long as it does not 'cross the line'; as soon as it does that then all spatial continuity is lost and editing becomes an exercise in confusion.

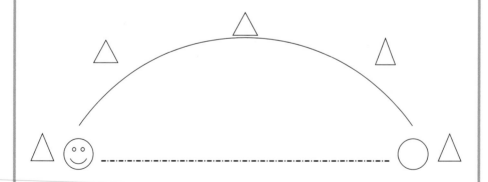

Post-production

Modern post-production is invariably carried out on a non-linear computer system (most commonly Avid, Final Cut, Pinnacle and Premiere) that ingests digitized material (and on some systems analogue material), and facilitates not only basic assembly editing, but also the addition of effects, sound editing, and the use of corrective tools such as grading. It is likely that a single editor will work through the shot material to produce a final cut of the sequence, and may be working from a storyboard, or more actively with a director.

The editor's role is one that should be governed by process in order for him or her to maximize their creativity. This process involves digitizing material and importing it into the chosen editing program; adding clips to a timeline to construct the sequence; trimming clips to tighten the sequence; laying audio tracks; laying any necessary video and audio effects; correcting any shot-to-shot problems (such as colour correction); creating title and credit sequences; and finally dubbing the finished product off to disc or tape.

Editors have a range of creative options open to them that determine the nature of the finished piece. Like all options these should be used sparingly to enhance the sequence and only when appropriate.

INFORMATION BOX – BASIC OPTIONS IN EDITING

- **Dissolve** An image fades out as another fades in, making a connection between the two (girlfriend fades out as mother fades in).
- **Fade** Often to black but can be to any colour. The duration of screen time given over to the fade and the end colour can suggest particular meanings.
- **Graphic Match** Two shots can be connected through shapes within the frame (a clock matched to a car wheel).
- **Match on Action** Two shots can be connected by the replication of an action across each (character begins putting drink down in seedy Soho bar, and cuts to drink reaching bar counter of Caribbean beach bar).
- **Montage** Placing one image next to another creates meaning (person's face with apple pie = hungry, person's face with coffin = sadness).

Reflective analysis

Reflective analysis can benefit from careful development, editing and drafting, and should consider how the identified micro element(s) focused on have been applied to the construction of the sequence. Ideally it should show a clear awareness of the audience and their reaction(s) to the finished work, and should do all this in approximately 750 words.

It is often worthwhile stating who the intended audience was for the sequence, as this then allows some element of testing (letting a representative of that audience – family member, friend, teacher – see the finished piece and express their responses to it) and then some reflection on their responses to the micro elements. This in turn can lead to a consideration of intended meanings and their production, which then focuses the piece on process and techniques. A personal response to the work can make a suitable conclusion to the reflective analysis.

ACTIVITY

- Show your finished extended step outline/storyboard/film to a group of people who are representative of your target audience. Try (if appropriate) to get a wide range of ages, genders and social groupings. Get them to discuss the work as a group, and shape the discussion with reference to the macro and micro focus of the piece.
- Revise the work in the light of their comments.
- Design a questionnaire to test the revised work on an audience. Focus the questions on issues raised in the previous discussion.
- Show the revised work to the same group, and get them to complete the questionnaire.
- Use the questionnaire results to inform any final revision of the work.
- Look at the finished work yourself and fill in one of your own questionnaires. How do your results compare with those offered by your audience?

INFORMATION BOX – EXAMPLE OF REFLECTIVE ANALYSIS: STORYBOARD *THE CROSSING*

I designed my storyboard for an audience of 18 to 25-year-olds as they are in the appropriate age group for thrillers and the content of the film is likely to mean that it will secure an 18 certificate from the BBFC. I titled it *The Crossing* as this has several meanings, including referencing the border crossing, double-crossing and the rite-of-passage crossing for the central character. I based this character on an amalgamation of several of my friends in an attempt to better reach my target audience. The key micro focus of my storyboarding activity revolved around cinematography and *mise-en-scène*, and though the latter was hard to achieve, what I could not place literally in the pictures I was able to describe in the accompanying shot descriptions.

I was endeavouring to use the conventions of 1960s British spy thrillers (*Ipcress File*, *Billion Dollar Brain*) and while using colour I still tried to achieve a high-contrast look with a strong use of shadow. Light and shade is important in conveying some meanings at a basic level and, when coupled with both diegetic sound and a non-diegetic music track, this meaning can be enhanced.

In terms of composition I tried to make the sequences interesting and varied while maintaining consistent thematic shooting. Colonel Inchalyka, for example, is largely shot either from on or slightly above the eyeline to bring the audience on to his level. Similarly I used several over-the-shoulder-shots to ensure the audience was brought literally on to his side.

I was quite surprised that when I showed the storyboard to representatives of my target audience the majority of people thought that Colonel Inchalyka was the bad guy – and yet I had worked so hard to signpost his honesty and integrity. Maybe I was too subtle, or maybe my audience have a genre-based response to such characters which means that they are automatically suspicious of them. Perhaps I should have made Colonel Inchalyka a woman instead? I suspect that the music theme I applied to him may have impacted on their view of him (in retrospect bad guys often have a theme).

To help me storyboard the sequence, I looked at several books, and found the Film Education booklet on storyboarding very useful in terms of working through the idea and structuring the shots. Making the characters seem real without letting them speak too much was difficult and I kept having to invent ways of showing, not telling. The gunfight sequence was fun to do and I decided to use the techniques I have seen in other films such as the work of John Woo and Sam Peckinpah, with lots of extreme close-ups crashing with long shots to create a sense of confusion and chaos in the audience.

continued

I also looked at Steve Katz's *Film Directing Shot by Shot* for some ideas on how composition works. I began to get interested in shot-to-shot structures and as a result designed several match shots. The oldest in my target audience felt that the match shots worked well and reminded him of the work of Orson Welles. I hadn't planned this, but in retrospect I can see a similarity with some shots from *Citizen Kane*. I am rather pleased with this, especially as it highlights the fact that audiences will read into images, irrespective of what the intended meaning is.

I worked through three drafts of the storyboard, showing each to my teacher (who is outside my target age group) and to a friend who is in my target audience. My teacher was able to offer some good advice, but my friend seemed to think each version was OK, and I didn't find much of use in his comments. Overall I am very happy with the finished piece and my use of micro aspects, and I feel I have learned a lot about the nature of making meaning and the structure of shot-to-shot relationships. I have also learned that I can apply learning from academic areas of the course to the practical areas, and this has increased my enjoyment of both.

(694 words)

References and Further Reading

Scriptwriting/step outlines

Gaffney, F. (2008) *On Screenwriting*, Auteur, London

Hicks, N. (1996) *Screenwriting 101*, Wiese, Oxford

Storyboarding

Begleiter, M. (2001) *From Word to Image: Storyboarding and the Filmmaking Process*, Wiese, Oxford

Fraioli, J. (2000) *Storyboarding 101*, Wiese, Oxford

Production

Jones, C. and Jolliffe, G. (1996) *The Guerrilla Film Maker's Handbook*, Cassell, London

Katz, S. (1991) *Film Directing Shot by Shot*, Wiese, Oxford

Useful Websites

http://www.script-o-rama.com (Drew's Scriptorama: script and screenwriting site)

http://w3.tvi.cc.nm.us/~jvelez/MMS170/storyboard (Storyboarding: history, purpose and techniques)

http://www.themakingof.com (The making of Hollywood's hit movies)

http://www.filmundergound.com (Film underground: DV filmmaking site)

http://www.cyberfilmschool.com (Cyber film school: pro-end DV filmmaking site)

part 2

BRITISH AND AMERICAN FILM (FM2)

4 THE AMERICAN FILM INDUSTRY

This chapter will:

- encourage you to see films as products of global industry dominated by Hollywood
- outline the stages that make up film production, or the actual making of the film
- outline the stages in the commercial process that come after the film has been made, essentially distribution, marketing and exhibition
- encourage you to try to follow through the process behind bringing one of your own favourite films to the screen

INFORMATION BOX   *i*

This section will be particularly relevant to FM2: British and American Film – Producers and Audiences for the WJEC's AS in Film Studies. This part of the AS course tries to help you to understand how, in addition to being viewers of films, or spectators, people who watch films could also be seen as consumers. And, in relation to this approach, how films themselves could be discussed in terms of being products made and designed to be consumed in particular ways.

The global and local dimensions

The film industry reaches right around the globe. In terms of making films they can be shot on location, or in film studios, all over the world. In terms of showing films, although they may initially be shown in one country or another with the right marketing and distribution back-up they can quite quickly be seen by audiences around the world.

ACTIVITY

1   Some films now have a global release date – they are available to be seen by cinema audiences around the world on the same day. Why has this come about?
2   Try to research this, remembering that potentially there might be more than one reason.
3   Produce your own short list of examples of films that have received a global release date.

In studying film, you should be intensely aware of this increasingly important global dimension to film; globalization is a process that in recent years has affected films and the film industry as much as any other commercial enterprise. However, you should also be alert to the fact that this global aspect to the industry is actually expressed and experienced locally. As a result we are able to give due consideration to the film industry as a worldwide phenomenon simply by paying careful attention to the presence of film within our everyday lives.

GLOBALIZATION: that process whereby the lives of individuals and local communities are affected by worldwide economic forces. It may also be seen as the idea that the world is becoming a single marketplace dominated by multinational companies. This is seen by some as a positive force enabling everyone to have access to the latest goods, technologies and communication systems. It is seen by others as simply the latest expression of Western domination over Third World countries.

Once again, your everyday experience of film and cinema is a valuable starting point for your studies. The magazines and newspapers we read, the TV we watch, the conversations we have with friends, the streets we walk in and the shops we visit, to say nothing of the DVDs we buy and the cinemas we attend, will all announce the presence of the film industry as a worldwide commercial fact.

ACTIVITY

1   If films do not receive a global release date the gap between cinema release and finding the DVD in the shops is getting shorter, particularly for Hollywood films. Why is this?
2   Try to undertake research to find out why this might be the case and then compare and discuss your conclusions with other people, if possible.

ACTIVITY

1   Compile a list of local cinemas within, say, five to six miles of either your college or your home. How long has each cinema been open? Can you find out brief details for the development of each cinema? Do any local cinemas have a particularly long history? How many screens are available at each cinema?
2   What sorts of films are shown at these local cinema(s)? If there are several cinemas, do they tend to specialize in any way? Is their programme dominated by mainstream Hollywood films? Do they show what might be called 'art-house' films at any time? If so, when are they screened and how often?
3   Find out the cost of tickets. If there are several cinemas, is there much difference between prices? If so, can you see any reasons why this might be? Are there special discount times or discount deals at particular cinemas?
4   Where are the cinemas situated and why are they sited in these places? Are they in town or out of town, and why? Are they easily accessible by road? Are there any bus and/or rail stations nearby? Is car-parking easily available?
5   Do they advertise their presence and what they are currently showing in local newspapers and/or on local radio? Do they offer press screenings of new films before they are shown to the public?
6   If you can, try to arrange a visit to a local multiplex (and/or smaller cinema) and an interview with the manager. Try to find out:

■   how the cinema decides which films it will be showing and for how long

continued

- what percentage of films shown would be classified as American
- whether they have any deals with particular distributors or studios
- how they decide which advertisements and trailers to show
- what percentage of their takings come from the box-office
- what percentage of their takings come from other sources, particularly food and drink.

(Perhaps you can come up with a further list of questions to ask before your visit.)

Hollywood

Alongside the type of film analysis we have undertaken with a variety of films in Part 1, as film students we need to remember that the films we see at the cinema and the DVDs we watch at home are the products of this massive ongoing industrial process. In the case of most of the films we have considered so far we have been dealing with products of Hollywood, that suburb of Los Angeles in California that has been home to the big American film studios since early silent movie days so that the place name has itself become a shorthand term for the American industry as a whole.

> **HOLLYWOOD:** as early as the 1910s the US film industry began to shift its base from the East Coast to what was essentially a place in the Californian desert, a rural area on the edge of Los Angeles. The name 'Hollywood' has, of course, become a term signifying something much more than simply a place in California.

ACTIVITY

1. Consider why Hollywood might have become the American centre for industrial filmmaking. What advantages might it have offered the business initially, and later as it developed as a filmmaking centre?
2. Discuss your ideas with other people, if possible.
3. Try to find time to undertake a little research to see if any of your ideas stand up to scrutiny. Basically you are trying to find out where the industry started in America and how it came to be located in Hollywood.

(The history of all of this is in a sense by the by; what is crucial is that you begin to think about film in business terms – why would a film industry interested in churning out as many film products as possible in as short a space of time as possible and for the greatest profit possible move to Hollywood? Begin to think in these terms and you will be well on the way to understanding this part of the Film Studies A level.)

Studios

Most famously Hollywood has been built around studios, well-financed big-name companies in the business of making films and in making money from films. *Casablanca* (1942), for example, the 'classic' wartime romantic drama set in what was seen as an exotic North African location, was made by Warner Brothers, one of the major companies operating during that phase of film history spanning the 1930s, 1940s and into the 1950s known as the Studio System. The perhaps most famous 'classic' text from the same period, *Citizen Kane* (1941), was made by another studio known as RKO (Radio-Keith-Orpheum).

INFORMATION BOX – *CASABLANCA* AND *CITIZEN KANE*

- *Casablanca* (1942) was filmed and then released just as the United States was entering the Second World War. It was made by Warner Brothers in an effort to encourage the country to take up the struggle against Hitler's Germany. It featured two famous stars from the period, Humphrey Bogart and Ingrid Bergman.
- *Citizen Kane* (1941), directed by and starring Orson Welles, is one of those films that always features near the top of the '100 best movies ever' lists that you tend to find at regular intervals in film magazines.

The first of these studios, Warner Brothers, will be familiar to most people since it is still very much one of the major 'players' in the industry. However, you may well not have heard of the second name, since RKO went out of business in 1955. It was the only one of the major studios from the period to go out of business in the face of the huge competition offered to the industry by the advent of TV. So to some extent studios come and go, although most seem to manage to be taken over or become involved in mergers rather than actually go out of business. (We will consider the studios based in Hollywood in a little more detail later in this chapter.)

Figure 4.1
Orson Welles
in *Citizen Kane*
(1941)

INFORMATION BOX – WARNER BROTHERS AND RKO

- **Warner Brothers** was formed as a production company in 1923 under Harry, Albert, Sam and Jack Warner. In 1927 the company introduced synchronized sound for the film *The Jazz Singer* and revolutionized the industry. They quickly took over a chain of theatres and also another production company, First National. In 1989 Warner merged with Time Inc which then merged with Turner Broadcasting in 1996 and then with AOL in 2000 to become one of the largest media entertainment conglomerates. (See how the history of this company is built upon mergers, and also the effort to use new technologies to obtain a commercial advantage over rivals whenever possible.)

■ RKO (Radio-Keith-Orpheum) was formed in 1928 through a merger between RCA (Radio Corporation of America) and the Keith, Albee and Orpheum cinema chains. In 1931 the company bought Pathe's studios and distribution outlets. At this time sound was just coming in and for obvious reasons RCA felt it had useful experience in this field. By 1955 the company had been wound down and most of its assets sold off. (See how this company starts at a time of change for the film industry and again demonstrates the usual process of mergers and takeovers that is symptomatic of the industry.)

ACTIVITY

1 Research the development of TV in both the United States and Britain. You may find it more interesting to try to complete this task with someone else rather than on your own.

■ What are the key dates for the development of TV as a commercial enterprise?

■ How rapidly did TV sets make their way into the home in both countries?

■ When did satellite and cable first appear, and again how rapidly did this new technology and the accompanying increase in available channels make its way into the home?

■ In what ways could TV be seen as a competitor to film and the cinema, and in what ways could it be seen as a useful parallel medium that could be used by the film industry in commercially advantageous ways?

2 Discuss your research findings with other people who have undertaken the same work. Take particular note of any ideas they have come up with that you missed.

(Try not to produce pages and pages of downloaded information. We want no more than two A4 sides of succinct typed notes – key points and ideas, and just a *few* dates and facts.)

The Internet clearly represents a wonderful resource for this sort of work, but here are two pieces of advice:

continued

TELEVISION: this may perhaps at first seem a strange choice of key term when considering cinema and film. However, TV is clearly in the business of screening staged film dramas and from this perspective is in immediate competition with cinema. On the other hand, since TV has provided a ready-made screen in every home as early as the 1960s the potential of a further space in which to show film products also becomes apparent. When we reach the era of video and later DVD we find that these products depend entirely for their success, or otherwise, upon people having access to screens within as many homes as possible.

films as commercial products

If you pick up a DVD copy of *Citizen Kane* today you will see that it is marketed by Universal and so, despite the fact that the company originally responsible for making it no longer exists, as a commercial product it continues to this day to be a valuable commodity capable of making money for whoever owns it. If you have more recent films at home and look carefully at the packaging, you will be able to see a logo or a series of logos proclaiming the company or companies responsible for distributing these products. For example, pick up a copy of *Collateral* (Mann, 2004) and you will see it has been brought to you by a company called Paramount, which as with Warners will in all likelihood be a familiar name to you.

ACTIVITY

1   Research the development of VHS and DVD in both the United States and Britain. Again, you may find it more interesting to complete this task with someone else rather than on your own.

- What are the key dates for the development of these two formats as commercial enterprises?

VHS: Video Home System, Matsushita's videotape format which became the norm for recording in the home after overcoming its commercial rival, Sony's Betamax system, in the 1980s.

DVD: Digital Versatile Disc, the system that has now almost totally replaced VHS. Discs can hold much more information than videotapes (providing the possibility for all sorts of 'extras' to be included alongside the main film) and offer a higher quality image. They are also much easier, and therefore much cheaper, to produce.

Adaptability of the film industry

Perhaps the key to understanding the success of Hollywood over the past 100 years is to recognize the way in which it has always demonstrated an incredible ability to adapt to changing business circumstances. At heart the mainstream American film industry has recognized that what it is offering the public is a product, and that its success depends upon adapting that product to a constantly changing market. Hollywood has continually managed to find ways to embrace new technologies such as those mentioned above.

On the Waterfront (Kazan, 1954), an early film starring Marlon Brando, was made during a period when the American industry was facing perhaps its major challenge. It needed to reorganize itself in the face of competition from the then stunning new technology of TV. Studios were beginning to use independent producers; they would finance a one-off project for one of these producers and then distribute the resulting films. This meant they no longer had the ongoing, week-in, week-out expense of staffing and running studio production facilities. The package of business arrangements (cast and crew to be signed up and paid for a given period, clearance for filming at various locations to be obtained, studio space to be booked for filming on set, editing facilities to be lined up) necessary

Figure 4.2 *On the Waterfront* (1954)

to complete the *On the Waterfront* project was organized by independent producer Sam Spiegel, who then released the finished product through Columbia. It was a relatively low-budget movie being made for just $800,000 on a tight 35-day shooting schedule but it grossed $9.5 million at the box-office when first released.

$2 million on a $20 million outlay is a much better percentage return and thus a better business proposition.) Often you will find that although on the face of it everything about Hollywood has changed over the years, in fact little has really altered. There are often parallels between what went on in the past and what happens today.

In the face of continued competition from TV and changing leisure patterns, the industry continued to lose ground during the 1960s and 1970s but in general Hollywood continued to maintain its recognition of film as a commercial product. In the mid-1970s during a time of continuing difficulties for the industry, *Star Wars* (Lucas, 1977) took more than $46 million during its first week.

This was achieved by coming up with a strong initial concept, marketing the film imaginatively and making a big play of releasing the film at the same moment to more cinemas than was usual at the time. The film became the first to gross more than $400 million at the US box-office and effectively changed marketing practices and release strategies for the industry.

The main thing to take on board is the fact that despite difficult times, in general Hollywood has been able to continually re-invent itself by seeing film as a commercial product that has to respond to a changing marketplace and take advantage of new opportunities offered by new technologies. At each moment in its history when the industry has faced the need to reorganize in the face of new competition, the effort has always been to reorganize in as effective a way as possible in order to continue to make money.

ACTIVITY

1 Research a few of the films mentioned in this chapter so far. Who were the main stars in each film? See what you can find out about the main star from each film. Who directed each film? Again, see what you can find out about these people.
2 Write a short 100 to 200-word biography on the star you find most interesting and another on the director you have found most interesting.

Figure 4.3 *Star Wars* lobby card (1977)

Change over time

As a student of film it is important to know a little about the history of Hollywood:

- to be aware of early 'silent' cinema and the change to 'talkies' around 1930
- to be able to identify differences and similarities between the Studio System of the 1930s and 1940s and contemporary Hollywood filmmaking
- to understand something of how the Studio System broke up in the 1950s before re-inventing itself during the 1970s with films like *Jaws* (Spielberg, 1975) and *Star Wars*.

To emphasize the point once more, the continuity link through all this time and the factor that it is most important to recognize from the outset is that film has always been seen by Hollywood as a commercial product to be made in as cost-effective a way as possible and to be sold for the greatest profit achievable.

Casablanca, Sin City and baked beans

So, when we enter our local DVD store and take from the shelf the film marked *Casablanca* or the film marked *Collateral* or *Sin City*, or *Pirates of the Caribbean: Dead Man's Chest* (Verbinski, 2006) it is not in some senses any different from entering a supermarket and picking up a can of our favourite baked beans. We will look at the labelling, paying particular attention to the maker's name and noting what the pictures on the box suggest about the item we are considering purchasing. We will decide if this is the product we want, buy it, take it home, open the package and prepare ourselves to enjoy what the advertising and marketing has told us to expect. Films in their DVD (and VHS) formats are packaged using visual images and wording in as effective a way as possible to tell us exactly the sort of product we are buying; or perhaps sometimes we might think in order to trick us into purchasing something that does not turn out to be half as good as the packaging suggested, or as the trailers and other adverts promised.

ACTIVITY

1   Look at your DVD collection when you get home and choose one or two with what you believe to be interesting, eye-catching packaging.
2   Analyse the ways in which the covers are 'working' to attract attention and convey messages about the product to potential purchasers.

■   What words or names are being used and why? How prominent are they and why? What colouring is used? What typeface is employed? Why?
■   How about the image? Why has it been chosen? Break the image down into component parts if possible: how does each work to create meaning for us?

3   If possible, take the DVD cover about which you feel you have the most to say to a meeting with other students studying film with you. Explain your understanding of your chosen DVD cover to them and compare your ideas with the ideas they have about the covers they have brought for discussion.

Films and the cinema

But of course films do not just come as DVDs. Films are usually first seen as new releases screened in cinemas (although you can buy made-for-TV films, and also films that go straight to DVD rather than having a theatrical release). Indeed, the ultimate financial success of any movie is usually determined by its level of success in the cinema. Here we are not just talking about final box-office takings for the year of release: it is usually true to say that by the end of the opening weekend analysts working for the studio concerned already have a pretty strong indicator as to the film's eventual level of financial success, or failure. Films shown in the cinema are sold to us via still images and wording in ways that are reminiscent of DVD covers, but in this case through the use of posters. In addition to this, you will probably be well aware of the way in which when we attend the cinema trailers work hard to attempt to persuade us to return in the future to see further films.

ACTIVITY

1   Choose a film poster you have seen recently and examine the way in which it has been put together. Is it effective or not? In what ways is it effective? In what ways do you think it is not effective? How do the layout, wording and images that have been chosen attempt to make the poster effective?
2   Write 600 words explaining how you feel the layout, wording and images work to attempt to sell this particular film.

ACTIVITY

■   What has been the most effective trailer you have seen recently at the cinema?
■   What made it effective? Was it something to do with the voiceover? Or the visual images selected? Or the style of the filmmaking? Or the challenging nature of the ideas that seemed to be examined by the film?
■   Do you think it would have been equally attractive to other cinemagoers, or is there a reason it was particularly interesting to you?

Films and TV

Films are also available for us to watch on TV of course and have been for around 50 years, but only comparatively recently has this space become so important for film sales. With the proliferation of channels brought about by the appearance of cable and satellite TV a massive new 'window' for the exhibition of film has opened up for the industry; previously there were only a relatively few terrestrial channels.

ACTIVITY

1   Research preview trailers on any pay-to-view channel. Analyse the ways in which these previews are 'working' to attract attention and convey messages about the product to potential purchasers.

■   What words or names are being used visually and why? How prominent are they and why? What colouring is used? What typeface is employed?

■   Do the previews use a voiceover? If so, how has the voiceover been constructed? What elements of the film are being emphasized in the voiceover script and why? Is there a particular tone of voice employed?

■   How about the images, why have they been chosen? Break the images down into component sections if possible: how does each work to create meaning and generate responses from us?

2   If possible, take a recorded copy of the preview trailers you have looked at to a meeting with other people studying film with you. Explain your understanding of your chosen previews to them and compare your ideas with the ideas they have about the previews they have brought for discussion.

Economics and the film industry

For now, the main thing to take on board is that a commercial film is the product of an industrial production process involving the use of a variety of technologies and human labour. The interrelated roles of industrial relations, markets, business agendas and issues of profit and loss accounting, for example, are all therefore of relevance to an understanding of how we as an audience come to be presented with the films we are. Perhaps you were not expecting to have to deal with these sorts of areas in studying film, but you have to appreciate that this is a multi-million-pound industry.

ACTIVITY

1   Organize yourselves into groups and either nominate one photographer in each group or agree to take turns in this role.
2   Go to your nearest town or city and take shots of as many film-related images that you can see on the streets as possible.
3   Before you go out on location, list specific places you know in the town/city where you might find images related to film (e.g. cinemas, bookshops, shops selling DVDs, DVD rental outlets, billboards).
4   Create a montage of images to be displayed in the classroom or on your school/college website if possible with the aim of showing just how inescapable a part of everybody's life film has become in recent years.

(If you wish to take shots inside any premises make sure you explain what you are doing and ask permission before clicking the shutter.)

Filmmaking: the process

There are, as we have seen, a whole series of ways in which we as consumers of film come into quite immediate contact with the industry in our everyday life. What will most likely be outside of our direct experience though will be the various stages involved in the making of commercial films.

There are three phases to the actual production, or making, of a film:

- **Preparation, or pre-production**: the initial idea is developed and written as a script, and funds are obtained.
- **Shooting, or production**: images and sounds are physically recorded and put on film (or digitally recorded).
- **Assembly, or post-production**: images and sounds are edited and put together in their final form.

Obviously each of these stages can be carried out on a very small scale, for example, within a school or college, and if you have taken part in the process you will be aware of how well you have to be organized and how carefully you have to plan each of these stages. But if we are looking at the commercial film industry, beyond the actual making of the film there will also be issues of distribution and marketing to be considered because once it has been made, the film has to find an audience and be placed in an accessible form before that audience. It has to be decided where and when the film is going to be exhibited.

Figure 4.4 Planning, filming, editing

- In what countries is it to be shown?
- Should there be a single global release date?
- Should some countries receive the film before others?
- In which cinema chains is it to be shown in particular countries?
- Initially, how many cinemas should it be released to in each country?
- How should this initial release be built upon in order to maximize the potential audience? How quickly is it to move on to DVD release?
- How long should it be before it is shown on satellite, cable and terrestrial TV?

In other words, what are the marketing and distribution strategies that should be followed for this particular product (bearing in mind that potentially each film may need to employ strategies individually tailored to the particular nature of the product)?

> **MARKETING:** the total package of strategies used to try to promote and sell a film.

Large distribution companies in charge of marketing will employ researchers to investigate the market for any particular film and enable them to keep abreast of shifting trends in consumer practices. They will also use focus groups (or members of the public) from the supposed target market to view and comment upon the film at various stages, with the idea of altering the script if necessary. Such early showings of the film behind closed doors are known as test screenings.

All of this will occur before those elements more usually associated with marketing (the screening of cinema trailers, the launching of a press campaign and the instigation of a poster campaign) come into play. Although, of course, the planning for each of these strands involving the development of a clear timetable for each stage of the marketing process will be underway even as the movie is being filmed.

(Today, where a big-budget Hollywood film is concerned, as one team of workers is involved in the production of the film another team will be working alongside them with the job of developing an accompanying computer game. The primary marketing for this will be the film itself, but there will also be a further distinct strategy being put in place by an additional marketing team. And, of course, as the game is being marketed, so also the film, and probably more importantly at that stage the DVD of the film, will be 'piggy-backing' that advertising and publicity.)

To some extent, if you have a big budget blockbuster marketing decisions are easy; if you can, you swamp every other opposition product through a saturation release that hits as many screens as possible from day one. But if you do not have a big budget, then a carefully planned release strategy may involve helping your film to create good 'word of mouth' through a limited opening release pattern, before opening to more cinemas in order to build on this initial positive response as what the business calls 'want to see' is created. In fact, of course, even if you are producing a very low-budget small-scale movie you will still be thinking in terms of some audience or other. It may be that you are only producing it for yourself and your friends to view or perhaps as a home movie for your immediate family or as a short to be put out on the college website, but still you will be aiming to engage the interest of your prospective audience. You will want to create a film that means something to them and generates some sort of previously envisaged response from them. Ideally, what the producers of commercial films are looking for is a film with 'legs'; that is, one that is going to keep on running, thereby making money at the box-office over an extended period.

> **RELEASE PATTERN:** this is the part of the marketing strategy that determines the number of prints of the film that are to be initially put out to cinemas, which cinemas are to receive the film to begin with, and how that initial release of the film is to be expanded and built upon.

A film might be given a 'general release' right across the country or it might have a 'select release' to a few cinemas in a few cities where the audience is felt to be right for this particular film. A 'saturation release' would indicate that the effort has been to put the film out immediately to as many cinemas as possible – to saturate the market.

A film is usually released first of all within its country of origin before moving out to other countries in a developmental fashion, although it is now possible for a big Hollywood movie to have a single global release date.

Whatever pattern is adopted, the key point to recognize is the way in which market analysts will have worked together to try to decide upon the strategy that will be best suited to maximizing box-office returns on their product.

So, a film (any film) may always be seen as going through:

- a production phase
- a distribution phase
- an exhibition phase.

Distribution

This involves making sure a release pattern is put into place that will enable the product to reach the widest and largest audience possible. Of course, film distributors may be small firms specializing in certain types of film or multinational corporations with global networks of offices, and the products they deal with and markets they focus upon will vary enormously. However, essentially, the distributor:

- acquires the rights to the film
- decides the number of prints to be made and released to exhibitors
- negotiates a release date for the prints
- arranges delivery of prints to cinemas
- provides trailers and publicity material for exhibitors
- puts together a package of advertising and publicity to promote the film
- negotiates related promotional and/or merchandising deals.

Marketing

This may be seen as three distinct areas: advertising, publicity and promotional deals worked out with other companies. Within an overall marketing budget possibilities within each of these areas will be considered in terms of the likely return on ticket sales weighed against cost. The big plus in favour of publicity is that it is essentially free, although there might be some associated costs such as expenses for one of the film's stars who is going to be interviewed on a TV show. Advertising, on the other hand, has to be paid for: so, if as a marketing executive for a particular film you succeed in getting a review on the film pages of a newspaper next to an advert for your film, the first of these will be free whereas the second will have to be paid for.

As you will be aware from your own cinema visits, a trailer is also usually put out several weeks before the release date in order to raise awareness of the product. Indeed, sometimes a series of trailers are now produced as the film moves towards its release date. These may begin showing months before the film is due out and must be carefully structured in order to build anticipation rather than turning the potential audience off through such a long lead-in period.

TRAILER: a short advert for a film put together by the distributors. It will usually comprise extracts from the movie in question with an added voiceover designed to sell the film. A shorter version of the trailer sometime before the film is due out is known as a 'teaser'.

ACTIVITY

- When you are next at the cinema watch one or two of the trailers that are shown particularly carefully and try to note the key points that are emphasized (either through words or images) about the film in question.
- If you get the chance, try to monitor any other trailers you see for the same films over the coming weeks before they are released.

Advertising

A range of media will be considered – newspapers, magazines, TV, radio – with a clear agenda to hit a specific target audience. The poster campaign is often the primary medium for advertising a film comprising the central image that will also feature heavily in the publicity campaign. Some films will have teaser posters before the release date, a main poster to coincide with the release date, and later a third poster with comments from critics. For other blockbuster films there may be still more posters but these will always retain unifying features that should make them instantly recognizable as part of the same campaign.

You will also have noticed how posters for any film often vary according to where they are 'placed'. For example, a poster designed to catch your eye as you are walking, cycling or driving will be different from one in a magazine where you are expected to have more time to take in information.

POSTER CAMPAIGN: a marketing strategy involving the use of a prominently displayed series of posters to promote a film. Each poster will be carefully put together to present what is seen to be a desirable image to be associated with the film and will be strategically placed in the press and positioned on billboards in such a way as to attempt to catch the eye of the film's target audience. The aim will be to present the public with a clearly defined notion of exactly what is special or particular about this film. This is sometimes referred to as the film's 'unique selling point' (USP).

ACTIVITY

1 Find your own examples of posters for one film that have been designed for a range of placements.
2 How do they differ? How are they constructed to fit their likely audience? Explore layout, text and visual images in detail, in relation to each other but most importantly in relation to the chosen outlet position.
3 Write a short essay (600 words) exploring the differences.

Publicity

Since they are essentially free, reviews, articles, interviews and photographs used in any of the media have a special importance for the success of a marketing campaign. Press kits are sent out comprising authorized stills, cast and crew credits, production notes, and biographies of cast/director/producer. There will be efforts to get key personnel, especially stars involved with any new film, on to as many TV and radio outlets as possible. Again, be aware of your own experience: you know only too well that when you start seeing a particular favourite star of

Figure 4.5 (above and opposite) Two different posters used to advertise the film *Hairspray* (2007)

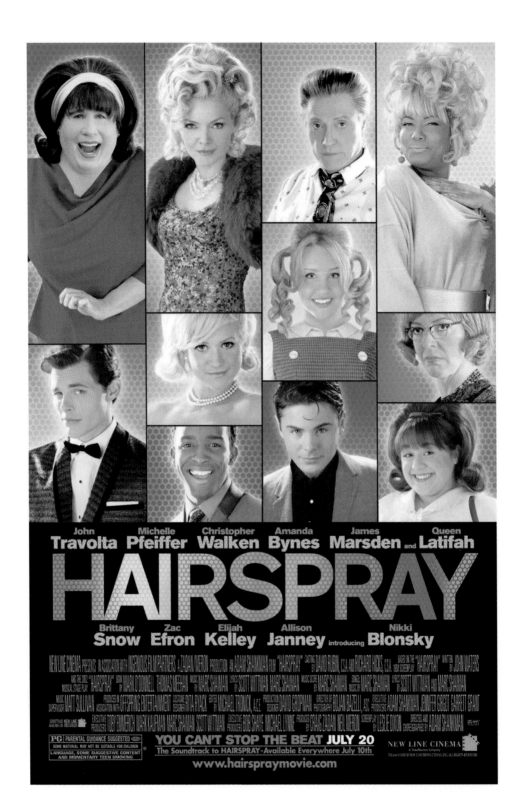

yours on TV on one programme after another it always coincides with the release of their latest movie (or the latest instalment of their autobiography).

ACTIVITY

1   Take a high-profile Hollywood film of your choice that is about to be released and, by looking carefully through the *Radio Times* or any other magazines or Internet sites with programme schedules, try to see whether the marketing team have been successful in gaining time and space to promote their company's new product.
2   Draw up a list of programmes with dates and times that are reviewing the film, interviewing 'the talent' involved in the project, and/or showing extracts from the movie.

'**THE TALENT**': a film industry term for the main creative players involved in the production of any particular film. It is often used to refer to the director, the producer, the screenwriter and the lead actors as a group of key personnel, but may include others such as the art director, director of cinematography and musical director.

Promotions

Special concessionary deals may be offered to sectors of the public believed most likely to be interested in the film being promoted; competitions connected to the film may be set up in magazines or newspapers, or on food packaging likely to be picked up by the target audience; and merchandise related to the film in some way may be given away or offered at special rates. In each case the effort will be to raise awareness of the forthcoming film among potential consumers within the profiled target audience.

ACTIVITY

1   Without researching the ways in which this film was actually marketed, choose a newly released film and decide what you would

Exhibition

Cinema exhibition has always tended to be controlled by a relatively small number
of companies, and often the major studios responsible for making films will have
considerable stakes in some of these companies that are responsible for showing
their products. If small independent exhibitors want to screen less well-known
films they need to know their local film-going market well, since they will be
working without the back-up of the major marketing campaigns that accompany
big studio productions.

But as was previously suggested, exhibition no longer refers simply to showing
films in the cinema. We can now see films on terrestrial TV, satellite and cable TV
(including specialist pay-to-view channels), on video or DVD using high-quality
home cinema set-ups, and now via the Internet and even mobile phones.

ACTIVITY

1   Research the ways in which the Internet is now used in relation to
film.

2   Find as many different sites as possible. These may be critical
magazines, fan-based sites, industry-organized sites or educational
sites.

3   Allocate one website per person to be explored in some depth.

4   Each person should prepare a short one-page A4 handout on their
website for everyone else, describing the main features and in
particular setting out what its role and purpose within the film process
might be said to be.

1   How many films are to be shown on terrestrial TV next week? How
    many hours of terrestrial TV scheduling do these films take up? How
    much does the terrestrial TV licence cost?
2   How many specialist film channels are available on satellite and cable
    TV? How many hours per day are films shown on these channels?
    How much does it cost to subscribe to these channels?
3   How many pay-to-view channels are now available to subscribers?
    How many hours per day are films shown on these channels? How
    much does it cost to purchase each film on these channels?

(You will obviously need to use either the *Radio Times* or some other
magazine showing programme schedules to complete this exercise. You
may like to work in groups to complete the task more efficiently.)

Film production, distribution and exhibition

Take any two films of your choice and try to trace their development through from
their initial inception as embryonic ideas to their box-office success (or failure).
Use the Internet to help you with your research, but be pragmatic about your
choice of films; look to see how much information seems to be available before
you make your final choice. The only limitation on your choice is that one film must
be from Hollywood and the other must be British. For each film you might try to
answer the following questions but do not treat these as anything more than
guidelines. You will not be able to find the answer to each of these questions and
you may well have ideas of your own for additional relevant information to include
under each phase of the industrial/commercial process.

1   What happened during pre-production?

   ■ Whose idea was the film? Did the idea start with the writer, or were writers
     brought in to develop a preconceived idea?
   ■ Where did the idea come from? Was it an original idea, or was it perhaps
     a book first or TV series or comic strip, or from some other source?
   ■ Who wrote the original script? Did other people become involved in the
     writing as the project progressed?
   ■ How easy was it to arrange the financial backing to make the film? Who
     were the financial backers?
   ■ How well known was the production company? What was its track record?
   ■ Who was the producer? How did he or she become involved?
   ■ Who was the director? How did he or she become involved?

2 What happened during the production phase?

- Was it an easy 'shoot'? If there were difficulties, what were they? Were there tensions between any of the key creative personnel, often known as 'the talent'?
- Was any part of the film shot on location? If so, where?
- Was any part shot in a studio? If so, which studio, where?
- Were there any difficulties with casting, or with acquiring the stars/actors the producer wanted?
- Was it shot within budget? Was it ever in danger of going over budget? What was that budget? Can you find a breakdown for the budget?
- Were there any changes to the script during production? How many changes or rewrites? Did the same scriptwriter(s) stay 'on board' all the time, or were some replaced?
- List as many people as possible making contributions to the production.
- If possible highlight some of their individual contributions.

3 What happened during the distribution phase?

- Who were the distributors? How well known was the company? What was their track record as distributors?
- How did the filmmakers decide where to release the film and when? What was the eventual release pattern?
- What deals were made for distribution abroad? How easily were these deals secured?
- Did they at any stage change their plans for the release pattern, and if so, why?
- What was the marketing and advertising strategy for the film? Was there a premiere, and if so, where?
- What outlets were used for advertising? Was TV used, for example?
- Were there any merchandising tie-ins?
- Was any additional publicity gained, and if so, how?

4 What happened during the exhibition phase?

- When was the film first released; also where and on how many screens?
- Was there a particular strategy attached to increasing the number of prints available?
- Were there any difficulties with the censors? How did the censors classify the film?
- Were there any other special restrictions placed on the exhibition of the film?
- What was the reaction of the critics to the film? Was it considered a critical success? Has it been reassessed since then?
- Did the film create any particular media debate, or make news headlines?
- How much money did the film take in its first year? Was it considered a commercial/financial success?
- Did it have 'legs'; that is, did it continue to run in the cinema for some time?

To make the point once more, there may well be questions here to which you cannot find the answer for your chosen film and there may be important points you would like to include that are not covered in the questions as set out. Remember: all this is only here to offer guidelines and possibilities; it is for you to work on tracing the development of your own chosen product from concept to the screen.

EXAM QUESTIONS

- To what extent are Hollywood films simply 'products' made to make a profit?

- How important is marketing in influencing people to watch Hollywood films both at the cinema and on DVD?

- How are billboard posters and poster-style advertisements in newspapers and magazines used to create audiences for films?

CONCLUSION

In order to study film it is important:

- to maintain a thoughtful and perceptive awareness of the fact that films exist as part of a film industry
- to realize that there is a complex commercial process to be gone through before a film reaches the screen
- to see films on one level at least as being sold to consumers and knowingly bought by those consumers as commercial products.

References and Further Reading

Abrams, N., Bell, I. and Udris, J. (2001) *Studying Film*, Arnold, London (ch. 2)
Corrigan, T. and White, P. (2004) *The Film Experience: An Introduction*, Bedford/ St Martin's, Boston, MA (ch. 1)
Gomery, D. (1988) 'Hollywood as industry' in Hill, J. and Church Gibson, P. (eds) *The Oxford Guide to Film Studies*, Oxford University Press, Oxford and New York

Kawin, B.F. (1992) *How Movies Work*, University of California Press, Los Angeles
and London (Part 3)

Kochberg, S. (2003) 'Cinema as institution' in Nelmes, J. (ed.) *An Introduction to
Film Studies*, Routledge, London

Lacey, N. (2005) *Introduction to Film*, Palgrave Macmillan, Basingstoke (ch. 3)

Miller, F. (1994) *MGM Posters: The golden years*, Turner Publishing, Atlanta

Nourmand, T. and Marsh, G. (eds) (2005) *Film Posters of the 90s: The essential
movies of the decade*, Aurum Press, London

(There is a range of poster books that are fairly easily available and are similar to
the two listed above.)

Useful Websites

www.imdb.com
www.variety.com
www.hollywoodreporter.com
www.filmfestivals.com
www.futuremovies.co.uk
www.radiotimes.com

(Websites such as those listed above may be of help if you're researching the
commercial development of recent films.)

www.filmfour.com
www.warnerbros.co.uk
www.thefilmfactory.co.uk (Buena Vista)
www.paramountpictures.co.uk
www.fox.co.uk
www.disney.co.uk
www.sonypictures.co.uk
www.pathe.co.uk
www.miramax.com
www.universalstudios.com

(Websites such as those listed above may be of help in looking at the ways in
which powerful studios promote their films.)

www.cineworld.co.uk
www.odean.co.uk
www.picturehouses.co.uk
www.screencinemas.co.uk
www.appolocinemas.co.uk
www.caledoniancinemas.co.uk
www.genesiscinema.co.uk
www.showcasecinemas.co.uk
www.myvue.com
www.screenroom.co.uk

(Websites such as those listed above may be of help in researching the exhibition
of films.)

5 HOLLYWOOD

This chapter deals with:

■ production, distribution and exhibition under Old Hollywood and New Hollywood
■ areas of continuity between Old Hollywood and New Hollywood
■ gaining a wider historical perspective on Hollywood

INFORMATION BOX *i*

This chapter will be relevant to FM2: British and American Film – Producers and Audiences for the WJEC AS level in Film Studies. However, you should note that the emphasis in the WJEC syllabus is on contemporary Hollywood and, strictly speaking, you are not being asked to investigate the Hollywood of the past in anything like the detail offered here. However, if you have the time for the reading and/or research, understanding where contemporary Hollywood has come from helps you to make greater sense of the current configuration of the American industry.

Difference and change within similarity and continuity

The production of a film followed by its distribution and then its exhibition is then the general process. However, there have been (and continue to be) changes to the way in which this basic pattern has been adapted and used by the industry over the years since cinema began at the end of the nineteenth century; and there have been (and continue to be) differences between the structure of the film industry in different countries.

Hollywood's greatest period of fame and cultural importance was arguably during the 1930s and 1940s in that period we have called the Studio System but which has also been described as The Golden Age of Hollywood or Classical Hollywood, and is sometimes known simply as Old Hollywood. In this one site of American industrial-style film development there were differences in the approach to the basic process of production, distribution and exhibition before and after this Golden Age and even changes during this period (including differences in approach from one studio to another).

In all likelihood, during your research into the phases of development of a Hollywood and British film at the end of the last chapter you will have noticed considerable differences within the basic framework between the processes bringing your two chosen movies to the screen. These differences may have been a product of the different strategies of different studios, the different cultural backgrounds of Hollywood and Britain, and perhaps most obviously as a result of differences in budget.

Old Hollywood–New Hollywood: a simplification

So, films have to be made, brought to the attention of the public and then shown. However, the relative importance of each of these three areas for Hollywood has been subject to change over time. Under the Studio System a few major companies tried as far as possible to make, distribute and show their own films, thereby effectively exerting direct control over all three stages of the process. But this system began to break up in the 1950s as the film business evolved different industrial strategies to try to meet new challenges, particularly those offered by the advent of television as a competitive medium and the movement of people out of town into newly developed suburbs and away from the old established cinemas. Old Hollywood came to be replaced by New Hollywood, with the major studios not so involved in making their own films but increasingly interested in financing independent productions and then controlling their distribution.

Of course, this is an oversimplification. The Studio System of the 1930s, 1940s and early 1950s was never static but was instead constantly changing, or evolving, whether in response to economic factors such as the Depression of the 1930s or external influences such as the Second World War. Within the general industrial framework known as the Studio System individual studios were also attempting different commercial strategies at different times. In the same way, so-called New Hollywood has followed a similar pattern, constantly adjusting to meet new challenges and take advantage of new commercial opportunities over the past 50 years.

Old Hollywood's unit-producer system

During the early years of the Studio System a few top executives such as Jack
Warner and Darryl Zanuck at Warner Brothers would oversee all film production,
effectively keeping a tight personal control over everything that was going on in
'their' studio. But in some studios this strong top-down management was later
modified into a 'unit-producer system' where a crew worked together under one
producer to complete six to eight films a year. These teams of workers, employed
directly by the studio, would sometimes specialize in a particular genre: examples
often given include Arthur Freed's unit at MGM which specialized in musicals, Val
Lawton's horror unit at RKO and Jerry Wald's unit at Warners, specializing in noir-
melodramas. (Try to find time to watch *Mildred Pierce* (Curtiz, 1945), since this
will provide you with an interesting example of noir-melodrama.) This was clearly
an economically sound way of working, since everybody on the team would
become a specialist on a particular type of film and therefore able to set up
equipment efficiently and effectively. Those responsible for setting up the lighting,
for example, could become noir-melodrama or musical or horror specialists and as
a result would be able to create the desired genre lighting effects with the minimum
of direction, thereby saving time and, most importantly, money.

ACTIVITY

1   Research any studio of your choice that was in business during the
    1930s and 1940s.
2   Try to sum up in note form the key developments in its evolution
    during this period using no more than one side of A4 paper.
3   Find other people who have researched other studios and exchange
    copies of your notes for copies of theirs in order to try to compile a
    package giving details of several studios from this period.

New Hollywood's package unit system

By contrast, in contemporary Hollywood there is what is known as a 'package unit' system at work: studio space is rented and personnel hired for the duration of the one project. Individual producers now have to put together a one-off package of finance, personnel, equipment and studio time for each film being made. The studios no longer have to be concerned with keeping busy what was effectively a factory-full of workers permanently on their payroll; instead arrangements can be made to film each one-off movie wherever is most convenient around the world, perhaps in places where union laws might be less stringent and rates of pay considerably lower. The main Hollywood companies were driven over to this system in an effort to cut expenditure in the 1950s in order to survive in the face of the decline of cinemagoing as a leisure activity.

ACTIVITY

You may like to try to look into the changes in leisure patterns and indeed home lifestyle that evolved in the USA after the Second World War. In what ways is it usually suggested that life changed for the majority of Americans at this time? Try to list as many features as possible of the new way of life that emerged post-1945.

Actors, directors and agents

Actors and directors have always been key personnel in the industry, but under Old Hollywood structures they were very much subservient to studio producers and executives. They were told to work on one project and then when that was

Figure 5.1 Shirley Temple – an Old Hollywood star – in *The Blue Bird* (1940)

finished they were assigned by their studio bosses to a new project: contracted to the studios they were quite simply at the beck-and-call of those studios. Stars sometimes tried to resist being typecast or undertaking a project that they did not feel was right for them in some way, but in doing so they risked being sidelined by the studio which effectively had the power to make or break their career.

ACTIVITY

Try to find one star from the period of the Studio System who had confrontations with his or her studio management. What were the disputes over and what were the outcomes?

Nowadays, both directors and stars have agents cutting deals for them and they (and their agents) have become relatively more powerful within the business, especially since they are no longer held under exclusive contracts to one particular studio as they were in the past. It could be argued that since perhaps the 1970s agencies have become the real power brokers in Hollywood, controlling stables of stars, directors, screenwriters, cinematographers, producers and other filmmaking personnel, and striking deals for clients in return for a percentage of earnings. A possible analogy would be with British football where there has been increasing concern in recent years that agents have become the most powerful behind-the-scenes people in the game: every footballer is signed to an agent and it is the agent who negotiates a player's contract with a club.

ACTIVITY

1   Find out the names of the major agencies in Hollywood. When were they set up and who now runs each of them? Can you find out what stars they have on their books?
2   Were there agencies around during the Studio System? If so, how powerful were they during this period and were there any particular limitations on their power?
3   When did agencies begin to have more power and what changes in the film industry brought this about?
4   If possible, share the information you find out with others, making sure you agree on the fundamental details and discussing your answers to 2 and 3 above to see if you have come up with the same basic ideas.

Producers

Finding themselves under the financial pressures outlined above in the 1950s, the studios were prepared to support the emergence of independent producers who offered them greater business flexibility, enabling them to pick and choose projects. The studios could back a particular production with these independent producers without any need to bankroll a workforce that stretched from stars to catering staff on a long-term basis. But this change also opened up the possibility of top creative personnel like stars and directors being able to negotiate freelance deals.

Under the Studio System producers exerted overall management control at any one time across a range of film projects that might be at various stages of completion. They would bring together a team of workers to complete each project under the supporting umbrella of the studio. With the end of the Studio System producers retained their importance with regard to each one-off film project, since they remained the linchpin executive needed to bring together the total package.

1 Take any film you have seen recently and find out who produced it. Then try to find out more about this person. What was their role on this particular production? What have they and others had to say about their involvement and contribution? What projects had s/he been involved in before?

2 Prepare a presentation on your producer and give it to a group of other students who may in turn be able to offer presentations on producers they have researched.

3 Can you arrive at a list of key factors or approaches that seem to feature in the careers and outlooks of all of these producers?

4 Discuss the lists you arrive at to see if everyone agrees on the key points. Facts, dates and lists of films are not as important as attitudes towards the industry, approaches towards the business of filmmaking, and thoughts on the industrial/commercial process.

The place of cheaper products within a big budget industry

The big players in the industry have of course always been interested in cheap-to-produce movies that were likely to offer good percentage profits. In the era of Old Hollywood companies such as Columbia and Universal invested in cheap B-movies (as opposed to expensive A-movies) from early in the 1930s. As the Depression hit America some cinemas began trying to attract hard-up customers by offering two feature films instead of one, creating a demand for these cheap supporting films. By the mid-1930s up to half of the outputs at Warners, Fox and RKO were also taken up with these movies.

At the same time about 10 per cent of studio output in the 1930s and 1940s comprised 'series pictures' such as those made by Warners using the 'Dead End Kids' or MGM's 'Andy Hardy' series starring Mickey Rooney.

Incidentally, it is often suggested that the market for films under Old Hollywood was much more homogenized; that is, that there was a single market to be catered for rather than a series of smaller market segments with differing demands. But 'series pictures' such as these show that the segmented nature of the market was recognized at the time with teenage audiences in particular being targeted by the 'Dead End Kids' films.

Figure 5.2 *Cat People* (1942) – a B-movie

ACTIVITY

■ See what you can find out about the 'Dead End Kids' series (or another series from the 1930s and 1940s of your choice). How many films were made in the series? How popular were they?
■ If you have the time, try to watch *Angels With Dirty Faces* (Curtiz, 1938) to see how the popular concept of the 'Dead End Kids' could be integrated into a bigger budget movie.

In more recent times there may not be B-movies but there are similar products such as made-for-TV movies or films that go straight to DVD. At the same time major studios have more recently recognized (especially on the back of the success of films coming out of the Sundance Film Festival for independent American movies, perhaps) the potential profitability of low-cost films, and have as a result set up arm's-length low-budget companies such as Fox Searchlight at Twentieth Century Fox.

Production: an overview

Although the film industry has clearly changed in many ways since the 1930s and
1940s, you could argue that it is the similarities which are most striking. For
example, the teenage market was recognized from quite early on, as was the place
within the industry of cheap, quickly made movies alongside films demanding larger
budgets.

Similarly, although it is true that the status and power of stars has changed, a
further constant factor within the business has been the way in which stars have
always been used to promote and sell the film product. One of the major types of

film on offer during the Studio System era was the feature film marketed and made as a 'star vehicle' to show off the qualities that made the particular star attractive to his or her target audience. In this environment stars signed to particular studios were seen as a hugely valuable resource. Nowadays, as we have said, stars receive massive salaries compared with their counterparts under the Old Hollywood structures but in fact this only reflects their continued importance in marketing and securing box-office returns: we could argue that they are being used by the industry in very similar ways to the 1930s and 1940s. (Although, on the other hand, it is true to say that stars are now often additionally important in securing finance for a project: if as a producer you can get a top star signed up to a project the other parts of the package are likely to begin to fall into place. Again, be aware of the fact that there is never a simple answer to any of these issues: for every point you make in favour of seeing things in one way it is probably possible to view the matter from an opposing perspective.)

Related to the role of stars there is also of course the way in which the 'star–genre' formula has been used in both Old and New Hollywood. At Warners during the Classical Hollywood period, for instance, it could be argued that the presence of James Cagney and Edward G. Robinson meant a cycle of crime dramas and gangster movies were likely to be inevitable products of this studio. The genre approach and linking of particular stars to particular genres has continued to be used by New Hollywood, since it seems to continue to work as an effective marketing strategy: in effect the 'star–genre' relationship means a known, tried-and-tested product is being guaranteed to the customer. The British actor Hugh Grant may have succeeded in creating something of a career for himself in Hollywood but it is on Hollywood's terms. Grant guarantees the re-production in movie after movie of a certain 'lovable young man, requiring mothering', a romantic comedy character that the industry finds particularly useful in attracting an audience (and therefore profit) for a certain genre of film.

Figure 5.3 *Love Actually* (2003) and *Music and Lyrics* (2007) – note the similar dress and actions required of Hugh Grant

ACTIVITY

- List your favourite Hollywood film actors and beside each note the genre (or genres) most usually attached to each.
- Make a note of any roles in which this actor has stepped outside of his or her normal character portrayal and genre framework.
- Consider whether these films that show the actor outside of his or her normal range were successful or not at the box-office. If they were relatively unsuccessful, reflect on whether you think the change in expected role for this actor could have had anything to do with his or her lack of success. If they were successful in terms of box-office takings how was the transition achieved? What was it that enabled audiences to make the move to seeing 'their' star in a different role? Was it the way in which this played directly against expectations and so was interesting, since it was always 'playing off of' this star's more usual performances? Or was it perhaps that the role, although on the surface something different, was actually not that far from what was usually expected of this star (think of Eastwood's western persona as Dirty Harry, for example)?
- Because of their increased power within the industry do contemporary stars have more opportunities to move outside of a small potentially typecasting range of parts than the stars of Old Hollywood? If possible, discuss this with a small group of other people studying film.

Distribution in Old Hollywood and New Hollywood

Despite having their production 'factories' located in sunny California (the sun of course meant that you could film outside for longer each day and for more days in a year), during the studio era all the major studios had New York offices that were the site of ultimate power. It was from here that finance, marketing and sales were controlled. The industry during this period was entirely market-driven and commercially motivated: today at this fundamental level nothing is any different. It is still within production, finance and distribution that the major studios hold most power, and in many cases we are still talking about the same companies that dominated the 1930s and 1940s: Paramount, Warner Brothers, Columbia, Universal, Disney and Twentieth Century Fox. The control of advertising and promotion networks guarantees a market for the products of these major corporations; and it is the distributor who dictates the terms of any deals agreed with both producers and exhibition outlets.

- Over a period of several weeks collect data on the top ten films in the USA and Britain (available in several weekend newspapers and film magazines).
- Note the distributors of each film, taking particular note of which names occur most frequently. But also look to see how much their films are taking, because one successful blockbuster movie could take more than the accumulated total made by several other films with less financial backing.
- Look to see whether films hold their position well in the charts over several weeks or whether they fall away quickly. See if there are any films that seem to start quite slowly but then hold their own in the lists reasonably well. In other words, do these films have 'legs' and do they seem to manage to achieve good 'word of mouth'?

Remember to be aware of the key strategic position occupied by the distributor. The producers of films can in theory make any films they want and as many films as they wish; however, if they cannot get the films out to the public (that is, they cannot distribute them), then their films will never be seen. Exhibitors can in theory show any films they like in their cinemas; however, in practice they can only screen films the distributors are willing to let them have. Therefore, in effect, if you have control over distribution you have control over the whole film industry.

Figure 5.4
Titanic (1997)

In the studio era, in addition to A-movies and B-movies studios also occasionally put out more expensive 'prestige pictures', such as MGM's *The Wizard of Oz* (1939), released in selected first-run theatres. Today, high-cost, potentially lucrative 'special attractions' such as Twentieth Century Fox's *Titanic* (Cameron, 1997) may be said to fulfil the same function; but now immediate saturation of the marketplace, flooding the film into as many cinemas as possible from the first weekend, would be the opening strategy.

In both eras the films make a statement about the power of the studios involved. Despite the costs involved it is still calculated in both cases that the film will make money, although it has to be said that Twentieth Century Fox studio boss Bill Mechanic is on record as saying that *Titanic* was definitely not meant to cost as much as it did with the director, James Cameron, apparently continually going over budget.

The recognition of films as viable commercial propositions

In America a key factor in the film industry's commercial success has been the way in which it has received backing from both the banks and the government. Wall Street bankers became especially important in backing the industry during the Depression of the 1930s while the government basically condoned the control over the industry operated by just a few powerful companies (by 1939 the Big Five controlled about 2,600 theatres, only about 15 per cent of the total but 80 per cent of the metropolitan first-run theatres). And although the studios were forced by court intervention to back away from vertical integration in the 1950s, this in fact only worked to strengthen their economic position within the changing circumstances of the period. They were able to reduce costs while reinforcing their control over distribution, the most important sector within the film business.

Today, the US government continues to show that it is fully aware of the worldwide importance of its film industry and negotiates to secure global trade deals that are as favourable as possible to Hollywood. The central international body regulating world trade, the General Agreement on Tariffs and Trade (GATT), which was replaced by the World Trade Organization in 1995, has since shortly after the Second World War worked towards 'the liberalization of world trade'. In practice this has meant opening up as many areas as possible within the global market to products from the rich industrialized countries of the West. In relation to the film industry, the USA has consistently argued that other countries should not be able to operate trade policies designed to defend their film industries against American competition. In Europe, France and Italy in particular have tried to limit the market for Hollywood products in their countries. In Britain at any one time more than 90 per cent of screens are showing American films.

ACTIVITY

1 In groups, choose one national newspaper each and for the next week photocopy any articles you can find that are in any way related to the film industry.
2 Spend time comparing the articles you have come up with. How many articles have you managed to find in each newspaper? Do some papers seem to give more coverage to film-related issues than others? Do they all cover the same issues?
3 Were there any articles in the business sections of newspapers? Remember, these could be about a parent company or multinational corporation that is involved in a wide range of media with film production, distribution and/or exhibition being only a part of their operations. Were there any articles that discussed world trade agreements?
4 Have any members of the group chosen articles that other people would not at first have thought were related to the film industry?

INFORMATION BOX

Reading an upmarket newspaper is probably one of the best ways to keep abreast of changes happening in the film industry. (It will also help you to improve your use of language, discovering new ways of structuring sentences and widening your vocabulary.) Start off by simply trying to find a couple of articles a week that seem interesting and perhaps in some way relevant to your studies.

Awareness of the importance of marketing

Marketing may be said to be an increasingly important area of the film industry with budgets for this part of the operation in some cases almost matching production costs (although in truth the importance of selling the product often as an escapist fantasy has always been recognized by Hollywood). For the studios, marketing (as discussed in the previous chapter) essentially involves:

- securing free publicity in the editorial sections of the media whenever possible
- devising eye-catching paid-for advertising

- obtaining tie-ins with other consumer products that will result in symbiotic promotional pay-offs for both products
- clinching merchandising deals that will create additional income but also further work to keep film product as a whole in the public eye.

Obvious summer, Christmas and spring holiday blockbuster seasons have now emerged; and movies are perhaps being reviewed by film critics with increasing seriousness as art as well as entertainment.

However, as suggested above, do keep in mind that this is nothing new for the film industry: gimmicky publicity stunts, merchandising, and magazines devoted to the stars and their movies were also features of the Studio System; the pressure to see film as an art-form as well as entertainment goes back to the silent era; and gossip-driven interest in the lives, loves and lies of stars has been a constant feature of the media.

ACTIVITY

1 Go through the *Radio Times* or a similar magazine showing next week's TV schedules and make a note of the film review shows available according to channel, day and time.
2 Record as many of these programmes as possible and watch them with a group of fellow students if possible.
3 How do the shows compare? Do they review the same films? Do they handle their reviews in similar or different ways? Are there features that make each show distinctively different? How serious-minded would you say each show is aiming to be?
4 Does each show seem to be targeted at a particular audience? Can you find out each show's ratings? Which is the most popular? From your viewing why would you think this is the case?

Willingness to integrate independents into the system

The major Hollywood studios have always it seems been willing to integrate independent companies into the industry. In a sense, in doing so they have only been responding to business pressures so that, for example, as the Studio System began to break up they were increasingly willing to use independent companies often almost as arm's-length production units. This attitude could be seen as further evidence of the sensible business pragmatism displayed by the studios for the most part since the earliest days.

There were several factors moving the industry towards using independent companies for film production during the 1940s and 1950s.

- With cinema attendance rising, there was increased demand for top feature films during the Second World War and this meant that studios were prepared to distribute independent movies to help meet this demand. Production facilities and financing as well as distribution expertise would be provided by the studio for these films. An example of this trend would be Frank Capra's *Meet John Doe* (1940) which was made with Warner.
- At the same time an increasing number of people within the industry also began to work as 'hyphenates'; that is, they fulfilled two major roles on any single film. This accorded them increased status and power within the industry: examples would be producer-director Mitchell Leisen and writer-director Preston Sturges at Paramount.
- In addition, the Screen Actors Guild (recognized by the studios in 1938), the Screen Directors Guild (1939) and the Screen Writers Guild (1941) emerged as collective organizations prepared to challenge total studio control. In this changing atmosphere top 'talent' such as Howard Hawks began to work on a freelance basis.

In a sense this trend has continued so that independent filmmakers like Spike Lee have established their own production companies. However, it still remains the case that these production companies depend for distribution on the majors: Paramount, Warner Brothers (Time-Warner-AOL), Universal Pictures (Matsushita), Twentieth Century Fox (News Corporation), Disney and Columbia Pictures (Sony), so that ultimate control of the industry remains with these organizations.

Often successful independents which go on to distribute their own films end up being taken over by one of the big names. New Line, for example, was quite successful in the early 1990s but was taken over by Turner Broadcasting which became part of Time Warner in 1996. Miramax, another successful independent from the period, was taken over by Disney in 1994.

Importance of the overseas market

It is also the case that from its inception as an industry the American film business recognized the importance of the overseas market. The domestic market was large enough to sustain the industry independently and yet there was still a willingness to consider in particular possibilities offered by the European market. By the late 1930s Hollywood derived more than 30 per cent of its revenue from overseas markets with 45 per cent of this coming from Britain and a further 30 per cent from continental Europe. Today, although other areas of the world (especially Japan) have become increasingly important within the US overseas market, the essential fact remains the same in that a huge onus is put on securing global sales with blockbusters now regularly grossing more abroad than in the USA.

Willingness to adapt to new technologies

When radio in the home posed an alternative to cinema for family entertainment in the late 1920s the industry quickly adopted sound. When television posed a similar threat in the 1950s the industry quickly adopted colour, widescreen and other new technologies in an effort to beat off the new rival. Clearly, TV sets used small screens and were initially only available in black and white, so adopting colour and widescreen were obvious ways of marking out the cinema experience as something special.

In its battle against TV the industry was certainly not entirely successful, with the decline in cinema attendance through the 1950s and 1960s mirroring the uptake on TV sets in the home. But it still remains the case that overall the cinema industry has always been responsive to potentially alternative new technologies intruding into their marketplace.

Although initially perceiving new technologies as a threat, the industry especially in recent years has been quick to make use of them for their own ends. Hollywood has capitalized on new markets in the home and at the multiplex, using cable and satellite film channels to get TV viewers to pay for films they watch at home. (It is worth stopping to consider carefully the extent of the use the film industry now makes of television, which was initially seen as such a threat.)

The industry eventually made similar use first of videos and then DVDs. By 1986 video sales surpassed box-office takings in the USA, and by the 1990s the rentals and sales market was worth more than $10 billion; and yet seemingly this did not detract from cinemagoing, with 20 million a week visiting multiplexes in the USA by the early 1990s.

What the industry has come to recognize is the importance of co-functioning media (other media that may be used to support and magnify the impact of film). Particularly from the late 1980s the studios began to realize that the way forward was to position film as the central focus of a multimedia business. Multinational multimedia corporations eventually came to dominate the industry (for example, Time-Warner-AOL and News Corporation), effectively reintroducing vertical integration in a magnified form. Smaller, supposedly independent filmmakers are often in fact owned by multinationals (e.g. Miramax (Disney) and New Line (Time Warner)). What the industry uses now is a special form of business energy known as synergy.

The theatrical release is still the key commercial moment for any film in the sense that success or failure here determines the profitability of any deals that are going to be secured for the release of the product into other 'windows': you can obviously charge cable and satellite suppliers, terrestrial television companies and overseas distributors more for the rights to a film that has been a success on its initial release. But the key factor is that there is now an array of further marketing opportunities for any film over and beyond its cinema release.

ACTIVITY

1   The balance between box-office takings and income from DVD rentals and sales can obviously change each year. From research (perhaps on the Internet, where the UK Film Council website would be a good starting point), can you find out the current situation? Can you find out the trend over recent years?

2   How does the number of cinema tickets sold in a year compare to the number of DVDs rented and sold?

3   What happens when you include illegal DVD sales? How accurate are 'guesstimates' in this area?

Control of exhibition outlets

Eight companies dominated the 1930s and 1940s: five corporations (Paramount, Loew's (later MGM), Fox Film (later Twentieh Century Fox), Warner Brothers and Radio-Keith-Orpheum (RKO)) which each ran a studio, undertook marketing and distribution, and owned a chain of cinemas, and three smaller companies (Universal, Columbia and United Artists) owning no cinemas but cooperating with the 'Big Five' to control the industry. Films went to cinemas owned by the 'Big Five' for first-runs (Paramount owned over 1,000 cinemas during the 1940s) and only then to independent theatres. These independents often had to accept 'block booking' of a corporation's output and 'blind buying'. This system was known as vertical integration, meaning that the main studios operated within each of the three main areas within the industry – production, distribution and exhibition.

> **BLOCK BOOKING:** means you have to agree to take all of the films produced by a studio in a year, including the lesser films, in order to get the major productions.

> **BLIND BUYING:** means you have to take the films on offer without having a chance to first view them to see if you want them or not.

> **VERTICAL INTEGRATION:** refers to the way in which studios in the 1930s and 1940s integrated the whole process from making to screening films under their control.

Although this oligopoly situation was broken in the 1950s, following a 1948 court ruling against Paramount which found that such extensive control of the industry was illegal, the industry giants seem to have re-established similar if not stronger control today, although it is true to say that they have not returned to a situation of having direct control over exhibition. Cinemas in the USA and UK are now largely owned by companies that are only involved in exhibition. Despite being forced to divest themselves of cinemas in the 1950s, the majors had interests in 14 per cent of US and Canadian screens by the late 1980s with four cinema circuits controlling almost 30 per cent of exhibition outlets in the USA and the top 12 cinema circuits controlling 45 per cent of cinemas. National Amusements (linked to Paramount through the parent company Viacom) currently has 1,500 screens in North America and more than 200 screens in Britain, but in both cases this is only a small part of the total number of screens.

> **OLIGOPOLY:** term used to describe the situation in which a small group of companies exerts powerful, almost exclusive control over the business being done within any particular industry.
>
> (Please note: this is not the same as a monopoly which is where just one company dominates a whole industry.)

Target audiences

It may be argued that target audiences have changed since the Studio System days, with major companies such as AMC (American Multi-Cinema) in the USA with well over 5,000 screens aiming to locate their multiplexes in 'middle-class areas inhabited by college-educated families'. Perhaps audiences were much more predominantly working class in the 1930s and 1940s.

It may also be argued that the market is now much more strongly divided into segments with a range of screens catering to a range of tastes. And yet, genre and star categorizations of product always meant that the Hollywood product was in fact carefully differentiated for specifically targeted market segments. So, perhaps the audience was not really that much more homogeneous in the Classical Hollywood period.

Domination of the major studios over distribution means that they effectively continue to control exhibition, since no exhibitor is going to jeopardize retaining a major source of income. In addition, of course, the Hollywood product has the advantage of massive financial resources for marketing and production.

Cinemas and multiplexes

The multiplex has perhaps made the cinema experience somewhat different from that of the 1930s and 1940s, although even then the effort was often to sell the total experience of the evening out rather than simply the film. Just consider the picture palaces of the 1930s and 1940s. These were huge, cavernous spaces, palace-like in their dimensions and in their décor. Compare this with the homes that most of the punters were coming from. Remember also that the clients would be waited on by uniformed ushers and usherettes and then you will realize that the idea of selling 'the whole experience' is nothing new in the cinema business. All of this is not to say that the multiplex has not played a major role in reviving cinema fortunes in the UK: the year before the opening of the first multiplex in Milton Keynes in 1985 attendance was down to 52 million admissions per year, but by 1996 that figure was up to more than 123 million.

Conclusion: difference or continuity?

The simple fact is that the major studios continue to dominate the film industry with takeovers and mergers within the wider media entertainments industry ('horizontal integration') only serving to further reinforce this control. It could be argued that in the 1960s and 1970s there was some loss of control for the major Hollywood studios but it could also be argued that since the mid-1980s the major studios have regained the sort of overall level of control over production, distribution and exhibition that they enjoyed in the 1930s and 1940s.

The major difference is that now the income of these studios is no longer so dependent upon immediate box-office takings. Cinema exhibition is important and initial success here means guaranteed profits in every succeeding sales window associated with the film. However, powerful marketing, global distribution and the ability to sell essentially the same product again and again in a variety of 'windows' around the world means losses can generally be avoided on even the biggest box-office 'flop'.

The American presence around the world as an imperial power, particularly after the Second World War, has given additional access to global markets (e.g. Germany and Japan). At the same time American companies have become multinational companies in a process that has gone on alongside the globalization of American-English as a first international business language, further assisting market penetration. In addition, the level of financial resources available to these massive corporations crucially means that they are able to absorb greater levels of risk than smaller companies and therefore have inevitably achieved business longevity.

Figure 5.5 (opposite) A modern multiplex and a traditional picture palace

BRITISH AND AMERICAN FILM (FM2)

CONCLUSION

In order to study film it is useful:

- ■ to have some awareness of the historical development of the film industry in Hollywood
- ■ to be able to compare Old Hollywood with New Hollywood; that is, former processes used in Hollywood with more contemporary processes.

The key to understanding Hollywood as a whole is:

- ■ to realize that filmmaking in Hollywood has always been seen as a commercial process.

References and Further Reading

Abrams, N., Bell, I. and Udris, J. (2001) *Studying Film*, Arnold, London (chs. 1 and 4)

Balio, T. (1996) 'Adjusting to the new global economy: Hollywood in the 1990s' in Moran, A. *Film Policy*, Routledge, London

Balio, T. (1998) 'A major presence in all the world's important markets: the globalization of Hollywood in the 1990s' in Neale, S. and Murray S. (eds) *Contemporary Hollywood Cinema*, Routledge, London

Belton, J. (1996a) 'Technology and innovation' in Nowell-Smith, G. (ed.) *The Oxford History of World Cinema*, Oxford University Press, Oxford and New York

Belton, J. (1996b) 'New technologies' in Nowell-Smith, G. (ed.) *The Oxford History of World Cinema*, Oxford University Press, Oxford and New York

Finler, J.W. (2003) *The Hollywood Story*, Wallflower, London and New York

Gomery, D. (1996a) 'Transformation of the Hollywood system' in Nowell-Smith, G. (ed.) *The Oxford History of World Cinema*, Oxford University Press, Oxford and New York

Gomery, D. (1996b) 'The new Hollywood' in Nowell-Smith, G. (ed.) *The Oxford History of World Cinema*, Oxford University Press, Oxford and New York

Gomery, D. (1998) 'Hollywood corporate business practice and periodizing contemporary film history' in Neale, S. and Murray S. (eds) *Contemporary Hollywood Cinema*, Routledge, London

King, G. (2005a) *American Independent Cinema*, I.B. Tauris, London and New York (ch. 1)

King, G. (2005b) *New Hollywood Cinema: An introduction*, I.B. Tauris, London and New York

Lacey, N. (2005) *Introduction to Film*, Palgrave Macmillan, Basingstoke (ch. 3)

Maltby, R. (1998) 'Nobody knows everything: post-classical historiographies and consolidated entertainment' in Neale, S. and Murray S. (eds) *Contemporary Hollywood Cinema*, Routledge, London

Moran, A. (1996) 'Terms for a reader: film, Hollywood, national cinema, cultural identity and film policy' in Moran, A. *Film Policy*, Routledge, London

Parkinson, D. (1995) *History of Film*, Thames and Hudson, London and New York (chs 4 and 6)

Schatz, T. (1996) 'Hollywood the triumph of the studio system' in Nowell-Smith, G. (ed.) *The Oxford History of World Cinema*, Oxford University Press, Oxford and New York

Smith, M. (1998) 'Theses on the philosophy of Hollywood history' in Neale, S. and Murray S. (eds) *Contemporary Hollywood Cinema*, Routledge, London

Useful Website

www.ukfilmcouncil.org.uk

6 THE BRITISH FILM INDUSTRY

This chapter asks:

- What is distinctive and different about the British film industry?
- What measures are employed by the industry to prosper on a world stage?
- How the UK Film Council are engaging with developing the British film industry

The British film industry controls a powerful medium that tells British stories, and shapes how the British see themselves, how the world sees them, and how they see the world. It offers reflections on and explorations of British life (and the lives of other nations from a British perspective), and adds to a sense and construction of a national identity.

British film serves many diverse cultural purposes, engaging British society with issues that impact on their lives and the lives of those with whom they may not have direct contact but nevertheless share common ground within that society. It reflects the make-up of society, offering representations of self and others, and thus plays an important role in defining social debate, and relationships between groups within society. In reflecting society it plays an equally important role in enriching the spectator, by exposing the range of cultural experiences available within their own society. In recent years British film has become confident in expanding its range to include a wider cross-section of ethnic groupings, gender groupings and cultural groupings, and as such is promoting the diversity of regional identities and from this diversity is offering a more representative and inclusive national identity.

A distinctive and different cinema

In her paper 'Government and the Value of Culture', Tessa Jowell, Minister for Culture and the Arts, made no mention of film as a significant medium of culture, and in doing so indicated that she does not perceive film as being in the same kind of cultural arena as other art-forms (theatre, for example). Perhaps this is due to British cinema being a victim of its own success, with increasing numbers of indigenous film being produced and cinemagoing reaching record levels (or at least levels not seen since the 1940s). UK cinema admissions are currently in an upward trend, seeing them increasing on average between 8 per cent and 12 per cent each year for the past four years. With in excess of 180 million tickets sold (a figure that was inconceivable 20 years ago), much of the credit should go towards the cinemas themselves, as they have inwardly invested significant proportions of their profits to improve the cinemagoing experience. If government sees a successful, thriving economy generated by British film then it is likely to be blinded to its artistic and cultural significance, concentrating instead on other cultural arenas that do not see such large audiences or levels of economic success.

What the government does not see from admissions figures is that approximately 80 per cent of UK box-office come out of mainstream films distributed by American distributors and that in comparison with other EU countries Britain is exposed to a limited range of films, with American product squeezing out indigenous exhibition.

Other than the product that British film delivers (in artistic terms of story), which is often centred around British 'themes' and values, the 'little Englander', or the Englishman abroad, and may well be classed as a 'heritage film', it is the structure of the industry here that makes it distinctive and different, and which is both a boon and problem to its success.

In America the film industry realized (a long time ago) that it is in international distribution where the serious money is to be earned (up to 80 per cent of a film's profit can come through this source), and so they invest heavily in this end of the market. Retaining the distribution rights to their films also means that these films continue to offer potential profits for many years to come, thus ensuring a continuity of cash flow. Additional profit can be reinvested in the creation of product, and as such distribution successfully 'pulls' production.

The British market however has evolved from an historic position of being production led, with entrepreneurial producers determinedly 'pushing' their films through to completion and distribution. This distribution is almost invariably through an American company, and in order to complete the film the producer may have agreed a disadvantageous pre-sale of the distribution rights (e.g. cinema, DVD/video, pay-per-view, satellite TV, terrestrial broadcasting, alternative platforms), meaning that any money made is likely not to be reinvested in British production, being instead diverted overseas.

The British film industry has been compared to a 'cottage industry' when seen in relation to the industrialized American model, and this, coupled with its inability to deliver a production line of products and in so doing mitigate risk by having a large enough slate of films to ensure failures do not have such a devastating effect, appears as a disincentive to potential investors. Integrated support from the broadcasting industry is deceptive as it appears to play a significant role, yet the BBC spends approximately 1 per cent of its revenue on filmmaking, while the other broadcasters (with the notable exception of Channel 4) spend even less per year.

This cottage industry is also reflected in production where many companies are established to produce one film, and may well disappear after its completion (whether successful or not), resulting in an industry that is continually re-inventing itself, and never establishing the fixed financial structures, systems and infrastructures that may be used and exploited continually into the future. With 95 per cent of production companies in Britain employing fewer than ten people, it is no surprise that they are unable to compete with American, or indeed other, national cinemas. Forty-three domestic British films were produced in Britain in 2003 and 27 in 2004 (there were only two made in 1982 however), whereas by comparison Bollywood's output is approaching 1,000 per year. With limited distribution these British films did not fare well at the box-office either in Britain or internationally, with the most successful production of 2004 in terms of box-office receipts being *Shaun of the Dead* (Big Talk/Studio Canal/WT2/Working Title 2004, Director: Edgar Wright), the comedy zombie movie spoof. Worldwide demand for film has exceeded all records, with growing audiences and diversity of exhibition platforms to meet that demand. The British film industry however has not been in a position to successfully and vigorously respond to this demand and (since in 1984 it was celebrating its ability to produce 20 features) currently appears to be sinking back to a position it was in over 20 years ago.

This is in clear contrast to the American model where the film industry has diversified to strengthen and develop links with other media and other delivery

Figure 6.1 *Shaun of the Dead* (2004)

platforms, and in so doing has created vast media empires, conglomerates that maximize the profit from a single film through owning and controlling the rights to every element in it. Thus even a weak film will eventually come into profit without damaging the parent company.

However, it did produce such cinematic gems as *Enduring Love* (Film Four/Film Council/Pathe/Free Range/Inside Track/Ridgeway 2004, Director: Roger Michell) and *Bullet Boy* (BBC/Film Council/Shine 2004, Director: Saul Dibb) in the same year, both of which exceeded their box-office expectations considerably. Each was connected solidly with contemporary city life and each reflected the landscape and architecture of London as a vibrant, diverse, multicultural melting-pot, updating the stereotype and rewriting London and indeed Britain once more. Both films presented a London that was known and real to the English audience, and as such this may have prefaced their respective successes.

ACTIVITY

■ If Britain cannot compete on the world stage, and retiring to a 'cottage industry' style of production is not moving the film industry forward, what approach should British film take? Consider developments in production, distribution and exhibition.

continued

Surviving in the shadows

The picture is not all negative however. The amount of international awards that British filmmakers have won (particularly in the past 20 years) is notable and is significantly out of proportion to the size of the British film industry on the world stage. As Alan Parker noted in his 2002 presentation to the UK film industry entitled 'Building a Sustainable UK Film Industry':

> **First. We have outstanding creative skills. We've got superb writers, directors and actors – not to mention the creators of hugely valuable intellectual properties like Harry Potter. Richard Curtis, for instance, has written British films which have grossed over a billion dollars at the world box office.**
>
> **Second. We have outstanding studios and facilities companies, world-class costumiers, camera companies and digital post-production houses – studios and facilities which have been a magnet for inward investment, principally from the US.**
>
> **Third. We still have – just about – the finest technicians and craftspeople anywhere – although their numbers are diminishing at a worrying rate.**
>
> **I could also add a fourth: we have the English language – not just the same language of American movies, but that of the Internet.**

In fact, in terms of the rest of the world, the British film industry is in good shape and is seen as one of the most dynamic in the world. With the global market for film estimated at $63 billion in 2002 – and the American industry taking an 80 per cent share of this global market – the British film industry took 5 per cent, a figure that may superficially seem low when compared with the 80 per cent American share, but when compared with the rest of the world it means that Britain has 25 per cent of the non-American share, a healthy figure by any standards. Britain is now in fact the world's third largest film market against revenue (after America and Japan).

The British government has been fundamental in creating the conditions for this success, and one particular piece of tax law – the Section 42 tax break (which offers producers about 10 per cent of their budget back in the form of a tax break, and which makes Britain a very attractive place in which to shoot a movie) has proved incredibly useful in attracting filmmakers to British shores in the face of stiff competition from Eastern Europe, South Africa, Canada and New Zealand, and has promoted Britain as a destination that is high on the priority lists of many of the world's filmmakers.

Distribution is changing, with the Film Council taking determined measures to develop and support indigenous distribution companies that can compete on the world stage. Distribution is currently controlled by America through a number of powerful distribution companies, who preference their own and other American product above British releases, creating the situation where British films find it hard to reach their audiences. The American-owned Buena Vista, which distributes Disney and Miramax films, has the largest share of the British distribution market, with another American company UIP following hot on their heels. With players of this size and strength dividing up the market between them it is perhaps surprising that running a reasonably close third is an independent British-owned company Entertainment, which has brought a remarkable slate of successful films on to the market and has had considerable commercial success.

The Film Council is also looking at ways of improving the balance in ownership of Britain's cinemas, and is already piloting a number of schemes designed to offer support to the great number of independent cinemas that dot the country. The landscape has changed for the major players also in recent years, with cinema chains being acquired by venture capitalists who see them as reliable investments.

The Odeon and UCI chains were bought by a venture capitalist group, *Terra Firma*, in August 2004, and the Warner Village chain was purchased and rebranded by *Vue* (another venture capitalist group) in May 2003. The American Blackstone Group bought both Cine UK and the UGC chains at the end of 2004, which means that in terms of British exhibition the American production conglomerates now own very little. With the advent of digital acquisition, distribution and exhibition in cinemas, which is being advocated and supported by the Film Council, it is possible that controlling interests in British cinemas could return to British industrial control for the first time in over 50 years.

ACTIVITY

- Look at the strengths outlined by Alan Parker (above). Which do you feel is the most important to maintain? What other strengths would you add to this list?

continued

- The market for exhibition is changing rapidly. Find out who owns your local cinemas. Are they independent or part of a chain? What are the practical differences? List the advantages and disadvantages of each – which one comes off best?
- Visit the Film Council website and look at the papers there on digital futures. In a group, discuss the potential that digital distribution and exhibition offers the British Film Industry. Do you think it will impact on broadcasting? What overall effect do you think it will have on the British film industry?
- How well do you think the British film industry is surviving in the shadow of Hollywood? What can it do to ensure this survival continues?

References amd Further Reading

Goldsmith, B. and O'Regan, T. (2005) *The Film Studio: Film production in the global economy*, Rowman & Littlefield

Useful Websites

http://www.filmcouncil.org

The Economic Contribution of the UK Film Industry (UK Film Council/Pinewood Shepperton commissioned report) http://www.ukfilmcouncil.org.uk/ information/ downloads/?subject=39

The Economic Impact of the UK Screen Industries (UK Film Council commissioned report) http://www.ukfilmcouncil.org.uk/information/downloads/?subject=40

http://www.skillset.org/film

7 SUPPLY AND DEMAND

This chapter will deal with:

- ways in which audiences as both fans and consumers may be seen to have a role within the filmmaking process
- ways in which audiences as both fans and consumers can put pressure on the film industry to produce the products they want to see
- ways in which the film industry is able to exert pressure to try to create fans and encourage consumption

INFORMATION BOX

This chapter will be particularly relevant to FM2: British and American Film – Producers and Audiences for the WJEC AS level in Film Studies. Although the particular focus will be on audiences as fans and consumers of films, we will need to explore the roles of both producers and audiences, since the dependent relationship between the two is crucial to the industry.

The early cinema experience – the creation of demand

As the initially perhaps rather strange nature of film came to be accepted during the early 1900s, so too the practice of going out to watch movies as a form of entertainment came to be accepted socially and thought of as a normal, everyday experience. However, in studying the film industry it is as well to remember that the experience of going to the cinema is, in fact, a socially engineered practice found only in societies where the culture has embraced not only film technology but also the concept of film as a commercial proposition. In order to make money from the movies the early exhibitors of film had to attract the public to a venue where people could be charged for watching the products on offer. In doing so they were beginning to engineer a situation in which the public could be encouraged to become consumers of film products on a regular basis.

The commercial development of the idea of cinema

Early cinemas were primitive affairs – perhaps a former shop that had been cleared and filled with chairs or a fairground tent erected in one town after another. However, by as early as the 1910s and 1920s in some areas in America the concept had been developed to the stage where cinemas were such grand places that they were known as 'picture palaces'. These venues to all intents and purposes were like 'palaces', with rich drapes, thick carpets, intricate plasterwork, magnificent entrance halls, expensive chandelier lighting, sweeping flights of stairs and uniformed ushers whose job was to treat patrons with the respect due to their betters. It is often said that multiplex cinemas were such an important innovation for the film industry in Britain in the mid-1980s because they recognized the need to give the public not only a choice of films but also an appealing social experience. Yet the importance of the 'total experience', the recognition that what was being sold was not just the film itself, was appreciated just as strongly by the exhibitors who invested money in building the 'picture palaces' in the early years of cinema. They were part of a large group of entrepreneurial businessmen in the United States who recognized early on the commercial possibilities for film.

Figure 7.1
A picture palace

The popularity of the cinema experience

Of course, the presence of a large domestic market looking for cheap entertainment helped to make the possibilities clear to the business community. In particular, it has been suggested that with large immigrant communities in the United States lacking a good command of English, silent cinema was an especially appropriate form of entertainment that was always likely to become instantly popular. By 1930 Americans were making 80 million visits a week to cinemas across the country – a figure that equated to 65 per cent of the population going once a week. This percentage dropped off a little during the economic Depression of the 1930s but still held steady at around 60 per cent. Clearly such popularity places a huge onus on the industry to supply this demand for product.

In terms of sheer numbers, the cinema was at the height of its popularity immediately after the Second World War with 90 million visits a week being made to cinemas in America and more than 30 million a week in Britain. Today, despite increases in attendance over the past 20 years, those figures are down to 27 million a week in the USA and just over three million a week in Britain.

ACTIVITY

1   Try to find older members of your family or family friends who are willing to be interviewed about their cinemagoing experiences. Draw up a series of questions before you sit down to interview them but do not feel restricted to these areas if you find the discussion developing in unexpected but interesting directions. Think carefully about ways that might ensure you obtain a useful interview. Can you find a time and place where both you and the person you are interviewing will feel comfortable and relaxed, for example? Interviewing parents and grandparents (or people of equivalent ages) would be particularly useful because setting their views alongside your own would give you some insight into the experience of three generations.
2   Obvious questions would include:

   ■ where and when they first went to the cinema
   ■ how regularly they went to the cinema when they were in their teens and early twenties
   ■ which films they particularly remember seeing and why
   ■ how popular cinemagoing seemed to be among their friends during this period
   ■ why they think people went to the cinema at that time

   continued

3 Try to put the ideas and perspectives you obtain from the interviews into the form of a comparative table showing how the different people you have interviewed have responded to the same sorts of questions.

4 Discuss the responses you have obtained with other people who have undertaken the same exercise. Bring your final table of responses with you in order to help you to look for similarities and differences between the results of your interviews and those conducted by other people.

The nature of the cinema experience

And yet, at the same time, in a way how strange is the idea of going to the cinema. We choose to venture into a dimly lit, soon-to-be-darkened auditorium with a group of strangers and sit in front of a large screen in order to share with these people we have never met a lightshow display of 'magically' created images of the real world or even of distinctly unreal imaginary worlds.

On the other hand, perhaps this is not so strange; the gathering together of communities to listen to specialist members of the group given the job of telling stories has always been, it would seem, a feature of human society. In the years prior to film projection, magic lantern shows (which involved storytelling and the projection of images on to a screen) would be taken from town to town. And audiences were used to gathering to watch live performances on stage in these years whether it was 'highbrow' plays in upmarket theatres or 'lowbrow' vaudeville acts (comedians, singers, dancers, acrobats and the like) in dance-halls.

ACTIVITY

■ Why should communities always have gathered together in this way? What do the individuals concerned gain from the experience? What does the society or community gain from allowing the activity to take place?

■ Why have storytelling and performance always seemed to be important during such gatherings? What do audiences gain from listening to stories and from watching performance?

■ If possible, discuss your answers to these questions with others.

- Think about your own cinemagoing patterns. Do you ever go on your own? Do you tend to go with the same people to the same sorts of movies? How does the experience differ depending on whether you are on your own or with particular friends? How do you decide what you are going to see and who you are going with? Do you simply go to watch the film at a set time or do you combine this with some other activity (or activities), such as shopping or eating out?
- When did you first go to the cinema? What did you see? Who took you? What can you remember about the experience (not just the film but the event of going to the cinema as a whole)?
- Note your own ideas in response to these questions before discussing and comparing your responses with others.

ACTIVITY

- What do the terms 'highbrow' and 'lowbrow' mean? Would you say that in your experience going to the cinema is a 'highbrow' or 'lowbrow' pastime? What we are really asking is: What type or class of people do you believe go to the cinema? Does this vary depending on the film, and/or depending on the particular cinema in question?
- Note your own ideas in response to these questions before discussing and comparing your responses with others.

Changing patterns of consumption

All of the above, of course, neglects to take account of one factor of which you will be well aware from your own experience: films are no longer solely or even mainly consumed in the cinema. Young people in particular increasingly watch films on small screens using various models of DVD players. Cinema admissions in Britain fell 4 per cent in 2005, and in the USA the box-office was down 9 per cent. Figures recorded across Europe were even worse (see www.ukfilmcouncil. org.uk/information/statistics/yearbook).

This trend towards home consumption really began in the 1960s when studios started to realize that they could use television to show films long after they had passed their sell-by date for cinema exhibition. By the following decade home

Figure 7.2
DVDs

video systems began to be cheap and lightweight enough to be marketable on a commercial scale and rental outlets began to supply feature films to this expanding market. By the late 1980s satellite technology was beginning to be used to broadcast to domestic receivers, and specialist film channels began to offer feature films some time in advance of their video release. What we are now witnessing in the high street is the rapid disappearance of videos as they are pushed from the shelves by a deluge of DVDs. These are easier and cheaper for distribution companies to produce than videos and therefore provide good profit margins, but they are also easier and cheaper for the public to copy. Hence there are growing concerns in the industry about the illegal copying of DVDs.

ACTIVITY

1   Undertake a survey among 20 to 30 young people to try to find out how they watch films. Questions you may like to ask could include:

- how often do they go to the cinema
- how often do they watch films on terrestrial TV
- how often do they watch films on satellite or cable channels
- how often is this a pay-to-view channel
- how often do they watch films on DVDs
- where do they do this and on what types of DVD players.

The role of the audience in the filmmaking process

So, in general terms, what exactly is the role of film audiences within the film industry? At its simplest the role of producers is obviously to create product, in this case films, and following this line of thought the role of the audience is to turn up and watch the films; but more importantly from an industry perspective the audience has to be prepared to pay money for the product on offer. In order for this to happen the audience clearly have to see the product as being worth the price being asked. If they are unsure of this and marketing is unable to convince them, then the whole business of filmmaking on a commercial scale is no longer viable.

The power of the audience within the film concept-to-screen process becomes clearer if we bear in mind from the start that the industry could churn out as many films as they wish, but unless the punters materialize in the cinema the products on offer will never come to represent a commercial proposition. Hollywood spends millions of dollars trying to persuade audiences to queue up at the box-office and no multinational corporation is going to do that unless it feels the returns are likely to make that marketing outlay a sound investment. Clearly audiences coming to a movie in their droves or staying away in equal numbers can either make or break a film as a commercial proposition.

ACTIVITY

1   Draw a diagram to show the relationship between audiences and the film industry. This can take any form you choose but you should aim to include as many factors as possible that contribute to the relationship. You may choose to put the film as product at the centre of the diagram and then try to show how producers and audiences relate to this central focus as well as to each other. Above all you

continued

should be looking to show how the producers can work to attempt to influence audiences to buy their product and how audiences can exert pressure on producers to come up with the sorts of products they wish to see available (among your ideas here you may like to consider how the Internet has altered the possibilities for audiences).

2   If possible, show your diagram to other people and in turn consider their efforts to complete the same task. Note similarities and differences in the diagrammatic forms chosen but above all look for points of agreement and disagreement over the strategies employed by both groups. (Using diagrams is often a good way to think your way through (or think your way towards understanding) these sorts of complex relationships. Incidentally, they can also be useful as a revision tool, since diagrammatic/pictorial representations can often be more easily recalled than simple lists of ideas.)

The pleasures of cinema

There is also a very real sense in which those of us studying film need to enjoy the experience of the cinema ourselves, or we will never be able to understand its power and position in our culture. The primary effect of a film on an audience has to be recognized as being that it 'pleasures' the members of that audience in some way so that they are enticed to spend time watching it (and the primary prerequisite for being a Film Studies student is that we find that films give us pleasure). However, there is also a very real sense in which if we are unable to detach ourselves and analyse what is happening to ourselves and others as we watch (that is, how particular effects are being made on the audience), making us at risk of being controlled (and perhaps even manipulated in dangerous ways) by what is undeniably a pleasurable experience.

VIEWING PLEASURE: there is the simple human pleasure of looking, or scopophilia (seen by Freud as one of the infantile sexual drives), and voyeurism, the act of watching others without their knowledge, both of which have been explored in film theory in relation to the act of watching films in a darkened room. But there are also pleasures derived from aspects of the film-viewing experience such as being able to solve mysteries, to follow a causal chain of events, to identify with strong characters, to recognize narrative patterns or genre features seen before, to be surprised or even shocked by images or portrayed events, to be able to experience fear in safety and so on.

ACTIVITY

1   In groups, undertake a survey of up to 20 people and try to find out what it is they find pleasurable about films. First of all you need to compile a list of questions for the survey. The first might most usefully be: Do you find films pleasurable? From here you can then ask a further series of questions to attempt to pinpoint what it is that is found to be pleasurable. You will need to decide (and agree) on these questions as a group. It might be useful to ask a final, more open question that allows the respondent to put forward any of his or her own ideas for what is pleasurable in films that have not been covered in your questionnaire.
2   When you have completed the survey analyse your results and present your findings briefly to the rest of the class, accompanied by an A4 sheet summarizing your key points.
3   As a class, try to compile an agreed rank order list showing those aspects of film that are found to be the most pleasurable.

ACTIVITY

1   Why do you watch the type of films you do? Is it that you like particular genres or types of storytelling? Is it that you follow the work of a particular star or director? Do you choose to watch different films at different times for different reasons, sometimes wanting material that is going to make you think and at other times wanting relaxing entertainment, for example?
2   Do you ever watch anything other than fictional narrative film? Why do you think more documentaries seem to have been made for the cinema in recent years than used to be the case?
3   If you have seen the film, what did you think of the use of animation in *Kill Bill, Part 1* (Tarantino, 2003)? Did you enjoy it? Was it successful, in your view? What other films have you seen that use animation in a similar way?
4   While you are thinking about Tarantino, if you have seen the film, what did you make of *From Dusk Till Dawn* (Rodriguez, 1995), in which he played the role of the psychotic desperado Richard Gecko?

continued

In particular how did you react at the moment of this film's transformation into a vampire movie? List any other films you have seen
that use different genres or combine genres in this or in similar ways.
5 If possible, discuss the ideas you have come up with on these points
with others taking especially careful note of where their ideas might
differ from yours.

Box-office takings and breaking even

When evaluating the relationship between audiences and the industry it does have
to be said that in the long run there are so many money-spinning possibilities
attached to a big budget Hollywood product along with such levels of marketing
expertise and funding that even a box-office flop, say, *Waterworld* (Costner, 1995),
is likely to eventually turn in a profit, however slender. There will be box-office
takings from around the world; distribution rights can be sold in countries around
the world; satellite, cable and terrestrial TV channels around the world will all
pay to show the film at some stage; and the DVD will go on selling and being
repackaged and resold at appropriate moments. So, *Waterworld* that cost a
reported $175 million to make took only $88 million at the US box-office and was
heralded as an expensive flop, and yet managed to make a further $166 million
abroad. Box-office takings are clearly important and the relative success or failure
of a big budget Hollywood movie in terms of profits will become clear over the first
weekend of a film's release. But there are a series of further commercial
possibilities beyond immediate box-office takings that attach to any major film and
enable studios to recoup their outlay.

ACTIVITY

1 Research the takings made by any recent film that has been
considered to be a relative box-office flop. Try to find out the costs of
production and marketing and then weigh these against the money
taken. Draw up a list of possible further revenue sources that are
either still in the future for this film or about which you have been
unable to find any data.
2 Present your information in brief (no more than half a side of A4
paper). If possible, exchange copies of your findings with other
people.

Figure 7.3 *Waterworld* (1995): a flop?

Films as entertainment for audiences

Of course, unless the creative personnel involved in making a film ('the talent' as they are referred to within the industry) are prepared to simply make the films they like for their own satisfaction and with no view to showing their efforts, they must always have some sense of audience in mind during the production process. If the director, the actors, the cinematographer and others want people to see their efforts they must create something that is in some way a commercial product; the bottom line is that it has to sell. Their perspective may be somewhat different from the pure business perspective on audiences found among studio executives which is solely focused upon whether people can be persuaded to pay money to watch a particular film, but it at least has to take account of this perspective.

As a form of entertainment competing with all the other forms of entertainment on offer, film must inevitably pay attention to its intended audience. The whole notion of entertainment implies an awareness of an audience that is to be entertained. The film industry does all it can to provide audiences with the stories they like framed within the genres they like. The producers of film make every effort to provide audiences with intrigue, spectacle, tension, suspense, surprise, shock, gratification and pleasure. Test screenings before an invited audience from the general public can even result in scenes being re-shot or endings to films being changed. Cinema chains invest huge sums in providing high-quality exhibition facilities for audiences in order to further accommodate the desires of the audience. As a business, film must take careful account of the paying public, since

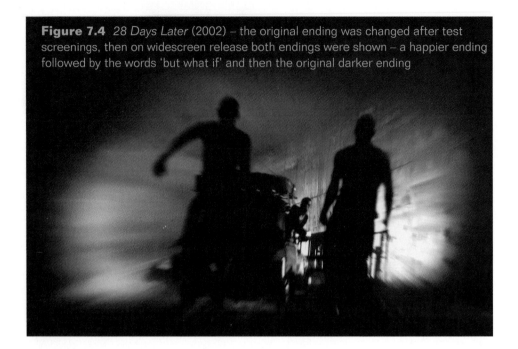

Figure 7.4 *28 Days Later* (2002) – the original ending was changed after test screenings, then on widescreen release both endings were shown – a happier ending followed by the words 'but what if' and then the original darker ending

these are the people who will either agree to consume the product on offer or not. All of this, of course, suggests once again that audiences are powerful players within the filmmaking process.

ACTIVITY

1 Find the official websites of any two major Hollywood studios and analyse and compare the layout of the sites. You should aim to explain how you see each element of the two sites as operating in relation to potential audiences. How do the visual images chosen, the written words and the sounds used work to grab the attention of the visitor to the site and perhaps attempt to turn him or her into a consumer?
2 Write 600 words comparing and contrasting the two sites. Explain ways in which they use similar techniques and any ways in which the two sites seem to adopt different approaches.

External limitations on supply – films as dangerous influences on audiences

An alternative view of audiences has often seen them as weak-willed, and easily manipulated or even corrupted by films. All types of mass media from dangerous new musical forms to children's television have been seen as having the power to bring about antisocial behaviour, especially among the working class and the young. As a result it has always been deemed necessary to try to monitor the content of films (and the media in general) in order to control the potential audience response.

As early as 1922 an industry-based organization, the Motion Picture Producers and Distributors of America (renamed the Motion Picture Association of America in 1945), was set up by the Hollywood studios in effect to agree a level of self-censorship that would obviate the need for any government interference. Most famously under Will Hays during the 1930s, when it became known as the Hays Office and adopted the Hays Code, this organization imposed strict censorship particularly over sexual morality. The code stipulated the maximum length of on-screen kisses, for example, and limited bed-scene possibilities by stipulating that at least one partner had to have one foot on the floor at all times.

Moral campaigners (at the time of the Hays Code it was the Catholic Legion of Decency) have repeatedly seen the media as being run by those who wish to challenge traditional morality. Some theorists have used psychological explanations to suggest that there is a direct cause-and-effect relationship between violence on film (or in the media generally) and acts of violence in society; watching too much violence makes people violent goes this line of argument.

ACTIVITY

1 Find a film from the past (pre-2000) that has been opposed by groups and/or individuals on the basis that it was likely to have some adverse effect on society (and perhaps in particular the young). For example, if you were interested in the early 1970s, films you could use would include *A Clockwork Orange* (Kubrick, 1971), *Straw Dogs* (Peckinpah, 1971) and *The Exorcist* (Friedkin, 1973). However, you have the whole history of film from which to choose, so try not to feel limited to a particular period: one of the recurring features of films is the way in which they constantly address taboo subjects (perhaps indeed this is some part of the role of storytelling within any society during any historical period).

2 Research your chosen film and if possible make a short (3–5-minute) presentation to others showing your findings. Try to use handouts and visual aids to show your audience exactly what was being said about this film at the time of its release. You may like to undertake this exercise in pairs or small groups.

External limitations on supply – moral panics

At frequent intervals every society seems to become worried that some group within the community (often, it seems, the young) is being corrupted in some way by a certain arm of the media. At this stage what have become known as moral panics break out, ironically within the media itself, as those who in some way see themselves as guardians of traditional values feel that social attitudes they believe in are under threat. Stories proliferate in newspapers and magazines, and on TV and radio, about the latest trend that is offering a threat to society. There was, for example, a panic in the 1980s in Britain around films released on to VHS that came to be known as 'video nasties'. Often these moral panics have focused on the idea of the supposed way in which vulnerable sectors of the public are being either desensitized to violence or are losing sexual inhibitions that have long been in place.

ACTIVITY

1   Conduct your own research using newspaper websites to see if you can find any articles on films currently causing controversy (or alternatively films from the recent past that have been viewed as in some way dangerous in their potential effects on audiences).

2   Download an article that deals with one such film at some length and analyse the argument being used. What is the attitude of the article towards the film in question? What are the main points put forward in the article? What evidence is used to support key ideas? Are any 'experts' quoted and, if so, what is their perspective on the relationship between films and audiences?

3   Do you personally find the line taken by the author to be convincing? Try to outline your main reasons for finding it either convincing or unconvincing.

External limitations on supply – censorship and classification

The British Board of Film Classification (BBFC) is a non-governmental body funded by the industry through fees charged to those submitting films, videos and DVDs for classification. The main role of the BBFC, which used to be known as the British Board of Censorship, is to classify films into a range of categories in order to prevent young people from seeing material not believed to be suitable for them. The following categories are used:

Figure 7.5 BBFC classification logos are trademark and copyright protected. Source: BBFC. Reproduced with permission

7.5a
U – 'Universal' – films suitable for everyone.

7.5b
PG – 'Parental Guidance' – films anyone can see but with a warning that they may contain material thought unsuitable for children.

7.5c
12A – films containing material suitable for those who are 12 years old or over but only for children under this age who are accompanied by a responsible adult.

7.5d
15 – films containing material suitable only for those who are 15 years old or over.

7.5e
18 – films containing material suitable only for those who are 18 years old or over.

There are a few other categories used alongside the ones above for videos:

7.5f
Uc – video releases thought particularly suitable for pre-school children.

7.5g
12 – releases containing material suitable only for those who are 12 years old or over.

7.5h
R18 – releases that can only be sold in licensed sex shops (or shown in specially licensed cinemas).

ACTIVITY

1   Do you think this is a useful classification system? Do you agree with the categories or are there any you think should be changed? In your experience is it effective?
2   Why do we have a classification system? Does it help audiences, and if so in what way? Could it be said to help those involved in making, distributing and exhibiting films, and if so in what way? Does it help those who are selling videos and DVDs?
3   What system of classification is used in the USA? List the categories used there. In what ways is this different from and in what ways similar to the British system?
4   Try to find out what other categories have been used in the past in Britain (and obviously what they meant). Why has the way in which films are classified changed over the years? How many factors can you think of that might contribute to this?

Fan power – demand dictating supply

It is often said that the critical factor for any film is whether or not it manages to obtain good 'word-of-mouth'; essentially whether or not those people who initially go to see the film come out singing its praises and telling their friends to go. But of course, in addition to good 'word-of-mouth', a film can also receive bad 'word-of-mouth' and probably what is even worse, indifferent 'word-of-mouth'; at least bad 'word-of-mouth' means the film has roused some sort of impassioned response. What is interesting about 'word-of-mouth' is the increasing speed and intensity with which it can now be delivered by fans. Websites, e-mail, mobile phones and text messaging now mean that verdicts on any new release can be communicated instantly and with increased potency.

Furthermore, with new technologies at their disposal fans are much more able to interact and maintain an ongoing fan base for particular types of film product whether that is with a genre, director or star focus, or taking some other per-spective as a starting point. Fan clubs and conventions have traditionally been maintained via newsletters and paper-based fanzines, but now e-mail newsletters and website fanzines magnify and intensify the possibilities. Fans have always been able to create slow-burning cult classics out of films that have initially flopped at the box-office but perhaps there is now greater opportunity for this sort of activity.

Industry power – supply dictating demand

But if fan power is potentially on the increase as a result of new technologies, then as a result of these same new technologies and a movement towards business globalization the power of the film industry to exert control over the public is also growing. As a result of mergers and takeovers media companies are increasingly coming together in single stables or conglomerates of media interests.

Through working under the same umbrella organization these media companies are able to support each other in a reinforcing symbiotic exchange. A single multinational could have subsidiary companies:

- making, financing and distributing films
- reviewing films in newspapers or on TV/radio stations
- publishing film scripts and distributing film soundtracks
- screening films via cinema chains or satellite TV.

With this sort of interconnected involvement in the film industry the power of such a global enterprise becomes clear.

Media ownership it seems is quite simply becoming increasingly concentrated in a handful of laterally and vertically integrated multimedia conglomerates. And these companies are powerful; you only have to look at the engaging quality of their official websites to see just how they might be able to use their resources to influence the cinemagoing/DVD-buying public.

- In 1989 Time Incorporated purchased Warner Communications to form Time Warner. In 1996 Time Warner merged with Turner Broadcasting to form the world's largest media conglomerate. In 2000 Time Warner merged with America On-Line to form the $350 billion corporation AOL-Time-Warner. This company has interests in cable television, film and television production and distribution, book and magazine publishing, the music industry, and now the Internet. All this is in addition to owning Warner Brothers film studio, New Line Cinema and being one of the largest cinema owners in the world.

- Rupert Murdoch's News Corporation combines film and television production with distribution at Twentieth Century Fox, has invested in lower budget film-making at Fox Searchlight and runs Fox network television. It also has worldwide cable and satellite television interests including ownership of BSkyB in Britain and Star TV in the potentially huge Asian market. In addition, this conglomerate has book-publishing interests and controls a portfolio of newspapers that includes the *Sun* and *The Times* in Britain.
- In 1993 Viacom bought Paramount. This conglomerate is now involved in both film and television production and distribution, owns cable channels such as MTV, VH1 and Nickelodeon, controls television stations, has interests in book publishing and runs the Blockbuster video rental chain. In association with another company, Vivendi, it owns a chain of cinemas worldwide.

ACTIVITY

1   Use an Internet search engine to find the websites of AOL-Time-Warner, News Corporation, Viacom and/or other big players such as Disney or Sony.
2   Find out as much as you can about the media interests of these organizations, paying particular attention to areas that you feel could be related to film, noticing how (as has already been suggested above) many areas could in fact be relevant in some way or other.
3   Compile diagrams in your own chosen style to show the interrelated business interests of each of these multinational conglomerates in as much detail as possible.

Globalization

These multimedia multinationals would be prime examples of the much discussed move towards 'global capitalism', or globalization. Each of them is able to use resources from around the world, most importantly perhaps cheap labour, during the making of media products. So, for instance, you might find that Hollywood movies are being filmed on location in places where union regulations protecting wage levels are not as tight as in some Western countries.

Having made the best use of global resources to keep down costs, these multi-nationals are then able to access global markets when selling the resulting products. So, there is a demand for Hollywood films right around the world that maximizes profit on a global scale rather than simply within North America. The commercial extent and financial power of these corporations enables them to contribute towards setting the agenda for the worldwide development of capitalism. So, if trade discussions are underway between countries, governments will be lobbied by these huge companies to try to make sure the resulting trade deals are advantageous to their future development.

One way of understanding what is happening here would be to suggest that it is the emergence of a whole series of new technologies (satellite TV, the Internet, mobile phones) that has led to this increasing media globalization and the formation of what has been dubbed 'the global village'. This concept of a global village amounts to the suggestion that as a result of new technologies the world has effectively shrunk to the size of a village; the vast distance between places has in effect disappeared, since it now takes only an instant to flash an e-mail from one side of the globe to the other.

GLOBALIZATION: a perceived economic trend towards the whole world becoming a single market so that major multinational corporations are increasingly able to control trade on a global scale.

ACTIVITY

1 If possible, discuss the ideas of 'global capitalism' and 'the global village' with a group of other people.
2 Before you begin the discussion jot down your own thoughts on these ideas and try to work out your own personal perspective on each. Do you, for example, believe that there is definitely a trend towards 'global capitalism' or 'globalization' taking place in the world? Do you think the concept of the global village is a useful way of looking at one aspect of the change that is taking place?

'Windows' and 'synergy'

Two key terms now for this area of Film Studies are 'windows' and 'synergy'. A film may now be viewed not only in the cinema but in a variety of ways, that is, via a series of 'windows'. We can attend the traditional cinema or a multiplex to watch a film, we can rent it on DVD (or video), we can buy it as a DVD (or video), we can view it at home via satellite or cable pay-to-view channels or dedicated film channels, or if we miss these opportunities we can catch it a little later on terrestrial TV. Furthermore, each of these 'windows' needs increasingly to be seen within the context of the global market discussed above rather than simply the domestic market.

Increasingly, media corporations are now in effect able to give publicity to, advertise and promote films made by their film production arm via their own newspapers, magazines, radio stations, TV stations, satellite or cable channels, or through the Internet. Increasingly, important financial spin-offs from films are contained 'in-house' as it were: film-related books can be published by a company that is part of the media corporation's stable of companies, TV or satellite rights can be sold to a company within the same group, soundtrack CDs can be put out by another company within the group. In these sorts of ways the business energy of any single company is magnified, even multiplied, and 'synergy' is created.

Less than 20 per cent of total film revenue now comes from the domestic box-office. So, although a good first weekend is crucial in giving a film that vital initial impetus, there is now a whole range of ways of subsequently recouping the financial outlay involved in making films.

ACTIVITY

How do you view the consumer of films? Is he or she using this form of entertainment for escapism, or companionship, or entertainment? Is he or she the victim of advertising and marketing when making choices of what to see, or is he or she perfectly able to make his or her own choices?

CONCLUSION

In order to study film it is important:

■ to maintain a thoughtful and perceptive awareness of the fact that the film industry attempts to put the public under considerable pressure to buy their products;
■ to realize that as fans and consumers the public may be able to in turn exert considerable influence over the film industry.

References and Further Reading

Abrams, N., Bell, I. and Udris, J. (2001) *Studying Film*, Arnold, London (ch. 3)
Bennett, P., Hickman, A. and Wall, P. (2007) *Film Studies: The essential resource*, Routledge, London and New York (ch. 12)
Corrigan, T. and White, P. (2004) *The Film Experience: An introduction*, Bedford/ St Martin's, Boston, MA (ch. 1)
Gledhill, C. and Williams L. (eds) (2000) *Reinventing Film Studies*, Arnold, London
Kochberg S. (2003) 'Cinema as institution' in Nelmes, J. (ed.) *An Introduction to Film Studies*, Routledge, London
Lacey, N. (2005) *Introduction to Film*, Palgrave Macmillan, Basingstoke (ch. 3)

Useful Websites

www.bbfc.co.uk (The British Board of Film Classification)

www.bfi.org.uk (The British Film Institute)
www.newscorp.com
www.timewarner.com
www.thefilmfactory.co.uk (Buena Vista)
www.paramountpictures.co.uk
www.fox.co.uk
www.disney.co.uk
www.sony.net
www.sonypictures.co.uk
www.pathe.co.uk
www.miramax.com
www.universalstudios.com
www.disney.co.uk or disney.go.com

(Websites such as those listed above give a powerful sense of the global reach of such corporations and in several cases an immediate visual impression of the range of interlocking media owned by each of them)

www.cjr.org (up-to-date information on who owns what in the media entertainments industry)

8 CONSUMPTION

This chapter deals with:

- the historically ongoing and continually developing relationship between the film audience and new technologies
- ways in which new technologies have affected consumers' experience of film
- what opportunities new technologies have offered to producers of films
- an overview of the relationship between new technologies and the cinema experience

INFORMATION BOX

The previous chapter has considered in part the consumption of film, looking at both the cinemagoing experience and the increasing popularity of DVDs. This chapter considers film consumption in relation to new technologies. It is again directly relevant to FM2: British and American Film – Producers and Audiences for the WJEC's AS level in Film Studies.

ACTIVITY

1 Undertake a survey among as many people as possible to investigate their use of modern film-related technologies. Try to bracket your

continued

responses into groups according to age and sex. You should put together your own carefully thought-out questionnaire but aim to find out the answers to the following sorts of questions:

- How many have access to satellite or cable TV and how many subscribe to the film channels? How many satellite or cable TV films do they watch in a week? How many pay-to-view films do they watch in a week?
- How many have a DVD player? How extensive is their DVD film collection? How many DVD films do they watch on average in a week?
- How many use the Internet to download films? How many use the Internet to read film reviews or other film-related material?
- How many have digital cameras? How many have or have used a film-editing software package?

(Remember to modify these questions and add to them as you see fit: this is an important part of the exercise, since it is asking you to think for yourself, and that is the key skill above all others that you should be aiming to cultivate.)

2   Display the results of your survey using a series of graphs of whatever type you believe best show the information.
3   Write a short report (600–800 words) explaining what your survey shows about modern-day use of film-related technologies.

Film and technology

Behind any discussion regarding exactly how we are going to define the 'film' in Film Studies there must be the question of technology: without the necessary technology film is impossible to make and impossible to watch; it is a form of expression that is intimately related to technology. Mainstream films are so closely connected to an industrial process that it is perhaps difficult for some people to consider film as a form of artistic expression. Everything we have been investigating in this part of the book would be leading us to see film as a commercial product rather than anything else. Indeed, one of the most interesting aspects of Film Studies is the way in which we are driven to see film texts as both creative works and profit-driven enterprises.

As a student of 'film', at least part of your studies must involve the need to consider in some detail the relationship of the film industry to new and changing technologies. In the process we should remember above all that this is not a new relationship but one that goes back to the early days of cinema. Cinema itself was clearly a stunning new technology in the late 1890s and early 1900s: when the

Lumière brothers, for example, set up their first screenings of 'actualities' in a basement in Paris in 1895, people were fascinated by the representations of life in moving images offered by this new technology. To begin with the sheer novelty of what was offered by this new technology was enough to draw audiences.

ACTIVITY

- Select a recent Hollywood film you have on DVD and watch a few scenes you know reasonably well with the TV adjusted to show black and white images.
- How does this change the experience? Does it feel strange? Can you imagine a world with only black and white television, where the only place you could see colour images would be at the cinema? Ask any older people you may know if they can remember this period before 1970 in Britain.

ACTIVITY

- Find a copy of a short silent film from the early period of filmmaking. It will probably come with a musical soundtrack which may well not have been originally written to accompany the film. Turn this down and, if possible, find someone who is a skilled musician (and hopefully is also studying film) to provide a live accompaniment to the film.
- Watch the film in this way with a group of other people. As you are doing so, try to imagine the experience of early cinema audiences. Make sure you find time to discuss the experience afterwards.

The key thing to notice as you undertake research into the relationship between film and new technologies is the way in which these new technologies are rarely adopted immediately they become available. Every new technology involves a (usually large) set-up cost for the industry. Therefore, if the new technology is to be adopted, either sizeable profits have to be seen as virtually guaranteed or the industry has to feel itself to be under such threat from an outside force that adopting the new technology is seen as the only way to maintain cinema's current share of the leisure market. Colour and widescreen technologies, for example, were available well before the 1950s but were not widely adopted until the advent of TV meant that cinema audiences were in steep decline and some additional

Figure 8.1 *Becky Sharp* (1935)

attraction was needed to woo the public back to the darkened auditorium experience. The first colour film is often said to be *Becky Sharp* (Mamoulian, 1935) but there were colour processes being used as early as the silent period, using labour-intensive hand painting of individual prints, for example. However, why would you spend money on expensive colour possibilities if the public was continuing to pay good money to come to a black and white experience and there was no competitive edge to be gained by the change to a new technology?

ACTIVITY

- Watch extracts from *Man With a Movie Camera* (Vertov, 1929) and then discuss with others what this film has to say about filmmaking and cinemagoing in the early 1900s.
- In this film you will see centre stage being given over to the movie camera itself. You will also see the cameraman and the editor at work, and have several glimpses of audiences in a cinema auditorium. The

film was made in Russia under very particular circumstances and by filmmakers interested in the avant-garde possibilities of the medium; nevertheless, it does give some insight into how film technology was viewed and used in the period.

Film and technological change

The film industry has always used new technologies relating to the making and showing of films (although crucially, as already mentioned, this has not always occurred as soon as the technologies have become available). A brief list of crucial technological moments in the history of cinema would include:

- the projection of moving images to create the original silent movies in makeshift cinemas in the late 1890s;
- commercially unsuccessful attempts to introduce colour processes and synchronized sound within a few years of the first screenings in the early 1900s;
- the financially successful introduction of sound (the 'talkies') in the late 1920s/early 1930s which led to massive changes in the industry;
- the widespread adoption of colour and widescreen in the 1950s in an effort to combat the competition from television caused by the mass production of TV sets, changing leisure patterns, and the movement of much of the population out to newly built suburbs following the Second World War;
- the gimmicky, ultimately unsuccessful efforts to offer the public three-dimensional film in the same period, again in an effort to offer the public something different from television;
- the increasing use of television from the 1960s as a medium for showing films with the accompanying realization that in this way old films could effectively be recycled or resold;
- the advent of VHS rental and recording from the 1970s opening up the possibility of again reselling old films but also effectively re-releasing relatively new films to a new 'window' after a period at the cinema;
- the introduction of satellite and cable channels from the 1980s which again offered a further 'window' for both old and relatively recent films (main package channels, premium subscription channels and pay-to-view channels of course effectively further subdivided this 'window');
- the increased marketing of the 'home cinema concept' from the 1990s so that with technology allowing larger screens and surround sound something approaching an analogous cinema experience becomes possible;
- the limited use of IMX and other large-screen formats from the 1990s which, because they would cost the industry so much to introduce on a wide scale, have so far never been used to offer anything more than the occasional theme park-style experience;

- the move to DVD technology from the late 1990s which with the use of 'extras' and an enhanced experience encourages consumers to replace their old video film library with the latest disc format;
- the increasing use of the Internet from the late 1990s, for marketing initially but also increasingly for downloading films;
- the advent from around 2000 of digital filmmaking and digital projection facilities in cinemas;
- the current 'format war' between HD DVD and Blu-ray Disc to become the successor generation format to DVD.

Each of these moments of technological change for the industry are essentially concerned with the viewing experience, but it is also true that there has been a parallel series of technological changes in the making of films. For example, when sound is successfully integrated into film then the cameras have to become silent in order that their mechanical noises are not picked up and obviously sound technology has to develop quickly in order to enable voices to be picked up clearly; in fact a whole new field of production and creativity opens up. Perhaps we have currently reached a similar turning point because the big question now is what impact new digital possibilities for filmmaking and exhibition are going to have on the industry.

ACTIVITY

- Working with others if possible, research the current development of digital filmmaking and projection. Find out only in very broad terms how the new technology works but make sure you obtain some estimates as to how costs compare with old methods.
- Try to form a clear picture of the advantages of the new digital technology but also an idea of obstacles in the way of introducing full-scale change.

(The key factor to bear in mind is the cost of replacing/discarding old cameras, editing equipment and projection facilities that are currently in use.)

ACTIVITY

Research the 'format war' between Blu-ray Disc and HD DVD to replace DVD. Which companies have backed which technology? Are there any possible alternative disc technologies?

New technologies and the consumer

New technologies might be said to offer consumers:

■ an improved overall qualitative experience as a result of better sound and/or image reproduction;

■ a heightened emotional experience as a result of a stronger sense of empathy with characters who in some way seem more real;

■ enhanced spectacle perhaps through the sheer overpowering size of the screen or the impact on the senses of a surrounding wall of sound;

■ improved ease of access, or ease of use, for instance, through enabling people to own their own film collections in various formats;

■ new, easier and intensified ways of using film to pleasure themselves, for example, IMAX would seem to offer an intense 'fairground ride' for the senses;

■ an enhanced intellectual experience through the provision of increased knowledge or understanding, for instance through the use of commentaries by directors on DVDs;

■ the chance to use new, ever cheaper and more compact devices to make films for themselves.

ACTIVITY

■ Try to add to the above list, if possible by discussing the idea of new technologies and the consumer with others. You may even want to cross ideas off the list given here if you do not agree with them (for example, the second point seems at least worth debating carefully).
■ Apply each of these ideas to the various new technologies mentioned so far in this chapter. What will each new technology offer the consumer? You should consider sound, colour, widescreen, surround sound, TV, VHS, satellite and cable, DVD including 'extras', home cinema, the Internet and any other technologies you think are important.

New technologies and the film industry

New technologies offer the industry:

■ the possibility of an improved opportunity to create profits (the costs or required expenditure involved in bringing in the new technology will be carefully balanced against the projected additional income before any new technology is introduced);
■ a way to protect current market share in the face of new potential competitors (in this case the costs will be set against the potential loss of income arising if the new technology is not adopted);
■ the chance to repackage and resell old products, especially cult and 'classic' movies, thereby establishing a new audience base, or even fan base, for an old product (note that this is even true of an older technological change like the move to sound);
■ an opportunity to place products for sale in new 'windows', thereby lengthening the commercial life of each film (a film may now be sold to consumers via the cinema, satellite and cable TV, DVD and terrestrial TV);
■ the chance to encourage multiple purchases of essentially the same product (so any one consumer might pay to see a film in the cinema, then later pay to watch the same film on pay-to-view, before later still buying his or her own copy on DVD);
■ a means of still managing to make a profit or break even on films that initially perform poorly or below expectations at the box-office (such products can be repackaged, remarketed and resold through a succession of 'windows');
■ overall, enhanced production, distribution and exhibition possibilities.

ACTIVITY

- Try to add to the above list, if possible by discussing the idea of new technologies and the film industry with others.
- See how many of the ideas from your list can be applied to each of the various new technologies so far mentioned in this chapter. What has each new technology offered the industry? Why has the industry (and essentially we are talking about Hollywood here) decided to introduce each new technology at its particular chosen historical moment? You should consider sound, colour, widescreen, surround sound, terrestrial TV, VHS, satellite and cable TV, DVD, home cinema, the Internet and any other technologies you think are important.
- This may involve considerable research. Try to work in groups with each person taking one area to work on. Then present your findings to the rest of the group, supplying everyone with a one-page handout summarizing your research.

New technologies and the cinema experience

It could be argued that new technologies have always added to, rather than detracted from, the cinema experience. The size and/or quality of the spectacle have been enhanced by each new development adding to the unique nature of the cinematic 'event' (even the advent of television in a sense only highlights the difference and in particular the spectacle of the cinema experience).

The experience of the cinema itself cannot be easily replicated or replaced but the alternative experiences of pay-TV, or home cinema, have their own attractions particularly in terms of flexibility of viewing. The advent of TV and changed leisure patterns ended the social dominance of the cinema as a source of entertainment and information (remember this was once the only place you could see visual images of news events). The cinema experience has made something of a comeback, although attendance is never going to match the heights attained in 1946 in both the USA and Britain.

As with studying the content of the films themselves, what we find is that the industry and its technological base always have to be seen within social, economic, political and historical contexts. Towards the end of the Second World War and immediately after, cinema attendance peaked, as without the presence of television sets in the home people sought news images and perhaps some sort of collective, community-enhancing escape. The nature of cinema attendance at this moment was determined by the nature of the historical moment, and this is always the case. Our job is to try to understand how changes and developments within the film industry might be connected to the contexts of the period in which they take place.

Figure 8.2 New technologies make watching films at home an increasingly attractive option

New technologies: an afterthought

We have given some initial consideration to the importance of new technologies to the film industry but we may be able to take those thoughts a little further. Some theoretical approaches that claim to give an insight into understanding society would see the development of new technologies as fundamental in determining the shape of society. Technological determinism not only assumes that progress is inevitable but also suggests it is technological development that essentially shapes society.

Supporters of the Internet suggest that this form of communication marks a new era of democratization and freedom of choice empowering ordinary people to produce and receive information and entertainment from all over the world. Others such as some Marxist critics might suggest that this development, by isolating consumers from face-to-face human interaction, enables them to be more tightly controlled and manipulated. Other critics note the increased access to pornography and extreme right-wing propaganda available on the Internet, or point to an increasing gap between information-rich and information-poor populations (less than one in a thousand black South Africans, for example, own a phone).

ACTIVITY

- How do you see the Internet? Is it a positive or negative development?
- Draw up a list of ways in which it could be considered to be (1) positive and (2) negative.
- In groups, compare your ideas with each other.
- What does all of this have to do with Film Studies? Discuss this in your groups and then as a whole class.

ACTIVITY

Undertake further research if necessary, and then write an essay (1,000–1,500 words) on the continually evolving relationship between the film industry and new technologies. You should aim to consider the introduction of sound, colour and widescreen to cinemas as well as more recent technologies.

CONCLUSION

New technologies:

- have always been of vital importance to the film industry;
- have only ever been adopted when the industry has been sure of their commercial importance.

References and Further Reading

Abrams, N., Bell, I. and Udris, J. (2001) *Studying Film*, Arnold, London (ch. 5)

Allen, M. (1998) 'From Bwana Devil to Batman forever: technology in contemporary Hollywood cinema' in Neale, S. and Smith, M. (eds) *Contemporary Hollywood Cinema*, Routledge, London

Bennett, P., Hickman, A. and Wall, P. (2007) *Film Studies: The essential resource*, Routledge, London and New York (ch. 12)

Lacey, N. (2005) *Introduction to Film*, Palgrave Macmillan, Basingstoke (ch. 3)

McKernan, B. (2005) *Digital Cinema: The revolution in cinematography, postproduction and distribution*, McGraw-Hill, New York

Neale, S. (1998) 'Widescreen composition in the age of television' in Neale, S. and Smith, M. (eds) *Contemporary Hollywood Cinema*, Routledge, London

Sergi, G. (1998) 'A cry in the dark: the role of post-classical film sound' in Neale, S. and Smith, M. (eds) *Contemporary Hollywood Cinema*, Routledge, London

Webster, C. (2003) 'Film and technology' in Nelmes, J. (ed.) *An Introduction to Film Studies*, Routledge, London

9 GENRE AND STARS

This chapter deals with:

- viewing stars as commodities or products of the film industry
- seeing genre as a marketing tool for the industry
- understanding stars as having commercial value
- seeing stars and genre as embodying certain social or cultural values and ideological perspectives

INFORMATION BOX

i

This section will be directly relevant to FM2: British and American Film – Producers and Audiences for the WJEC AS level in Film Studies.

Your experience of stars

When studying film it is always best to begin by considering carefully your own experience. Therefore, when starting to look at the idea of stars and their role within films and the wider film industry this is the place to open your investigations. Try some initial questions:

- Who are your favourite stars? Whose latest film do you really look forward to seeing?
- Why? What is it about their work that you really like? Is it something about the sorts of characters these people play that really engages your interest? Is it something to do with the subject matter their films deal with, or the attitudes they put forward through their characters?

■ Have the stars you like most changed over the years? Are there stars whose films you used to be interested in but no longer are? Have you recently taken an interest in the work of stars who never used to interest you? Why have these changes occurred?

Your experience of genre

Naturally, the same premise of beginning with your own experience holds true with the concept of genre and its importance within the commercial context of the film industry. So:

■ What is your favourite genre? Which genre films do you make a particular point of looking out for when you read reviews?
■ Why is this your favourite genre? What is it about it that you really like? Is it to do with the types of characters at the heart of this genre? Is it to do with the subject matter these films deal with, or the attitudes they tend to advocate?
■ Have the genres you like most changed over the years? Are there genres in which you used to take an interest but no longer do? Why have these changes in taste occurred?

Stars: the concept

In the early days of Hollywood the studio bosses who ran the film industry were not too keen on the idea of 'stars'. And, since you are now so aware of the fact that films are not so much an art-form as a business (or at least, as much a business as an art-form), you will immediately see why: quite simply, anonymous actors are not able to command large salaries; it is only when you become famous and have a public waiting to see your next movie that you are able to ask for more money to play the part. The first star known to her fans by her name is usually said to have been Florence Lawrence. Before 1910 she was simply known as 'the Biograph Girl' because she was seen in so many of that company's films (in 1909, for instance, she performed in 81 short films!), but when she moved to the studio that was to become Universal she was named in the credits for the first time. She made the first ever personal appearance of a film star at St Louis in March 1910 and other studios followed suit, with actors and actresses making a variety of media appearances.

The moment you turn actors into stars you implicitly acknowledge that they are a commercial asset to your business and that their presence is capable of attracting more paying punters than might otherwise come to see your film. At this point you potentially have to start paying at least the going rate and perhaps an inflated rate to obtain the leading man and/or woman you want for your film. Studios recognized the chance to boost the ratings of their movies by creating stars but they were also being driven by the public demand to know the names of these actors they kept seeing (and enjoying) in successive films. This suggests the

Figure 9.1
Florence Lawrence – the
Biograph Girl

importance of actors in the filmmaking process but also, of course, the importance (even from the earliest days of cinema) of fans – the passionate consumers of the industry's products.

ACTIVITY

1   Find a poster for a film that uses a star of your choice as its central visual image. Analyse both the visual image itself and the overall layout of the poster in relation to the star.
2   How does the title of the film combined with any words used to describe the film relate to the public perception of the star in question? Does it seem to be the sort of film in which most people would expect to see this star? How does the title and/or other words used reinforce (or contradict) the notions people might have of this particular star?

continued

3   How does the visual image given of the star work to create meaning and generate responses from us? Consider the posture or positioning of the body: Is he or she standing, sitting or lying down? Why has this positioning been chosen? What does it suggest? How are other aspects of body language and facial expression, including eyes and mouth, working to create potential meanings? What about costume, hairstyle and any objects placed nearby or being held by the star? Do not forget to consider the camera angle being used, particular colours being employed (or perhaps it is in black and white) and lighting. Remember that each of these elements of construction will have been carefully chosen. Do they work to reinforce (or again, possibly contradict) certain ideas normally embodied in this star's image?

4   When you are sure about all of these things in your own mind, explain your understanding of the poster and the image of the star that is being conveyed to other people. Ask them if they would agree, or perhaps disagree at certain points, with your analysis and discuss the ideas that come up.

Around 100 years after actors' contributions began to be acknowledged via film credits the industry seems to have taken to the concept of stars with some enthusiasm since the cash paid to them is now often the largest component part of any top Hollywood film's budget. Furthermore, it is not unusual for big name stars to receive the script from the studio even before a director has been appointed to the film project and then to be asked if there is a director with whom he (and it still is predominantly 'he' rather than 'she') would like to work. This suggests that getting the right star name attached to a project is often seen as more important than obtaining the services of a particular director.

INFORMATION BOX *i*

Tom Cruise was paid a reported $75 million for *Mission Impossible II* (2000), $25 million plus a percentage of the profits for *The Last Samurai* (2003) and a straight 20 per cent of the profits for *War of the Worlds* (2005).

Genre: the concept

Genre may be viewed in terms of film form with each genre having characteristic features of style. So, for horror films there will be typical elements of *mise-en-scène*, cinematography, editing and sound which when packaged together become recognizable as denoting this genre. For example, there might be a shot of a single dark house on a hill in moonlight that because of the camera angle seems to loom over us while ominous music plays on the soundtrack. In addition, there will be recognizable aspects of the narrative that again help to inform the audience of genre; typical characters, character relationships and storylines. All of this can be critically analysed to assess the extent to which the normal characteristics of the genre in question are being used in a stereotypical way and the extent to which they are being used in new and exciting ways while still retaining the genre in a recognizable underpinning form. However, we are not interested in this sort of analysis in this chapter.

Here, we are interested in the way in which because genre makes a film instantly recognizable as a certain type it can be used as an effective marketing tool. As with stars, genre is like a label on the package that announces what is to be found inside, and thereby calls to the target audience announcing that this is a product they might wish to purchase. With so many products on the shelf the film business needs ways of enabling the consumer to be able to distinguish one product from another. Genre offers one way of achieving this.

When customers enter a DVD store they need to be able to pick up products that will be the sort they might buy. Any random DVDs that are taken off the shelf to be studied further by potential customers are chosen according to the packaging, essentially the title and the keynote image provided, and what the packaging announces above all is genre.

ACTIVITY

1   Select a poster for a film of a genre of your choice. Analyse both the visual image and the overall layout of the poster in relation to the idea of genre.
2   How does the title of the film combined with any words used to describe the film relate to the public perception of this genre?
3   How does the visual image work to create meaning and generate responses from us? Consider the location or setting that has been selected, the props and costumes being used, colour and composition of shot being employed, and any actions being undertaken. Each element of construction will have been carefully chosen. Do they reinforce (or possibly contradict) certain ideas normally associated with this genre?

continued

Figure 9.2 A poster for *300* (2007)

4   When you are sure about all of these things in your own mind, explain
    your understanding of the poster in genre terms to other people. Ask
    them if they would agree, or perhaps disagree at certain points, with
    your analysis, and discuss the ideas that come up.

Genre is crucial for the marketing of all films but has been used particularly effectively by Hollywood. For low-budget movies coming out of Hollywood it has been recognized as being particularly crucial, since usually on these projects there are no high-profile stars to attract audiences. Fox Atomic, a subdivision of Twentieth Century Fox, was created in 2006 and focuses on action and horror. Universal's Rogue Pictures works in the same area. Both are attempting to mine the young adult target market and a critical part of their strategy is clearly the use of genre to give a guarantee of a certain product to the carefully targeted audience.

INFORMATION BOX   *i*

With a production budget of $20 million, *Disturbia*, distributed by Paramount and made by DreamWorks, had made $85 million worldwide within less than two months of its release in April 2007. In fact it opened in almost 3,000 cinemas in the USA and took more than $22 million in its opening weekend.

Within a month of its release in May 2007 *Spider-Man 3*, distributed by Sony/Columbia and costing $260 million to make, had taken almost $850 million worldwide. It opened in 4,300 cinemas in the USA and took $150 million in its first weekend.

These films from either end of the Hollywood market in terms of budget were roughly equally profitable. The percentage return on *Disturbia* by the beginning of June 2007 was a little better than that achieved by *Spider-Man 3* but, on the other hand, it had been out a little longer. What is common to both is that they have used genre as a key marketing tool.

(See http://boxofficemojo.com)

Stars and studios

The relationship between stars and the studios has never been an easy one: studios, aware as always of the financial bottom line, have not been keen to agree to increasing star salaries unless they have been forced to do so in order to protect the market share for their product. On the other hand, studios were quick to realize that stars could help to sell their product: Charlie Chaplin, for instance, may have been an artist in front of the camera and a perfectionist as a director behind the camera but to the studio employing him he was first and foremost a guarantee of financial success. There is film of Chaplin, who was from East London, returning to the city and being mobbed by literally thousands of people such was his popularity. And it is that popularity that is the key to the issue of stars because it equates to power, the power to make money by guaranteeing the financial success of commercial films.

In the 1930s and 1940s under the Studio System stars were held under the control of the studios by the use of tight contracts: each star had to take the projects offered or risk having their careers sidelined by the big movie bosses running the studios. Stars were loaned out from one studio to another for the making of one-off films in exchange deals, and their public image was carefully manufactured and then controlled by studio image-makers. Some did, of course, try to take more control over their careers: it was, for instance, Chaplin who with two other mega-stars from the period, Mary Pickford and Douglas Fairbanks, and the first Hollywood star director, D.W. Griffiths, moved to create their own production company, United Artists, as early as 1919, in order to distribute their own films and escape studio interference in the creative process.

Figure 9.3 United Artists (1919)

The power may now have shifted in favour of the stars (and, very importantly, their agents) compared with the situation during the Studio System but the struggle between studios and stars has always been there as part of the equation of filmmaking. While studios have basically always wanted stars to reproduce the same winning formula that has proved successful in previous films, the stars themselves have often wanted to try to take on the challenge of playing different sorts of parts.

AGENTS: not only actors but also directors, screenwriters, producers, cinematographers and others involved in commercial filmmaking have agents. The system under which these people would have been kept on full-time contracts to the studios came to an end during the 1950s, and from this point agents became especially important within the industry, as they had the power to continually renegotiate one-off film deals for those on their books.

The role of agents representing top stars is particularly powerful. If as a studio you believe it is the stars who really sell movies you will be prepared to pay a large percentage of your budget to secure the services of the star you believe will best embody the image required for your film.

ACTIVITY

1   List your favourite six stars and for each one describe, in no more than two sentences, what it is about them that you like. See if you can find out how much each of them was said to have been paid for their last movie. What percentage of the budget for the whole film did this amount to?
2   Exchange your lists with others. See if there are any stars who appear on several people's lists. If so, how are they described? Are the same star qualities attributed to them by everyone in the group who has nominated them? Are these facets of their image the features that make them generally popular with fans?
3   Are there any actors put forward by one person that other people in the group would not describe as stars? If so, why? Discuss what it is that particular actors may lack which means that, in your opinion, they would not qualify as stars.

continued

4 Compile a collective list grouping the stars according to whether they are male or female, black or white. Which group within each of these two splits contains the most names? Discuss why this might be.

(Your most useful starting point for this activity will probably be the Internet Movie Database (www.uk.imbd.com), a superb resource for this area of Film Studies.)

ACTIVITY

1 Working with others if possible, undertake a little research into the history of black actors in Hollywood. Your starting point will be to discuss how you are going to divide up the workload among members of the group.

- Who was the first black actor who could really be described as a star in your opinion? What can you find out about him or her?
- What sorts of roles did black actors have in early American cinema before 1920? What about under the Studio System through into the 1950s?
- Why did the status of black performers in Hollywood begin to change a little during the 1960s? What is the overall name given to the black political movement of the period in the USA and what can you find out about it?
- Which actors would you describe as the major black stars in Hollywood today? Can you find any short quotes (no more than two sentences) that seem to you to sum up their star image?

2 Prepare an illustrated wall display (or perhaps a web page) to display your findings.
3 Discuss with others why Hollywood today has African American stars and the use you see the industry as putting them to.

Stars as cultural products and media creations

In essence a star is a media-constructed image: Brad Pitt the actor, for example, has become something more than that which he started out as in the film industry; he has become a multimedia presence within Western, or perhaps that should be within a now global, culture. A star is created from a range of activities: the succession of roles taken up in films is of course critical, but there is also advertising, promotional work and media coverage to be considered as part of the process involved in the construction of a star. A star is not a person but a complex representation: in effect a cultural product. As spectators of his films we know the performances of Brad Pitt the actor. As fans we also know Brad Pitt as a star who appears in our newspapers, in our film magazines, on our DVD extras and occasionally on our TV screens. But neither as simple viewers of the films nor as fans do we know Brad Pitt the human being or the man.

ACTIVITY

1 Take one contemporary Hollywood star and research the roles they have played throughout their career. Is there any sense of continuity between the roles? Do the types of characters played have any similarities? Has the way in which the actor has played these roles involved the use of similar character traits? Are there any particularly significant roles that have created this actor's star image? What would you say is physically distinctive about the way in which this actor is shown in their films? Is their anything distinctive about the delivery of lines, or about the body language employed from film to film?

2 Collect as much information as possible about your chosen star from current newspapers, magazines, fanzines, industry-based websites, fan-based websites and books over a period of a month.

3 Examine your material carefully to see how the media has worked over this period to construct the star's image. What are the key features of the media image of your chosen star? How are words and photographs used in the articles to construct this image? How important to their image as a star are their physical attributes (physique, bodily proportions, facial features)? How important in the construction of their star image are the attitudes and approaches to life attributed to them? How important are events in their personal life?

Stars as commercial products

So stars, rather than being individuals, might be seen as 'media constructs' with a specific role to play within the film industry. But if we consider stars to be controlled by big business organizations then we might also see them as commodities being produced to create profits as a result of consumers buying the image they embody. From this perspective it is not Brad Pitt the person we need to understand if we are to gain insight into the role and place of stars within the film industry but 'Brad Pitt' the constructed media image. In financial terms, a star represents to the studio a certain capital outlay upon which a return is expected.

INFORMATION BOX

Figure 9.4
Brad Pitt in *Ocean's Thirteen* (2007)

William Bradley Pitt, the only person to twice be voted the 'Sexiest Man Alive' by *People* magazine in the United States, has spent plenty of time in the media spotlight. One of the stars of *Troy* (2004) and *Ocean's Twelve* (2004), he has been romantically attached to Gwyneth Paltrow, Geena Davis and Juliette Lewis among others as well as having been married to Jennifer Aniston for four years. He was first in *Company* magazine's '100 Sexiest Men' in 2004, sixth in VH1's '100 Hottest Hotties', fiftieth in *Premiere* magazine's 'Greatest Movie Stars of All Time' and thirty-second in a similar poll in *Empire* magazine. For his first feature film in 1988 he was paid $1,500 a week for a seven-week shoot: for *Mr and Mrs Smith* in 2005 he received a reported $20 million.

In keeping with this financial perspective stars are marketed in ways that deliberately emphasize particular facets of their constructed image in order to sell films. At the same time this market image also operates as a labelling mechanism denoting a particular type of star-related product to be found within the range of such brands available. So, if we go into a DVD rental outlet or walk past a cinema and see a certain star's name on a product on the shelf or on a poster outside the cinema door we will know what to expect if we choose to take this film home or go in to watch the movie. In this respect stars may be seen to work as one further means of organizing the film-related marketplace. Bruce Willis on a poster or DVD cover guarantees something different from Brad Pitt who in turn guarantees something different from Tom Cruise or Jude Law.

Stars and lifestyle choices

This process of using stars to market and sell not only their films but perhaps certain associated life choices has intensified in recent years with the development of new technologies and the creation of a multimedia entertainments industry. But essentially the process itself is no different from the way in which film stars of the 1940s (and before) were also used to sell cigarettes, cosmetics or other lifestyle choices through and alongside their films.

ACTIVITY

- Do stars influence the way in which ordinary people live their lives? Look back at all the material you have collected on stars through work you have done for this chapter so far. How might any of this material suggest stars could be influencing, or attempting to influence, the lives of people watching them or reading about them? What sorts of choices could the images portrayed of these stars encourage people to make in their own lives?
- Consider carefully your own ideas on this before discussing your thoughts with other people.

Today, film stars may be said to have to compete with a much wider range of celebrity figures, from television and sport in particular, to gain coverage in the newspapers and magazines devoted to the lives and loves of stars. On the other hand, the proliferation of television channels and the arrival of the Internet means there are now many more spaces waiting to be filled with images of, and details about the lives of, stars.

Interestingly, although stars are now said to have more power and influence within the industry than they did in the past, because of their dependence upon the media and the use to which their image is put to sell goods they may be argued to be just as tied into promoting the capitalist ideology, or worldview, as they have ever been.

IDEOLOGY: a person's or a society's set of beliefs and values, or overall way of looking at the world. The Western world in general is said to be built upon a belief in capitalism, or the idea that what is best for society, or what brings the greatest benefits to a society, is for business to be given free rein to operate without restrictions in an open, competitive market.

Stars and the nature of their power

What is being suggested here is that the only 'power' stars have is the power to make money both for themselves and for other people. Out of a range of potentially commercially viable projects they may be able to determine which gets 'green-lit' but they do not have *carte blanche* to get any film they please with any messages and values they like up and running. Their power, such as it is, depends upon a status that is derived directly from their place within the media entertainments industry; if they lose (or choose to begin to abandon) the Midas touch that has enabled them to become one of the chosen few A-list stars, then their options for their next film project immediately diminish. The size and site of the 'soap-box' available to them from which they may occasionally back what they see as 'worthy' causes is a precise reflection of their value as a commercial asset.

ACTIVITY

Do you agree with the above point of view completely, partially or not at all? If possible, discuss your thoughts on this with others. Try to decide how you see the power of stars. How much power do they have within the film industry and how far does it extend? Do you know of any examples of stars who have been able to exert a serious influence on any of the film projects in which they have been involved?

(This is a difficult issue. You are being asked to think about something you may well not have previously considered. We tend to simply take for granted the nature of the world around us, but the questions being raised here hopefully require you to go beyond this. You are being asked to question the whole basis of the way things are within the Hollywood-dominated film industry.

At this stage, you are not expected to necessarily come up with any final conclusions; you are simply being asked to consider the questions being raised seriously for yourself and to listen carefully and thoughtfully to the responses of others.)

GREEN-LIT: this is a jargon term used within the film industry for obtaining the 'go-ahead' for a film project to move from being a concept to actually starting production.

ACTIVITY

1 Research the work of two recent stars, such as Sean Penn or Tim Robbins, who have been politically outspoken and radical in their views.
2 List the films they have worked on, outlining for each the storyline and any messages you believe the audience is supposed to take away.
3 How have your chosen stars been presented/treated by the film industry and the media? What projects or political issues have they been involved in outside of filmmaking, and how have these been presented in the media?
4 For each of them, define what you see as being their political stance (200 words).
5 Name two or three films for each in which you believe you can best see their political stance embodied. Try to identify particularly strong scenes as evidence.
6 Show one of your chosen scenes to the class and explain the thinking behind your choice of star and film clip.

Genre as a marketing and production strategy

Genre conveniently operates as a marketing and production strategy, enabling the audience to establish the type of product on offer and therefore to purchase its favoured flavour of film. When the customer enters a DVD rental outlet or a shop selling DVDs, posters and the DVD boxes themselves announce the genre of the products on offer. If a particular day on the national calendar is approaching it is likely that there will be a special display offering products deemed relevant for the occasion and the products on display will have been chosen largely according to genre. So, if Fathers' Day is just around the corner certain products will be on offer on the special display and these will be distinctly different from those that were put out for the Mothering Sunday display three months earlier.

It is also worth noticing how in production terms clearly marked-out genres enable the economic organization of materials and workers to take place, as seen, for example, in the production of a whole string of gangster movies in the 1930s by Warner Brothers or a whole string of British comedies by 'the makers of *Four Weddings and a Funeral*'. Remaking the same film (with some differences) enables sets, locations, costumes and other elements of film fabric to be reused and helps to set up easily reproducible working patterns in which little time is lost in preparation because the cast and crew have essentially done it all before.

Stars as embodying social values

Each star has a specific relationship to film audiences; they are known by audiences for the types of characters they portray and for the attitudes and values their characters seem to embody. (They may also be said to have a further, more intense, relationship to those individuals within these audiences who chose to become fans.) Within their roles in films, each star may be said to carry certain meanings, to endorse or reject certain lifestyle choices.

In addition, since audiences often consume stars for the meanings they represent in their films (but also in their lives as displayed in the wider media), this can be a powerful way of ensuring that the public buys into a certain range of perceptions and outlooks. Essentially what is suggested here is that film, like all other media, has the power to influence the ways in which we live our lives: one of the ways in which we can be brought to understand and see things in certain ways is through the influence of stars.

Gender, race and stardom

Female stars from Marilyn Monroe to Jennifer Aniston are often presented on and off screen in such a way as to reconfirm male ideas of the sexual woman. Sometimes, however, in the roles they play in films they may be seen to threaten or challenge male notions of sexuality and dominance. Men may like to look at women in films (and elsewhere) in certain ways but they may in reality feel rather threatened by the sexual power exuded by the very personifications they desire to see.

ACTIVITY

1   Research the work of any contemporary female star. What sorts of roles does she play? Is she strong, powerful and independent, or weak, manipulated and at the mercy of others? What are the main themes and ideas to be found in her films?
2   Define what you see as being her main type of role (200 words).
3   Name two or three films in which you believe you can see her playing this central type of role. Try to identify particularly strong scenes as evidence.
4   Show one of your chosen scenes to the class and explain the thinking behind your choice of star and film clip.

Where would black stars fit into this pattern? Certainly both female and black actors occupy only a limited number of spots within the A-list of stars. Does this simply reflect a social reality? Or does it reconfirm (and work to perpetuate) the values of a male-dominated, essentially racist society? And, if it does, is this part of the role and function of the star system?

Obviously we can consider such issues for ourselves in relation to any stars we care to examine. The key point is that it is important for us not simply to accept such a phenomenon as 'stars and stardom' but rather to question and explore the basis on which it comes into being and continues to be of importance for cinema.

Figure 9.5 Halle Berry in *Die Another Day* (2002), recreating a famous scene in the Bond movie *Dr. No* (1962) in which a bikini-clad Ursula Andress emerged from the sea

Stars and ideology

Stars exist within a film industry that is owned and controlled by certain extremely powerful vested interests. As a result is it inevitable that stars have to adopt attitudes and assumptions that support the current status quo? Or can they in some way challenge current attitudes and ways of looking at the world while continuing to be allowed to operate within the industry? Can the process of reinforcing (and/or subverting) attitudes be seen at work both in the filmmaking process and within the resulting films themselves? Is it inevitable given the powerful position within society occupied by the major film studios, especially when they form part of some multinational conglomerate, that most films and most stars will reinforce attitudes approved by those studios?

Genre and ideology

Is all of this also true of genre? Do certain genres embody certain attitudes and ways of seeing the world? Despite the fact that certain horror films might show the demise of an evil male character have they not through the predominant focus of the film normalized the brutalization of women? Do war films perpetuate ideas of heroism and bravery that only serve to enable governments to lead the next generation of young people off to the next war? Do gangster films, again, glorify brutality and brutal people? Do melodramas reinforce the placing of women in subservient roles where the experience of being a victim is the norm? Or, can audiences use genres such as these to their own ends and not necessarily take projected values out into their wider lives? Can audiences in fact read 'against the grain' of a film so that they continue to see the world in ways that might be deemed to be in direct opposition to the values seemingly embodied in the film?

EXAM QUESTIONS

To what extent are star images controlled by the film industry?

To what extent are fans now able to determine the success or failure of individual stars?

What are some of the ways in which fans and the film industry work together to create a star's image?

CONCLUSION

In order to study film it is important:

■ to maintain a thoughtful and perceptive awareness of the fact that stars and genres may be seen as an integral commercial aspect of the film industry;
■ to see stars and genres on one level at least as capable of embodying social and cultural perspectives.

References and Further Reading

Abrams, N., Bell, I. and Udris, J. (2001) *Studying Film*, Arnold, London (ch. 11)

Bennett, P., Hickman, A. and Wall, P. (2007) *Film Studies: The essential resource*, Routledge, London and New York (ch. 3)

Butler, J.G. (1998) 'The star system and Hollywood' in Hill, J. and Church, P. (eds) *The Oxford Guide to Film Studies*, Oxford University Press, Oxford and New York

Dyer, R. (1986) *Heavenly Bodies: Film stars and society*, Macmillan, London

Finler, J.W. (2003) *The Hollywood Story*, Wallflower, London and New York

Gledhill, C. (ed.) (1991) *Stardom: The industry of desire*, Routledge, London and New York

Hayward, S. (2005) *Cinema Studies: The key concepts*, Routledge, London and New York

Lacey, N. (2005) *Introduction to Film*, Palgrave Macmillan, Basingstoke (ch. 3)

McDonald, P. (1998) 'Reconceptualising stardom' in Dyer, R. *Stars*, BFI, London

Roberts, G. and Wallis, H. (2001) *Introducing Film*, Arnold, London (ch. 8)

Useful Websites

www.entertainmentlink.co.uk
www.film.guardian.co.uk
www.imdb.com

10 NARRATIVE

This chapter:

- explains the terms *narrative* and *narrative structure*
- examines the role of the narrator
- explores the importance of stories in our everyday life
- outlines the expected or common features of stories
- considers ways in which we as viewers read film

INFORMATION BOX

This chapter will provide underpinning knowledge relevant to the study of British and US film in sections B and C of FM2: British and American Film for the WJEC's AS level in Film Studies.

Films mentioned

If you are working your way through the whole or parts of this chapter you will find it useful to have watched *Seven* (Fincher, 1995) and perhaps *Run Lola Run* (Tykwer, 1999), and helpful to have access to scenes, clips and single shots from at least some of the following films:

- *Pulp Fiction* (Tarantino, 1994)
- *Lock, Stock and Two Smoking Barrels* (Ritchie, 1998)
- *Lord of the Rings: The Fellowship of the Ring* (Jackson, 2001)
- *Four Weddings and a Funeral* (Newell, 1994)
- *Casablanca* (Curtiz, 1942),
- *High Noon* (Zinnemann, 1952)

- *Billy Elliot* (Daldry, 2000)
- *La Haine* (Kassovitz, 1995)
- *Ratcatcher* (Ramsey, 1999)
- *The Matrix* (Wachowski, 1999)
- *Donnie Darko* (Kelly, 2001)
- *Strike* (Eisenstein, 1924)
- *Moulin Rouge* (Luhrmann, 2001)

ACTIVITY

1   Summarize in 100–200 words the story of any film you have seen recently. Make sure you mention each of the central characters succinctly and that you give a clear sense of the beginning, middle and end of the story.

2   Exchange your synopsis with someone else if possible, and read each other's. Discuss the two pieces of work, looking for differences and similarities of approach. Which one strikes you on first impression as telling the story most effectively? What are the features of this piece of writing that seem to make it an effective retelling of the film's storyline? Does it follow a logical order? Is it using shorter, sharper sentences conveying information in a simple, straightforward way?

Narrative

Usually, although not always (we could consider documentaries, for example), our concern in studying film will be with works of fiction, narratives with characters and a setting that are told to us in a certain way and claim to represent the world to us. Given that this is the case, we are going to need to consider the fundamental nature of narratives, or stories, and the role and use to which they are put within human society.

To begin with, it might be worth noting that narrative seems to be integral to human experience of the world. We constantly use stories (and it seems we have always done so) to make sense and to create meaning out of our otherwise chaotic experiences. In telling stories we give order and shape to a series of events.

ACTIVITY

■   In pairs, tell each other the story of your life. (Before you do this you will need to plan it a little: write down the things you want to tell the other person and put them into an order you think is suitable and effective. You should only tell your stories to each other when you are absolutely sure you have shaped them as you want to.)

■ Remember things such as the need to immediately engage the interest of the person to whom you are telling your story, the importance of retaining that person's attention and the need to put things into an order that will enable the listener to make sense of what has happened to you during your life. (Notice as well that you have only been asked to tell the other person things you want to let them know about.)

■ One final condition: there is a time limit of ten minutes on the length of your story. (Notice that there seems to be some unwritten rule about the length of films you watch in the cinema: they almost always seem to run from 90 to 120 minutes. Why is this? What factors could have determined this length?)

Narrative structure

Narratives may be seen as particular arrangements of events within a structure. This structure may be the simplest one of relating events in chronological order, or it may be more complex. It could, for instance, involve the use of parallel episodes that form a deliberate contrast to each other, or the repetition of events seen from different perspectives, or the integration of symbolic events or images used in order to create significance.

> **PARALLEL EDITING:** this refers to moving back and forth between two or more narrative lines of action supposedly occurring at the same time.

If there is no apparent relation between the events in a film it is without plot (that is, there is no sense of a controlling order having been imposed on events) and it may be that what is being represented to us is the chaotic nature of human experience, or a lack of meaning in the universe. (Or perhaps we are dealing with a surrealist that aims to delve into the unconscious or the subconscious.) But such lack of structure is extremely rare, and not something that will be found in mainstream cinema; the very nature of storytelling is essentially that of giving order to events.

Even if the structure is extremely complex, involving unexpected time shifts and demanding that the viewer should keep elements of the story on hold until the bigger picture becomes clearer (think of Tarantino's *Pulp Fiction* (1994), for example, if you know it), order and shape will eventually be found. Indeed, the sense of achievement that comes from eventually recognizing and understanding the shape and form of the narrative is one of the pleasures offered by film. Through narrative we are reassured that any events that may happen are not random, and that the world we face is not a place of chaos but one of order.

The role of the narrator

Narration requires a narrator, someone (or more than one person) who tells the story. If you watch the opening to two films as different as *Lord of the Rings: The Fellowship of the Ring* (Jackson, 2001) and *Lock, Stock and Two Smoking Barrels* (Ritchie, 1998), you will find that both use the device of having a formal narrator's voice. However, often the narrator's role is in effect fulfilled by the filmmakers who position themselves outside of the story and decide what to include, what not to include and the order in which to place events. It is they who are narrating the story for us, but we will usually be barely aware of the filmmakers' presence as narrator.

If, as with *Fellowship of the Ring* and *Lock, Stock and Two Smoking Barrels*, the device of a narrator as a character or presence within the film itself is used it may be more obvious that the narrator has a particular perspective on events. If such a narrator is also a character within the story it will be clear that this person will see things from a certain perspective and will have his or her own relationship to events and characters. If an internal narrator is positioned outside of the main story and appears to be telling us what happened in an apparently objective way, he or she may be reliable or unreliable. The key point is that as readers of films we always need to ask ourselves who the narrator might be, what he or she can and cannot know about events within the narrative, and what his or her perspectives might be on any narrative event. For example, consider again the ending to *Seven*: why have the filmmakers decided to use Somerset's voiceover narration at this point?

ACTIVITY

- Try to find a contemporary film of your own choice that uses a narrator. What is his or her relationship to events shown in the story and how reliable a narrator should we take him or her to be? Are we expected to unquestioningly adopt his or her perspective on events, and if so, should we be happy to do so?
- How difficult is it to adopt a perspective outside of this narrator's viewpoint? If it is difficult, what makes it hard to achieve?
- Explain your film's use of a narrator (or narrators) to other people in a group, but only after you are absolutely clear as to your answers to the questions above. Do people who know the film agree with your analysis? If not, over what were there differences?

Plot structure

The story is the basic chronological order of events: the plot is the rearranged, highly selected chain of events in the film that has been given its own internal logic. By using narrative's ability to move backwards and forwards through time and space and rearranging the elements of simple stories, let us say 'Little Red Riding Hood' or 'Cinderella', we can create individual plot arrangements of the basic story events.

For example, we could start our story of Cinderella at the ball or our story of Little Red Riding Hood at the point at which she is about to be eaten, and then in both cases use flashback sequences to tell the story. In fact, we could start our narrative at any point within the chronology of the story that we chose. But what will always happen in a mainstream cinema narrative is that the plot will consist of a cause-and-effect flow of actions. You should be able to take any film and see how the sequence of events has been rearranged into a particular cause-and-effect chain.

Case study

FOUR WEDDINGS AND A FUNERAL (1994)

(Director: Mike Newell. Scriptwriter: Richard Curtis. Cast: Charles (Hugh Grant); Carrie (Andie MacDowell); Tom (James Fleet); Gareth (Simon Callow); Matthew (John Hannah); Fiona (Kristin Scott Thomas); David (David Bower); Scarlett (Charlotte Coleman))

continued

Figure 10.1 *Four Weddings and a Funeral* (1994)

This film would seem to be at least to some extent an exception to the rule in that it is almost a series of set-piece scenes. Can you think of any other films that might in some ways be said to not have a structure of cause and effect?

But is this film really an exception? Within each set-piece scene the events that take place always follow a cause-and-effect sequence, and there is in fact a sense of linkage between the individual episodes:

- Bernard and Lydia get together as a couple at the first wedding, and as a result constitute the occasion of the second wedding;
- we meet Carrie and her fiancée, Hamish, at this second wedding, thus leading naturally into the third wedding;
- Gareth has a heart attack and dies at Carrie's wedding, moving us logically by cause and effect to the funeral of the title;
- and from this gathering of the friends, the necessity pronounced by Gareth to marry, the increased calm of Henrietta, and Tom's telling Charles that he had never hoped for a blinding flash, all lead naturally to the final wedding.

ACTIVITY

1 Choose your own film and draw a diagrammatic representation of the ways in which cause and effect work within a single scene of your choice and within the structure of the whole film.
2 Explain your diagrams to a small group of other students who have undertaken the same exercise.

Characters

When approaching a film we should also consider carefully each of the main characters. Usually they will provide the filmmakers with a means of exploring various aspects of the human experience. Often they display particular commonly recognized traits of human nature, or complex inner conflicts of values and emotions. Often there will be contrasting, or parallel characters, that are used to highlight the oppositional possibilities open to human beings: love and hate, compassion and brutality, vengeance and forgiveness and so on. Sometimes characters are dramatized as unique individuals, and at other times they are presented as symbolic representations of what are seen to be particular types of character (perhaps a Christ-like character, perhaps a satanic character, perhaps something on that broad spectrum in between). Certainly characters and the relationships between characters will be a key element of any film's approach to storytelling.

ACTIVITY

■ Define the natures of the characters in any film you have seen recently. List what you saw as being the key features of each character.
■ Did you see them as being well-rounded, three-dimensional characters that you felt really could have existed, or as being rather flat, one-dimensional and ultimately unbelievable?

INFORMATION BOX

Flat and rounded characters are terms used by the novelist E.M. Forster when discussing literature in *Aspects of the Novel*. Rounded characters

continued

it is suggested have psychological depth, the complexity of real people. Often they are seen as being in some sense 'better' than flat characters that are underdeveloped or seem only to represent one aspect of human nature.

Stories in everyday life

Throughout our lives (or at least, from the time we are able to use language) we are surrounded by stories: fairy-tales, nursery rhymes, myths and legends, novels, histories, biographies, biblical narratives, plays, TV soaps, comic books, newspaper articles, songs, even conversation and, perhaps, dreams. Every day in almost every everyday situation in which we find ourselves it seems that storytelling plays a part. Eavesdrop on a few conversations and you will continually hear phrases that signal a story is being told: 'So, I said to her . . .', or 'I remember when . . .', or 'When we got there . . .' and so on.

ACTIVITY

- List the types of story with which you have come into contact so far today and expect to come into contact with later today. (Think carefully about this and you should find that stories are a much more integral part of your everyday experience than you might have at first realized.)
- Compare your list with that arrived at by at least one other person, if possible. See if anyone has thought of the sorts of stories missed by other people in the group. Try to arrive at as exhaustive a list as possible.

ACTIVITY

- What story do you remember above all others from your childhood? Write the story down, keeping as close to the original that you were told as possible.
- Think about the story: What was it about it that made it memorable to you? Who told you the story? Do you remember where? Were these factors important in your remembering the story?

- Exchange memories with other people and see if their experiences are in any way similar to yours.
- If you were to analyse the story what would you say were its key aspects: does it, for example, build tension, use suspense or surprise, involve colourful characters, or employ a repetition of events?

Storytelling expectations

All the evidence would suggest that the use of narrative is one of the fundamental ways in which we make sense of the world; stories could be said to bring order and structure to our otherwise chaotic experiences. As a result, as viewers who are already familiar with the storytelling conventions of narrative structure we approach film with definite expectations. We expect to see a range of characters, or character types, involved in a series of structured events that occur in certain places and at certain moments in time. There are likely to be problems and conflicts, and these are likely to be finally resolved in some way after having reached some climactic moment of confrontation.

NARRATIVE: this term is really quite simply used as another term for 'story'. But it can also be seen (perhaps more correctly) as a more technical term relating to attempts to theorize the principles by which stories are structured. Some theorists, for example, have suggested that all stories have 'deep-seated' underpinning common narrative structures.

The expectations we bring to a film's narrative are derived from our general experience of life, but also, just as importantly, from our previous experience of film and other narrative forms (we know, for instance, that both when friends tell us about something that has happened to them and when we watch films there is usually a clear sense of a beginning, middle and end to the story). Within this prior experience, our knowledge of genres (or different types of film and storytelling) will be responsible for the creation of a major component of audience expectation. So, if we are talking about storytelling forms in general we will know that fairy-tales, for example, tend to follow certain conventions while novels follow slightly different 'rules'. In addition, if we are talking about types of film we will know that the conventions attaching to horror might in certain ways be different from those associated with sci-fi films. Within each genre there is a slightly different set of rules of narrative construction at work, a slightly different language of narrative structure that is known to both the filmmaker and the audience. The filmmaker may follow these rules, or (and this is a major part of the pleasure of narrative for the audience) they may subvert our expectations, creating surprise for the viewer.

> **EXPECTATIONS:** the set of ideas each of us brings with us when we watch any film. These may be expectations to do with story structure, character development, or themes we anticipate will be dealt with; and they will be based upon our previous experience of these things.

> **GENRE:** this term has at least a double use here. It can be used to denote different general types of storytelling extending across a range of different media such as fairy-tales, plays and TV soaps; so, simply different types of storytelling. But it can also be used to refer to the classification of films into types such as horror, romantic comedy, thriller or science fiction.

ACTIVITY

- Think about a film you saw recently and jot down the outline of the plot structure (that is, what occurred in the order in which it happened in the film), perhaps in the form of a flow chart using arrows to show how one thing followed another.
- Try to decide what expectations you had when you went to see the film and whether the opening confirmed or challenged these expectations. Then, work your way through the narrative and decide at which points your expectations were fulfilled and at which points you were surprised by what happened next.
- How did your expectations change and develop as the film progressed, and what caused these changes?

Do all stories have the same basic structure?

Theorists interested in narrative structure have suggested that all films (indeed all stories) are structurally the same:

- we are introduced to a hero/heroine and shown the world in which they live
- the normality of this world is disrupted
- the hero/heroine sets out to restore order.

In basic terms we deal with a scenario of good versus evil, and a world in which order is set against chaos. Certainly experience would tend to suggest that all stories are founded upon the idea of a conflict between two or more central characters or groups of characters.

ACTIVITY

- Is it true in your experience that all stories seem to work around a central conflict and involve the basic features mentioned above?
- Discuss these ideas in small groups, considering a selection of films from different genres if possible. Do these general ideas hold true in all cases?
- What were, or who were, the representatives of good and evil in the narratives you discussed? Where could you see ideas about chaos and order at work? Was there always a point at which you could see the 'normality' of the given world being disrupted in some way?

Syd Field

It is not just theorists looking at stories in general who have suggested there are deep-seated structures at work. Syd Field,[1] advising on screenwriting, said good scripts comprised three clear acts. The first gave the set-up showing where the action was taking place, introducing who was involved and suggesting in broad terms what was going to happen. At the end of the first act there was a crucial point at which the direction of the whole of the rest of the film was set up. According to Field, this was followed by a second act with a key note of confrontation as the main character faced a series of obstacles to completing the central dramatic need of the film. At the end of this act there should be a further crucial point, he said, at which the central character would seem to have their goal in sight but would be faced with one final problem. And then in act three all the plots and sub-plots would be resolved.

ACTIVITY

- Take any film of your choice and try to apply Field's outline for a good script to it. Does it fit? Can you identify the two key plot points at the ends of acts one and two? Are there any ways in which your chosen film does not seem to conform to Field's suggested pattern?

continued

The simple story

Even a simple sentence, such as 'The cat sat on the mat', amounts to an observation of a subject within a particular environment and as such could well form the exposition (or opening) to a story. The tranquil ordinariness of normality has been set up and as such is ripe for disruption. If we add to this first sentence a second, perhaps, 'A mouse passed slowly before the cat', we have developed the situation and (because of the nature of the relationship between cats and mice) introduced a complication to the basic situation. Continuing with a third sentence, 'The cat pounced and pounced again, while the mouse dodged this way and that', we are building towards a potential climax that might come with 'The cat brought down its paw on the mouse's tail, held him fast and bared its teeth'. Our reader, because of her knowledge of narrative structure, will now be waiting for the resolution phase and perhaps a twist in the tale: 'The mouse smiled. The cat looked confused. The mouse pointed behind the cat. A large dog bounded into the room. The cat ran. The mouse continued slowly on its way.'

ACTIVITY

- Try to come up with your own short story comprising no more than 10–12 short sentences. The first sentence should set out a basic situation. The second should develop this a little and perhaps introduce some sort of complication. You should then move towards a climax before adding an ending that resolves the problem in your imagined world in some way.
- Alternatively, pass a sheet of paper around a small group of students and ask each person to write one sentence of a story. The first person sets out a basic scenario; the second introduces a further character or adds a complication, and so on. Aim to finish the story in 10–12 sentences and nobody is allowed to write more than one sentence at a time. Only read out the whole story at the end.

The use of time in stories

When we watch a film, we have to hold in mind at least three different time frames. There is story duration (the time frame in which we conceive of the story taking place), plot duration (the time frame within which we conceive of ourselves being told the story) and screen duration (the amount of time we are actually sitting in front of the screen). The story is the simple chronology of narrative events: the plot is the arrangement of these events within the film.

> **CHRONOLOGY:** the ordering of a series of events in time sequence. This is the simplest way of setting out a story and is important in films such as *Bloody Sunday* (Greengrass, 2002) involving the shooting of people taking part in a civil rights demonstration in Northern Ireland in 1972, where the development of events in sequence over a set period of time is a vital part of the whole creative enterprise.

Figure 10.2
Casablanca (1942)

In the classic romantic wartime drama *Casablanca* (Curtiz, 1942), through the use of flashback the story is able to cover a period of a year or more since Rick (Humphrey Bogart) met Ilsa (Ingrid Bergman) during the German occupation of Paris, but the plot takes place during just three days and nights as they meet again in Casablanca, and all of this occurs over a screen duration of only 98 minutes. Here flashback as well as the way in which stories leave out anything that is not essential to the progression of the narrative allows the compression of time to occur. Details given within the dialogue, such as Rick's involvement in pre-war conflicts in Spain and Ethiopia, although they have no visual presence within the film, enable us to extend story time still further into our characters' pasts. In the western *High Noon* (Zinnemann, 1952), in which we follow Gary Cooper's character, the sheriff, awaiting the arrival in town of the 'baddies', the screen duration of 85 minutes is the same as the plot duration since we experience his waiting minute by minute.

In *Billy Elliot* (Daldry, 2000) we essentially follow our central character over a period of about a year around the time of the miners' strike of March 1984 to March 1985. However, the story depends upon us being made strongly aware of the death of Billy's mother two years previously and includes a final scene some years later showing his ultimate success as a dancer. In *Orphans* (Mullan, 1999) set in a contemporary period in Glasgow, in a film that is 98 minutes long, we follow the stories of three brothers and their sister over the evening, night and morning before their mother's funeral. There is a clear pattern to the narrative structure with the four starting off together gathered around the coffin, dividing into pairs and then further splitting off as individuals before coming back together by the end of the film. In the French film *La Haine* (Kassovitz, 1995) we essentially follow the intertwined stories of three friends living in the working-class suburbs of Paris over a single day. The film opens the morning after a night in which groups of young people have been involved in violent confrontation with the police, and it follows the three friends through the day and night and into the early hours of the following morning.

INFORMATION BOX

There is absolutely no reason why you should have heard of any of the films mentioned in the two paragraphs above (although you may know of one or two of these films, at least by name), or in any other paragraph in this book. Gradually we hope you will widen your interest in films to encompass more and more different sorts, whether they are older movies, films from different countries, or films from genres you have not previously spent time watching.

> The key point with regard to the above examples is that you pick up the principles they are being used to explain and that you then try to apply these principles to films you know.

The use of imagined space within stories

In spatial terms watching a film involves us in exploring at least two spatial dimensions. There is screen space visible within the frame, but there is also off-screen space that we are asked to imagine or remember from earlier. In effect we are asked to contain a whole imagined world within our minds. So, in *La Haine*, we have some imagined spatial sense of the housing estate on which the three friends live and some sense of this as existing at a certain train journeying distance from the heart of Paris, and in *Billy Elliot* we have a strong sense of the mining community in which our central character lives. Similarly in *Orphans* there is a spatial sense of all of the events taking place within an imagined Glaswegian cityscape. *Casablanca* may have been filmed entirely in the Warner Brothers' studio in California, but as the opening image of the map of Europe and North Africa urges, we are expected to inhabit for the duration of the film the imagined spaces of Casablanca and Paris.

Time and space travel

Time and space could be said to operate as the two key dimensions for film narrative structure. The film's storyline moves us through time and through space, from one place to another and one moment to another, in order for us to follow a particular sequence of events that are set out in a specific sequence to tell the story.

This is at heart the 'magic' of storytelling and narrative film: we can be in Casablanca and then in Paris, in 1942 and then in 1940. However, do notice that this 'time travel' is not fundamentally based on the ability of the storyteller or filmmaker, the producer of the tale, to re-create other worlds and other times, but rather on the innate human ability to imaginatively occupy spaces outside of the here and now. The 'reader' of the film in other words is crucial to the successful realization of the imagined story.

ACTIVITY

1   Watch any of the films mentioned here alongside a film of your own choice that you believe has an interesting narrative structure. As you are watching make brief notes about where and when each scene takes place.

2   After you have watched each film decide what you would describe as being the beginning, middle and end to the film; in other words, its very basic narrative structure.

3   Without consulting with others try to draw a plan or diagram giving the pattern, shape or structure of the narrative.

4   For the films mentioned above in the text, if possible find somebody else who has watched the same film and compare your diagrams. Look for similarities and differences. Try to decide who has come up with the best outline plan and be very clear about why you think it captures the narrative structure most effectively.

5   For the film of your own choice, explain the narrative structure in detail to somebody else, using your diagram for that film to help.

(*Note*: there is absolutely no need to complete all of the tasks suggested in this book. This one, for example, will take time to do well and you may well not have the time. Activities are simply suggestions for things to do that will help you to make sure you understand the ideas being put forward.)

Cause and effect

As we are watching we expect each element within the narrative to be seen to have both cause(s) and effect(s); we expect events to be motivated in some way, to have been caused by something we have seen in the film and to have some discernible outcome. Without this all we would have would be a random series of unconnected scenes leading from nowhere to nowhere. By its very definition a story has an ordered series of events that leads to a conclusion.

> **CAUSE AND EFFECT:** this refers to the way in which mainstream films are moved forward by one scene or event having been caused by an earlier one and in turn giving rise to an effect which is seen in a subsequent scene or event. What this means is that everything we see has been motivated by something we have seen earlier and in turn motivates something we see further on in the film.

Resolution

To a large extent because of our experience of mainstream film, we expect issues that have been set up within the film to be resolved in some clear-cut way so that we know what finally happens. In most films this does happen, especially since this resolution of the issues at stake is often a means of confirming social norms and accepted consensual values. So, perhaps, in *Casablanca*, for example, it is the necessity in time of war of personal sacrifice and the placing of collective social aims over and above individual wishes that is asserted.

In *Orphans* it is the bringing of the brothers and their sister together as a united family around the graves of their parents in the final scene and what might be interpreted as their collective realization of the need to move on that gives some sort of answer to issues faced by the characters in the film. However, it could be argued that through the film (and specifically through the experiences of the central characters) we too have in some sense faced and gained a perspective on the important human concerns they have faced. In *Billy Elliot* a large part of the feel-good factor gained from the ending comes as a result of our feeling that Billy's goal of becoming a dancer has been achieved. But there is also satisfaction gained from the sense of 'family' unity achieved as a result of seeing his father, brother and best friend in the audience.

However, filmmakers can use our expectation that things will be sorted out by the end as a means of leaving us with uncertainty and ambiguity rather than answers. To some extent matters are resolved at the end of *Seven*, for example, but we are also surely left with a whole series of questions about both of our central characters, and certainly the issues raised by the film are left (necessarily) unresolved. In fact we could go further and suggest that the ending actually resolves matters in favour of evil in this film with John Doe's (Kevin Spacey) plans being fulfilled to the letter. This is very unusual, certainly for a mainstream Hollywood film, and is worth considering in some depth if you have seen the film.

At the end of *La Haine* we are given the basic outcome of the day's events for our three central characters, but the wider issues raised by the film are clearly unresolved. We have been given a whole set of possible reasons for the state of society and a further set of potential outcomes that might result from this, but nothing within this wider social context has been resolved. At the end of *Seven*

we can create our own possible future scenarios for Mills and Somerset: at the end of *La Haine* we can create our own possible future scenarios for a whole society. Both sets of filmmakers have in one way or another refused to totally close down the possibilities and left room for reader interpretation. Some spectators may feel themselves deprived of the comforting sense of satisfaction that a story with all the loose ends tied up may offer; others may be excited by the challenge offered by such final disconcerting uncertainty.

> **RESOLUTION:** the final phase of a narrative film that quite simply resolves all the storylines that have been set running. Films may of course leave some matters unresolved.

ACTIVITY

- Take any scene within a film of your choice and work out a list of the effects and consequences that arise from that scene.
- Look back in the narrative and try to list the events that have caused your chosen scene to take place.

> **EXPOSITION:** this is the opening to a film, which can often be in *medioreum* ('in the middle of things'). It sets up expectations and possibilities, and introduces key characters, locations and ideas.

Goal-orientated plots

In goal-orientated plots a character takes steps through the narrative to achieve a certain well-defined end. Such plots commonly revolve around searches, quests and journeys. *Billy Elliot*, for example, has already been referred to as having a goal-orientated plot: we essentially follow Billy's journey. Or plots can, as with detective stories, centre on the investigation (or search for information): *Seven*, for instance, works to resolve the mystery revolving around not only the identity of the 'Seven Deadly Sins killer' but also what his motivation might be.

Figure 10.3 *Seven* (1995)

ACTIVITY

Can you think of any films you have seen that do not have clear goals, or objectives, set out? Is it the case that this is a feature of all narrative films?

Films that focus strongly upon the psychological state of a central character can internalize this search or investigation so that what we have is this character's inner struggle for meaning or some understanding of the self. This may be said to be true in relation to all three central characters in *La Haine* and at least two of the brothers, Michael and John, in *Orphans*. The ending, as we have said, may represent a closed resolution of the problem(s) faced by the main character(s), or it may be left more open to interpretation.

Narrative structure and the spectator

The narrative is, of course, also taking the viewer on a journey. Patterns of development within the plot will engage the viewerr in the creation of expectations, which may be immediately fulfilled, delayed in their fulfilment or cheated; that is, the filmmaker engages in gratification, suspense and surprise. The interesting point is that each of these storytelling strategies is found to be pleasurable for the viewer.

Furthermore, however the storyline is structured it seems that because of our underpinning knowledge of narrative (whether inherent in some way to human beings or culturally learnt), we as the spectator have no choice but to actively engage in attempting to make logical narrative sense of what is unfolding before us. We are complicit in a vital way with the creative storytelling act; we willingly engage in the process, giving of ourselves both emotionally and intellectually.

ACTIVITY

- Watch *Ratcatcher* (Ramsey, 1999), if you have the time. Perhaps this is a film that could be seen in relation to a central character's journey or search.
- How would you define the goal being sought by James in such an interpretation? Would the ending suggest that James achieved his goal, and if so, in what way(s)?
- Decide on your interpretation or understanding of the ending and then discuss your ideas with others. Did everyone have the same interpretation?
- After discussion did you agree on one interpretation or did people still hold on to their individual understandings?

(Similar activities could be undertaken using a range of other films. *The Matrix* (Wachowski, 1999) and *Donnie Darko* (Kelly, 2001), for example, would be possibilities.)

The position of the reader

The view of events offered to us as we watch a film may be unrestricted; that is, we may be permitted a godlike overview enabling us to know more than any single character or even all of the characters; or our view on things may be restricted; that is, we may only be able to see events from one character's perspective. In *Orphans* we occupy a privileged position of being able to see what is happening to each sibling as they pursue their own individual narrative trajectories, but at the key climatic moment, as John sets out with the shotgun to avenge his brother's stabbing, it is vital that information is withheld from us in order to achieve the required shock effect. As this example suggests, there is, of course, a whole range of possible ways films might use restricted and unrestricted narrative. Sometimes a single story incident may appear twice or more in the plot, sometimes multiple narrators may describe the same event (in the famous Orsen Welles' film *Citizen Kane* (1941) different narrators give their individual interpretations of Kane's personality and driving motivations).

As readers, it is useful to continually ask ourselves if we know more than, less than or as much as any given character. We may have greater knowledge than a character (this tends to lead to suspense – we anticipate events happening that the character cannot know about and wonder when these things will happen or whether our character will find out what we know before the anticipated event occurs), or we may have less knowledge than the character or be confined to that character's perceptual subjectivity (this tends to lead to surprise – we don't anticipate events but experience them in as unexpected a fashion as our central character). The director Alfred Hitchcock explained this in classic terms by using the idea of two people sitting at a table having a conversation with a bomb in a bag beneath the table. If we as the audience knew more than the characters and were aware of the presence of the bomb, suspense would be at work because we would be on edge wondering if it was going to explode. However, if we didn't know about the bomb and it went off, we would experience the filmmaker's use of surprise.

We may also usefully ask ourselves as we are watching a film exactly how well we know any given character's thoughts, feelings and perception of the world. How sure can we be that we 'know' our chosen character? How confident can we be in their assessment of any given situation? Most films consider that there is an objective narration (a position of detached, balanced judgement) to which we return from more subjective episodes; but some alternative approaches may see such objectivity as unattainable or at least as severely problematic. There was much debate among the filmmakers over the way *Seven* should end. The ending that we have maintains Somerset's status as the reliable voice of reason and his concluding words as a narrator (despite the fact that a narrator has not been used throughout the rest of the movie) are justified because of this position of balanced judgement he has occupied throughout the film. But you may want to look at the alternative endings that were mooted and discuss this point further.

INFORMATION BOX

When you begin to consider these sorts of issues and look at the range of possible positions for the reader you begin to gain some awareness of the complexity of the reading process that is being undertaken as we watch a film. We are continually being expected to take up new perspectives, engage in new understandings, and shift our position in relation to new information.

Hollywood narratives

Hollywood narrative tends to focus on the psychological causes for actions or events that take place, for the decisions or choices that are made, and for individual character traits that are revealed. Often the narrative is driven by some form of desire, with the central character wanting to achieve some end; and there is usually a counter-force preventing him or her from achieving that end, perhaps a character that embodies an oppositional outlook or goal. So, in *Seven* we are continually being asked to understand events in terms of the psychology of our three central characters: the young rookie cop who believes in attempting to act as a force for good, the cynical older cop who believes nothing will ever change, and the insane psychopathic killer. (This sort of approach is very different to a narrative such as that used by the famous Soviet director Sergei Eisenstein for *Strike* (1924), where events are seen to be caused not by individuals but to come about as the result of massive social forces embodied in whole groups (or classes) such as workers and factory owners. However, films that do not see events as motivated by the psychological make-up of characters are rare.)

ACTIVITY

1   Consider these ideas in relation to a contemporary Hollywood film of your own choice. What are the psychological causes for each of the central character's actions? What are the psychological causes for the central character's key decisions or choices? What ends does each central character wish to achieve at various points in the narrative and what are the counter-forces working to prevent them from achieving these ends?

2   Explain your ideas briefly to a small group of other students if possible, perhaps using diagrams to illustrate your ideas.

In general, within Hollywood films of the 1930s, 1940s and 1950s there is a strong sense of closure with no loose ends being left unresolved, the moral message is clear and good triumphs over evil. However, it is also true to say that endings can rarely be entirely tied down and space is often left for the viewer to in part at least construct his or her own conclusion. At the end of *Casablanca* the German 'baddie' has been shot and the question of who gets the girl has been resolved for us, but what happens next to the characters we have followed throughout the film is to some extent unknown and open to conjecture.

Seven may have been made more than 50 years after *Casablanca* but fundamentally it works in the same way. We may be left feeling somewhat uncertain about the future for Mills and Somerset, but the story involving the seven killings has come to a definite close, and our initial questions about why these events were taking place have been answered. The difference, perhaps, is that far from being defeated, evil may even be said to have triumphed.

Chris Vogler

Chris Vogler[2] claims that any story about a hero undertaking a journey involves several stages:

- the hero's ordinary world is established and he is given a challenge or quest;
- the hero meets someone who gives him advice or he obtains something that will help in the quest;
- moving into the special world the hero faces tests/enemies, finds allies and learns the rules of this world;
- the hero faces his greatest ordeal, almost fails, achieves his goal, but still faces the return journey;
- the hero returns to the ordinary world as a changed person.

The importance of the reader or spectator

Finally, it is important to realize that as spectators in the cinema we are not inactive: narrative depends upon an interaction between the text and the reader. Throughout the process it seems that we are continually examining what has just happened and on the basis of our comprehension of that event within the context of the chain of events that have so far unfolded, we ask questions about what is likely (based on our previous experience of similar narratives) to happen next. Although of course the notion of 'asking questions' is not quite correct, since all of this seems to happen in a psychological flash.

Tzvetan Todorov

Todorov[3] sees narrative as following a common pattern of movement from a stable equilibrium to disruption of the equilibrium to a reordered equilibrium (achieved by action being taken against the force causing the disruption). You should be able to apply this template to the whole film and perhaps also individual scenes (do remember though that the initial balance may be suggested only very briefly).

ACTIVITY

- Choose a film and in a group work together to apply Todorov's narrative theory. (Obviously it will have to be a film that you all know well.) Alternatively, select a film that we have already considered as a case study.
- When you have done this try to do the same with Vogler's perhaps slightly more complicated suggested structure.

(This is a simplified version of Vogler's ideas. If you have time, research his ideas in more detail. In particular find out the names of the seven key characters (or archetypes) he claims are always present and see if you can apply these definitions to characters in your chosen film.)

ACTIVITY

- *Watch Run Lola Run* (Tykwer, 1999), making careful notes about the storyline, including characters and their relationships to each other.

Figure 10.4
Run Lola Run
(1999)

Narrative pleasure

One of the key functions of narrative is to deliver certain gratifications to us as an audience; films if they are to be successful in box-office terms must pleasure the audience in very particular, very predictable ways. We are 'pleasured' by knowing Todorov's pattern and seeing it unfold before us. We receive gratification from seeing our expectations confirmed but also from existing within the tension of wondering whether our expectations will be fulfilled or undercut. And perhaps we are most intensely 'pleasured' by finding the surprise of a new and unexpected twist that we are now able to add to our 'back-catalogue' of expectations. Another theorist, Barthes,[4] proposed that narrative worked through enigmas or the setting up of mysteries for the reader to solve. Again, the idea is that this is a process by which pleasure is provided for the reader.

Narrative dependence on oppositions

Taking a further possible approach, the work of Lévi-Strauss[5] is often taken as suggesting that narrative structure depends upon binary oppositions. This concept is essentially based around thematic concerns found in the text and suggests that for every theme you locate in the narrative its opposite will also be at work. So, if the notion of predator is attached to the scene with Marion and Norman in the parlour in *Psycho*, then the idea of prey will also be relevant. However, do be careful about linking a single idea too strongly to one character. For example, if Norman is associated with darkness and the night, then Marion will simply be linked to light and the day. Although in this case we might suggest this could be argued quite strongly, often the truth of a scene such as this is more to do with the good and bad in both characters (and perhaps ultimately in all of us).

In *Seven*, Mills and Somerset are clearly set up as binary opposites: the older, cynical, world-weary cop near to retirement and the young, enthusiastic rookie who wants to make a difference to the world. Interestingly though, this is far too simplified an analysis; for instance, it begins to emerge that they may be much closer to each other in their attitudes than such a binary opposition might at first suggest.

ACTIVITY

- In groups, take a film of your choice and try to draw up a list of oppositions within the text.
- For everything within the list you need to be able to show actual scenes that illustrate the oppositions.

Stories and society

The stories (legends, myths and sagas, for example) that are told in different cultures have often been seen as a means of coping with a society's experience of the world; from this perspective stories are seen as a way of making sense of a whole community's experience. Stories have also been viewed as the place where the collective memory or experience of the society is held and by means of which that collective memory and experience of the world is passed on to successive generations. Could film function in these ways? Could films be said to offer a society a way of negotiating its way through or making sense of contemporary experience and perhaps as a means of passing on that negotiated understanding to the wider community or next generation? How important might Hollywood prove to be in enabling American society to come to terms with the trauma of 9/11? How important was it in enabling that society to deal with the fractures within society that opened up around the Vietnam experience?

Case study

MOULIN ROUGE (2001)

(Director: Baz Luhrmann. Screenwriters: Luhrmann and Craig Pearce. Producers: Luhrmann, Fred Baron and Martin Brown. Director of Photography: Donald McAlpine. Director of Music: Marius DeVries. Cast: Nicole Kidman (Satine), Ewan McGregor (Christian), John Leguizamo (Toulouse-Lautrec), Jim Broadbent (Harold Zidler), Richard Roxburgh (the Duke).)

continued

Figure 10.5 *Moulin Rouge* (2001)

If we watch the first ten minutes of this film certain key elements of the narrative will already have been set up for us and we will have a set of narrative expectations about the rest of the film. This case study provides a framework for a narrative analysis which may be applied to any film of your choice.

The first prerequisite of any story is that it should grab our attention from the outset:

- How does *Moulin Rouge* seek to do this even before we have been introduced to any characters?
- What devices are used by the filmmakers to make the opening different from anything we have seen before?

And yet, at the same time, because of the musical refrains that are chosen, certain themes are already being suggested to us. What would these be?

- Is the hero clearly introduced? How do we feel about our hero? Have we, for instance, already started to identify with him? Do we have a clear sense of what he is like? What makes us fairly certain he is going to be the hero of the film? What possible complications or obstacles are already being set up for the hero?
- Which other characters are introduced in the opening sequence? What information do we find out about them?

- What information are we given about the world in which the film is set? Has the opening managed to create an imagined world in your mind? How has this been achieved? Can you apply the idea of equilibrium to this setting? What conflicts might cause a disruption to this world? Do we already feel we have some idea of what we think may happen?
- Have we been able to follow a clear cause-and-effect pattern between events in the opening? Has each event been clearly motivated so that we can understand why it has occurred?
- What questions are raised by the opening? How do you think these will be resolved by the end of the film? Are there mysteries or uncertainties about which we are keen to know more?
- Have goals been given or possible objectives suggested for the hero? Do we have any idea what he might find out about during the course of the film? Are there indications as to what his likely journey, search or quest may be?

Write an analysis of the ways in which the various aspects of narrative work to create meaning and generate audience response in the opening to *Moulin Rouge* (1,000–1,500 words).

CONCLUSION

One way of approaching films is to see them as stories. Essentially this involves analysing the various ways in which as stories or narratives they use certain common recurring features of storytelling or narrative structure.

Notes

1 Syd Field, author of a key screenwriting text *Screenplay*, who has worked as a consultant for Twentieth Century Fox, Disney, Universal and Tri Star Pictures.
2 Chris Vogler, author of another key screenwriting text *The Writer's Journey: Mythic structure for writers*, who has also worked for Disney and Twentieth Century Fox.
3 Tzvetan Todorov, a Bulgarian literary theorist interested in the structural principles underlying narrative.
4 Roland Barthes, a French cultural critic who through a varied series of approaches consistently rejected the idea that any sign simply worked as a representation of reality.
5 Claude Lévi-Strauss, a key exponent of structuralism, seeing apparently separate elements as only understandable when placed within the context of a system of relationships.

References and Further Reading

Armstrong, R. (2005) *Understanding Realism*, BFI, London (ch. 2)

Bennett, P., Hickman, A. and Wall, P. (2007) *Film Studies: The essential resource*, Routledge, London and New York (ch. 3)

Hayward, S. (2005) *Cinema Studies: The key concepts*, Routledge, London and New York

Lacey, N. (2005) *Introduction to Film*, Palgrave Macmillan, Basingstoke and New York (ch. 2)

Nelmes, J. (ed.) (2003) *An Introduction to Film Studies*, Routledge, London (ch. 4)

Phillips, P. (2000) *Understanding Film Texts: Meaning and experience*, BFI, London (ch. 2)

Phillips, W. H. (2005) *Film: An introduction* (3rd edn), Bedford/St Martin's, Boston (ch. 7)

Roberts, G. and Wallis, H. (2001) *Introducing Film*, Arnold, London (ch. 4)

Useful Websites

www.bfi.org.uk
www.filmeducation.org
www.thestoryispromise.com
www.philobiblon.com – non-linear narrative
www.aber.ac.uk/media/index

11 GENRE

This chapter deals with:

- defining the concept of genre
- genre as a means of giving pleasure
- acknowledging genres as dynamic and subject to change over time
- recognizing the possibility of seeing genre as a form of film language
- looking for similar thematic concerns across genres
- recognizing the use made of genre as a marketing strategy

INFORMATION BOX   *i*

This chapter will provide underpinning knowledge relevant to the study of British and US film in sections B and C of FM2: British and American Film for the WJEC's AS level in Film Studies.

Films mentioned

If you are working your way through the whole or parts of this chapter you will find it useful to have watched the whole of *Scream* (Craven, 1995). You will also find it helpful to have access to scenes, clips and single shots from at least some of the following films:

- *Psycho* (Hitchcock, 1960)
- *East is East* (O'Donnell, 1999)

- *Runaway Bride* (Marshall, 1999)
- *From Dusk Till Dawn* (Rodriguez, 1995)
- *The Ballad of Little Jo* (Greenwald, 1993)
- *Notting Hill* (Michell, 1999)
- *Nosferatu* (Murnau, 1922)
- *Blade Runner* (Scott, 1982)
- *Total Recall* (Verhoeven, 1990)
- *Independence Day* (Emmerich, 1996)
- *The Full Monty* (Cattaneo, 1997)
- *Collateral* (Mann, 2004)
- *The Big Combo* (Lewis, 1955)
- *Sin City* (Miller/Rodriguez/Tarantino, 2005).

Genre: the concept

Most often narrative films are classified by both the producers of films and audiences according to the concept of genre; that is, they are seen in terms of categories such as sci-fi, or musical, or western, or horror, or even sub-genres such as spaghetti western or 'slasher' movie. However, this way of classifying film is not usually analysed or examined in any way by most of us but is simply taken for granted.

If, however, we were to consider the issue we might recognize that each genre has its own iconography, that is to say characteristic props, costumes, settings and character types that act as visual signifiers alerting us to the appropriate category within which we can expect to pigeon-hole any particular film. There will also be musical signifiers (characteristic features of the soundtrack) and verbal signifiers (characteristic dialogue features), that is to say in general terms sound signifiers, indicating the genre being used by the filmmakers.

ICONOGRAPHY: as explained above, this simply refers to characteristic features of a genre, the things you expect to see and sounds you expect to hear that taken together collectively tell you the type of film, or genre, you are watching.

Again, as with all other film terms, knowing the name and what it means may be useful but it is not essential; it is recognizing the characteristic features that are signalling to you that this is a specific genre and being able to identify them at work in particular scenes within particular films that is important.

Case study

(Director: Wes Craven. Screenwriter: Kevin Williamson. Cinematography: Mark Irwin. Music: Marco Beltrami. Cast: Drew Barrymore (Casey Becker), Neve Campbell (Sidney Prescott), Skeet Ulrich (Billy Loomis), Courtney Cox (Gale Weathers), Rose McGowan (Tatum Riley), David Arquette (Dwight 'Dewey' Riley).)

Figure 11.1
Scream (1996)

continued

257
GENRE

Watch the opening to this film. It should quite quickly become apparent what is being referred to here as the opening since it almost operates as a 'stand-alone' short film in its own right, concluding with a dramatic camera movement that propels us towards an equally dramatic image of a body hanging from a tree.

Assuming you were unaware of the film's genre when it first started, how quickly would you become certain of the genre? What main genre heading would you classify this as belonging to, and would there be sub-categories, or sub-genres, within this major classification that you would see this film as fitting into?

What would be the factors that would alert you to genre from an early stage? Do you initially become aware of an overall category, and then later sub-categories? If so, at what point do these two things become clear and what are the elements within the make-up of the film that make these categorizations apparent?

In practice, of course, an audience in a cinema, or people who had bought or rented the video or DVD, would already have a good idea of what they were about to watch. What factors prior to coming to view the film would mean the spectator was pre-warned about genre and had in fact probably made a conscious choice to watch the film on this basis? (The list of ideas you arrive at here will make it clear just how much use both audiences and the producers of films make of the concept of genre before the actual moment of viewing. Posters, trailers, critical reviews and the director's previous work, for example, should all be on your list.)

Work your way through the whole sequence, listing as many elements as possible that are used by the filmmakers to make the genre clear to us. One of the keys to completing as comprehensive a list as possible is to remember the work done earlier on film form. Use the headings *mise-en-scène*, cinematography, editing and sound, and note ideas beneath each for ways in which these elements of film construction are being used to signal the genre to us. You should also find factors relating to narrative such as character types, character relationships and plot structure that help in indicating genre.

Examples under each heading would include:

- the setting of the isolated house in the country
- the use of knives as props in the kitchen
- the change in Casey's (Drew Barrymore's) movements as she begins to realize the situation
- the way in which a tracking shot is used within the house to follow Casey

- the single shot of the raised knife
- the change in pace of the editing towards the climax of the scene
- the sound of the knife being replaced in its holder in the kitchen
- sudden violent uses of language within the dialogue
- the use of the attractive, blonde girl home alone

You should be able to add many more ideas to this list (especially if you are a fan of this type of movie). You will notice, for instance, that colour, lighting and music are not even mentioned here. Particularly if you are a fan of the genre, you may like to spend some time picking out the references that are made to other horror films not only in the dialogue but also in the ways the film is constructed.

Make sure you watch the sequence several times and that you find time to compare your list with those arrived at by other people. When you have done this you will in effect have completed a genre analysis of the opening to this film.

Research a list of films that are generally seen as having followed in the wake of *Scream*. (If you are a fan of the genre you will probably be able to come up with a very respectable list without doing any research.) You may like to discuss a sequence from one of these films, applying the same approach as suggested above for *Scream*. *Scary Movie* (Wayans, 2000) would be an interesting choice for this exercise because of the ways in which it references *Scream*.

Subverting audience expectations

As an audience we always need to be alert to the fact that our genre expectations may be subverted or undercut in some way by filmmakers who are well aware of the elements audiences normally expect to find in films from any particular genre. So, for example, prior to *Scream* we would have expected the actor playing what is apparently the central female role to survive beyond the opening scene; and watching in 1996 we would have been shocked by the way in which our comfortable certainty was torn from us. You will also notice, however, that once we have seen this particular shock tactic used it becomes part of the array of horror genre possibilities to which we are alert as we watch our next horror movie (see *Scream 2*, for example). In fact it becomes part of the genre, something we look out for in subsequent films. In this way genre, and more importantly genre expectations, change and develop as filmmakers play with the norms of their chosen genre. (If we are enough of a fan to know some old horror movies we may even recall that it was Hitchcock who had his heroine killed off in a similarly challenging way in the middle of *Psycho* (1960), and armed with this knowledge we might not be quite so shocked by the opening to *Scream*.)

In a similar way but in a very different genre, *East is East* (O'Donnell, 1999) is commonly seen as a comedy and yet if we approach it with too simplistic a notion of what a comedy can be then it will confront us with some particularly challenging dramatic moments. This is a comedy that examines physical abuse within the home and is prepared to take on the potentially tragic aspects of a fundamentally loving intercultural relationship. It challenges our notions of what a comedy can be, or should be.

ACTIVITY

- Choose any film you have seen recently and decide how you would describe it in genre terms (it might be a film that you see as related in genre terms to *Scream*). List the visual signifiers and sound signifiers that you believe confirm your categorization.
- Try to find time to compare your ideas with those of other people. Pay particular attention to similarities and differences between your ideas and those of anyone who has considered a film from the same genre as you.

Genre as a film language

The rules and conventions of genre constitute a type of language, or code, by which filmmakers construct film while at the same time also operating as a language, or code, by which the audiences read film. However, these rules and conventions are subject to change over time as social outlooks alter or filmmakers develop the genre. So, the horror 'rules' were changed by Drew Barrymore's character being killed off within the opening sequence to *Scream*, and this has now became part of the set of horror genre possibilities.

Gaining pleasure from the expected and the unexpected

Making choices within the conventional expectations of the audience for a particular genre will give that audience a certain comforting pleasure; we feel we know where we are and that we have been given what we have come to see. However, making choices outside of the conventional paradigms, or sets of possibilities, available within any given genre will create a surprise for the audience, which can be at least as pleasurable as fulfilling expectations.

The use of a black sheriff in *Blazing Saddles* (Brooks, 1974) or the use of a whaling harpoon as weapon of choice in *Terror in a Texas Town* (Lewis, 1958) challenges our expectations of the western but also in the process excites us as a result of the novelty of the take on genre conventions that is being offered to us. One of our central notions of what romantic comedies are all about is severely challenged by the idea that Maggie Carpenter (Julia Roberts) in *Runaway Bride* (Marshall, 1999) should fight shy of marriage rather than going all out to obtain it. As with the mask in *Scream* (inspired by the iconic painting of the same name by Munch) and a scene such as that in the garage in the same film, the effort is always to find new iconographic effects for the genre.

ACTIVITY

- Imagine that you were to change the actors playing the lead roles in any film you have seen recently. What might have been the most bizarrely inappropriate possible choices? Discuss your ideas with others if possible.
- Take a genre you know well and decide what events you can imagine happening that would most upset your expectations for that genre. Again, discuss and compare your ideas with other people.

In horror films the viewer knows that a series of killings is likely to be carried out but the hoped-for novelty of how, when and where remain to be discovered. Similarly, as we journey with Mills and Somerset and the killer towards the final scene in *Seven*, as viewers of psychological thrillers we know there is going to be some disturbing final twist, we know we are inhabiting the lull before the final storm and in one sense we await to have our expectations fulfilled, but our hope is that this will occur in an unexpected way that we have not previously experienced. In

Runaway Bride we have been startled by the opening concept of a woman who is fearful of marriage, but if we know the genre well we will probably hold on to the hope that the resolution will be a bringing together of the key characters in a heterosexual romance.

ACTIVITY

- Can you think of any films you have seen where your normal genre expectations have been challenged in some way, or where the usual formula has been given some powerful new twist?
- List your ideas and discuss them with other people, taking careful note of their ideas as well as your own.

Hybrid genres

The fun audiences derive from having their expectations on the one hand fulfilled and on the other subverted has been intensified in recent years by the way in which filmmakers have been happy to mix genres in order to create hybrid, or crossed, genres. In *Scream* there is a clear mix throughout the film of 'teenpic' with the 'slasher' movie; a mix which really creates something new, a 'teen horror'.

> **TEENPIC:** this is a film featuring teenagers as the central characters and aimed at teenage audiences. The stories focus on the sorts of problems and difficulties faced by young people of this age.

> **SLASHER MOVIE:** this is a type of horror film in which the story revolves around psychotic males with plans to murder a group of young people. This sub-genre was at its height in the 1970s and early 1980s with films such as *The Texas Chain Saw Massacre* (Hooper, 1974), *Halloween* (Carpenter, 1978), *Friday the 13th* (Cunningham, 1980) and *Nightmare on Elm Street* (Craven, 1984).
>
> (There is often a disturbingly strong focus on the brutal murders of teenage girls, but there is also usually a 'final girl' who heroically wins out at the end and has been seen as an empowering female character.)

To some extent this mixing of genres has always taken place: noir films from the 1940s and 1950s were always thrillers and often also detective films. And in *Seven*, dealt with as a noir film in a case study at the end of this chapter, you will recognize elements throughout that might well lead you to classify this too as a detective film or a thriller.

In a modern film such as *From Dusk Till Dawn* (Rodriguez, 1995) however, something genuinely different occurs; rather than there being a hybrid mix throughout there is a sudden moment when the film moves from being a road movie to becoming a vampire/zombie film. This is a much more dangerous strategy for filmmakers, since it breaks the unspoken pact between producers and audience under which the filmmakers have agreed to make a certain type of film that the spectators have agreed to watch. The break is so abrupt that it risks alienating the audience rather than delighting them.

VAMPIRE MOVIE: this is a horror sub-genre that owes a lot to Bram Stoker's novel *Dracula* (1897) and again tends to feature male characters preying upon female victims, on this occasion by sucking their blood.

Figure 11.2
Dracula (1958)

ZOMBIE FILM: this is a horror sub-genre in which the dead (the zombies) come back to life and attack the living. See *Night of the Living Dead* (Romero, 1968) and *Shaun of the Dead* (Wright, 2004) to compare older and more recent treatments of the genre.

Figure 11.3
Meat Market 3 (2006)

Genre and binary analysis

From the point of view of genre analysis, as an alternative to looking for tell-tale iconography that reveals film type it is also possible to list oppositions found within a film. Different genres are often concerned with different sets of oppositions, and as a result have different thematic concerns. These are known as binary oppositions (a term mentioned previously in the chapter on narrative).

- In romantic comedies there is often a sense of a difficult opposition between the two central romantic figures that needs somehow to be bridged if they are to be brought together. Often the woman may desire marriage while the man fights shy of such commitment.
- Westerns often focus to some extent on the tension between the untamed natural world to be found in the 'wild' West and 'civilized' city-based society in the East. (See Maggie Greenwald's *The Ballad of Little Jo* (1993) for a feminist perspective on this genre.)
- Film noir has classically often been concerned with the antagonism between a seductive (but deadly) female and a male character at the mercy of these alluring charms.
- Horror often focuses upon the opposed extreme possibilities of human nature with women as the embodiment of trusting innocence and vulnerability and a male figure as the personification of violent predatory desire: in short we inhabit a world that contains both good and, most frighteningly, evil.

For each of these genres it would be possible to trace the existence of a host of other related oppositions. In a romantic comedy such as *Notting Hill* (Michell, 1999), it is not just the sense that our two characters come from different social worlds but also that they represent in a sense England and America, and that these countries somehow stand for oppositions between perhaps an intellectual literary culture and a rather shallow popular culture founded upon fame and wedded to financial accumulation as a barometer of success. And, since *Nosferatu* (Murnau, 1922) in film terms, and beyond that back into gothic novels and ultimately folk-tales, the horror genre has explored the relationship of our comfortable, everyday experience of society to the hidden danger of the dark outsider lurking just beyond the pale; or, in an even more potent variation, the relationship of the community to the hidden monster lurking unnoticed within society.

ACTIVITY

- Consider any film you have seen recently from a particular genre and decide how you would view it thematically in terms of binary oppositions.

- Taking two strongly opposed characters within a film and listing their characteristics can sometimes help to make the central oppositions within the whole film clear.
- Think of other films you know in the same genre. Are the ideas you have come up with for your film generally used as oppositions within the genre?

The recurrence of themes and interests across genres

We might also explore the ways in which different genres find different ways of negotiating, managing, or dealing with the same fundamental social issues. The city, for example, that is a focus of noir films also often appears in science fiction films where it is frequently a place of dehumanized brutality and isolation not so different from the labyrinthine place of entrapment found in noir films (see, for example, *Blade Runner* (Scott, 1982) and *Total Recall* (Verhoeven, 1990)). In sci-fi it is usually very clear that it is human society which has brought things to this situation. It is not, as with horror, that there is some inexplicable evil at the heart of man but that governments or huge corporations have mechanized, depersonalized and regimented the human experience of life. The city in *Seven* is the dark, foreboding place of rain found in *Blade Runner*, but interestingly it is also the place of horror where evil lurks in human form as well as being the nightmare world of noir films. As we explore genres in more depth what is often most startling is the extent of the overlapping interests that emerge.

Romantic comedies deal humorously with misunderstandings between the sexes that get in the way of the achievement of harmonious heterosexual marriage. They focus on women who desire the state of matrimony and men who to begin with are none too sure it is what they want. But the reassertion of the role, value and importance of marriage (at a time, we might note, when more couples have been choosing not to get married) is not confined to romantic comedies. There is, for instance, a sub-plot that runs throughout the American 'feel-good' alien invasion sci-fi film *Independence Day* (Emmerich, 1996) that is entirely devoted to reasserting romantic love and the institution of marriage. This strand of the film comes to a climax worthy of the most romantic of romantic comedies when as one couple get married the second couple who had parted before the film began hold hands and we see the wedding ring that has been loyally worn by the man throughout the time of their separation. Similarly, at the end of a comedy such as *The Full Monty* (Cattaneo, 1997) that does not have a dominant romantic focus, one of the clear implications is the re-establishment of romantic links between each of the two central couples. The partners in each relationship have been estranged from each other for different reasons but the use of camerawork and editing visually reunites them for us in an emotionally gratifying way in the final scene.

The value of this sort of approach to genre is that by looking at films in this way we will be able to identify particular themes that are of central concern to a range of films that do not initially appear to be linked by an analysis based upon simple iconography.

ACTIVITY

- Can you think of any two films (or more) you have seen from different genres where the same thematic concerns or interests have been apparent?
- Take time to jot down any ideas you might have on this before discussing the issue with other people. Take careful note of their ideas as well as your own.

Genre as a means of bringing order

There is a sense in which genre is like narrative in giving a certain shape and order to events. Each genre may be seen as a set of rules that allow the shaping of the disorder of life into some sort of controllable order. Within film genres the insoluble problems and contradictions of life can be, if not resolved, at least shaped into manageable, understandable forms. By the end of *Collateral* (Mann, 2004) the psychopathic killer in our midst has been tamed by the ordinary guy who through the experience has somehow been elevated to the status of hero.

ACTIVITY

Consider any film you have seen recently from a particular genre and decide what sorts of 'dangers' might be said to be dealt with by the film. Are the 'dangers' you have come up with generally to be found within films from this particular genre?

CONCLUSION

- Genres have distinctive individual characteristics that enable us to distinguish one from another in a general functional way.
- Genres may be understood as being used by filmmakers, spectators and the film industry in a variety of ways.
- Often the boundaries between genres will be blurred and similar interests/concerns will be detectable across genres.

References and Further Reading

Abrams, N., Bell, I. and Udris, J. (2001) *Studying Film*, Arnold, London (ch. 10)

Altman, R. (1999) *Film/Genre*, BFI, London

Armstrong, R. (2005) *Understanding Realism*, BFI, London (ch. 3)

Bennett, P., Hickman, A. and Wall, P. (2007) *Film Studies: The essential resource*, Routledge, London and New York (ch. 5)

Cameron, I. (1992) *The Movie Book of Film Noir*, Studio Vista, London

Hayward, S. (2005) *Cinema Studies: The key concepts*, Routledge, London and New York

Lacey, N. (2005) *Introduction to Film*, Palgrave Macmillan, Basingstoke and New York (ch. 2)

Neale, S. (2000) *Genre and Hollywood*, Routledge, London and New York

Phillips, W.H. (2005) *Film: An Introduction* (3rd edn), Bedford/St Martin's, Boston, MA (ch. 6)

Scorsese, M. (1999) *A Personal Journey Through American Movies*, Faber, London

Useful Websites

www.filmsite.org
en.wikipedia.org
www.bfi.org.uk
www.filmeducation.org
www.aber.ac.uk/media/index

12 REPRESENTATION

This chapter:

■ considers key questions to be asked about the representation in films of race, class, gender, sexuality and national, regional, cultural and religious identity

INFORMATION BOX ⓘ

This chapter will provide underpinning knowledge relevant to the study of British and US film in sections B and C of FM2: British and American Film for the WJEC's AS level in Film Studies.

As you study your chosen British and American films you should aim to ask yourself the sorts of questions outlined here wherever and whenever possible.

film and ways of seeing the world

All films may be said to attempt to re-present what we might call the 'out-there' world or the world as it exists. In doing this they present to the audience a specific and particular way of seeing that world. Therefore, in reading films of all types we should consider the ways in which such concepts as class, gender, race, sexuality, and national, regional, cultural and religious identities are being addressed. With one eye on the so-called 'war on terror' and our experience of living with its consequences, we might also note that during any period of potential political intolerance ways of seeing the world become especially contentious.

Race

In considering representations of race and racial identity in films we need to decide how we would define the concept of 'race' and how we might consider racial identity to be acquired. We could then assess:

- whether any given film was defining 'race' in a similar way, or in a different way
- whether the film under consideration was showing racial identity as being acquired in any particular way
- whether it was seeing the concepts of race and racial identity as being fixed, or as varying between places and over time
- whether particular races were being given roles within the narrative while others were being excluded
- whether particular alliances between races were being shown
- whether racial stereotypes were being employed
- whether race was being shown as a means of oppression
- whether the racial difference of 'outsiders' was accepted within the film's narrative or not

Figure 12.1 *East is East* (1999)

Fundamentally, the concept of race is a means of categorizing people according to supposed biological characteristics such as skin colour or hair texture. Such an approach towards analysing films would naturally be particularly interesting and important in considering a film such as *East is East* (O'Donnell, 1999) which deals with the experience of a British Pakistani family living in Salford in 1970.

ACTIVITY

- If possible, go through the above list with a small group of other people. Consider each idea carefully and see whether any further possible questions occur to you.
- Try to feed back your ideas to the whole class if time allows and discuss any areas of difference or uncertainty.

Gender

In considering the representation of gender identities we need first to ask how we might define the idea of 'gender': what is it and how is it acquired? In particular we need to define the term 'gender' as distinct from 'sex' and 'sexuality'. Basically, a person's sex is denoted by their genital make-up or the biology of their body; a person's sexuality is defined by their sexual feelings and behaviour; and a person's gender is that male or female construction of self given to a person by the society and culture they inhabit. In considering gender in any given film we need to investigate:

- whether men and women are represented in particular identifiable ways;
- whether the film makes an assumption that gender is fixed, as opposed to recognizing that gender as a social construct may vary across time and between cultures;
- whether the dominant descriptions of femininity and masculinity presented to the audience are simply those that fit the standards of a patriarchal society, or a society built upon fundamentalist religious beliefs;
- whether men are shown as active and women as passive;
- whether men dominate the narrative while women tend to be marginalized.

This will be an especially important approach when considering a film such as *The Full Monty* (Cattaneo, 1997) in which the disruption of traditional gender roles forms the very heart of both the comedy and the narrative.

ACTIVITY

- Go through the above list with a small group of other people if possible. Consider each idea carefully and see whether any further possible areas for investigation occur to you.
- Try to feed back your ideas to the whole class and discuss any areas of difference or uncertainty.

Sexuality

In considering representations of sexuality we might begin by looking to see:

- whether sexual identity is seen to be fixed from birth or acquired via socialization;
- whether sexual identity is seen as being certain or something more fluid and ambiguous;
- whether there are clear representations of heterosexual behaviour, homosexual behaviour and/or bisexual behaviour;
- whether sexual stereotypes are being employed, and if so from where they might derive (whether for instance this is again a case of a patriarchal society displaying its machismo beliefs or fundamentalist religious attitudes);
- whether any particular sexual behaviours or feelings are being presented in a negative or positive light;
- whether there is any awareness of how sexual norms and expectations may have changed over time.

ACTIVITY

- Working with others if possible, decide on a list of films in which you believe consideration of sexuality might be especially important.
- Discuss these films and debate how you would see sexuality as being thematically important to each.

Class

In considering class representations, which is basically the idea that a society can be seen in terms of a hierarchy of stratifications with those in higher classes having more power, wealth and status than those in lower classes, we could investigate a film to see:

- whether class is seen as fixed from birth, or is used as a flexible concept;
- whether there are clear representations of working-class, middle-class and upper-class values;
- whether these are stereotypes, or more complex representations;
- whether these major class definitions are shown as subject to further subdivision;
- whether a hierarchical class structure is questioned, or simply accepted by the text.

ACTIVITY

Go through the questions posed here for sexuality and class with other people, and, as before, see if you can add to the lists.

'Britishness'

Similar approaches should be taken to issues of nation and national identity, and culture and cultural identity, paying particular attention to the issue of what may be said to constitute 'Britishness' and how this concept is presented in any given film. Again, this area will be particularly useful in relation to *East is East* where the issue of 'Britishness' and cultural difference is at the heart of both the comedy and what could be called the tragedy of the film. However, it is also especially relevant to the post-war comedies where in the absence of the multiculturalism of *East is East* the notion of national identity will be paramount. Often films attempt to suggest that a cohesive national identity exists within a country. Our interest is, first, in the exact nature of that representation of national identity and, second, in what relationship that representation might have to the social and historical reality.

> **NATIONAL IDENTITY:** a sense of national identity seems to depend upon some shared stock of images, ideas, norms and values, stories and traditions. Nations might be described as imagined communities or

communities that exist in the individual (and the collective?) imagination within, it seems, the physical borders of a nation-state. This affects the way we see both ourselves and others classified as existing outside of the 'in-group'. Yet, national identity does not exist in some singular, uncontested form; rather it is a site of struggle constantly undergoing a process of reaffirmation or redefinition.

CULTURAL IDENTITY: this can refer to personal identity chosen for yourself or an identity ascribed to you by others. You might choose to describe yourself as 'British Pakistani', showing your identification with what you feel to be an intertwined cultural background, while others might identify you as 'Asian'. However, notice this will in fact be only part of your cultural identity: the racial/national identity part. Your cultural identity will also be formed from your categorization within other cultural spheres such as class, gender and age. So, for example, the key foci of your cultural identity might be young, male, middle class, Christian, British Pakistani.

INFORMATION BOX i

The important point is that, while paying close attention to the details of the films it is vital for you to be questioning what you are seeing in relation to the nature of the world around you, or the nature of the society from within which the film is made.

References and further Reading

Benshoff, Harry M. and Griffin, Sean (2004) *America on Film: Representing race, class, gender and sexuality at the movies*, Blackwell, London

Hall, Stuart (ed.) (2003) *Representation: Cultural representations and signifying practices*, Sage, London

Lacey, Nick (1998) *Image and Representation: Key concepts in media studies*, Palgrave, London

13 HORROR

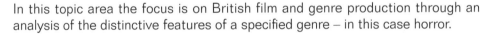

If you wish to study comedy rather than horror for your course, then there is an additional full chapter on British Comedy that can be found in the Resources section of our companion website at http://routledge.tandf.co.uk/textbooks/9780415454339/resources.asp

In this topic area the focus is on British film and genre production through an analysis of the distinctive features of a specified genre – in this case horror.

In studying a minimum of two films you will need to show knowledge of:

- The chosen films through detailed analysis of sequences.
- The importance of genre within the British film industry.
- How genres change over time.
- Narrative conventions.
- The way in which genres can represent social issues.

National cinema and the horror genre

It has been traditional (particularly in academic study) for British cinema to be defined in terms of a particular style and subject matter – social realism. This can create a distorted view of the nature of British national cinema both in terms of production and audience taste.

Consider the following points about the British film industry and genre production:

1   Some of the most financially successful recent British films (in the UK and the US) have been horror films.

Figure 13.1
28 Days Later
(2002)

- Budget: £4 million
- UK box-office: £6 million (318 screens)
- US box-office: £23 million (1,260 screens)

Figure 13.2
The Descent
(2005)

- Budget: £3.5 million
- UK box-office: £3 million (329 screens)
- US box-office: £13 milion (2,095 screens)

Both films are low to medium (in the context of British cinema) budget productions, funded by British companies (*28 Days Later* also received funding from the UK Film Council) with distribution deals with US film companies. The profit in addition to the figures above will include box-office returns across Europe, DVD sales and TV rights which mean that these are very successful films, unusually so for British cinema.

2   Hammer film studios (the production company most closely associated with British horror in the 1960s and 1970s) is one of a very few non-Hollywood studios which has an international recognition – or brand – Hammer Horror. This is apparent in the recent announcement (July 2007) that a Dutch consortium has bought the name and back-catalogue, and intends to restart film production under the Hammer Horror title. (It should be noted however that there have been previous attempts to restart Hammer film production which have come to nothing.)

3   Julian Richards, the director of another low budget British horror film; *The Last Horror Movie* (2005), stated that his application for funding from the UK Film Council was refused because horror 'wasn't really part of the culture of the British film industry' (Macnab, 2005)

ACTIVITY

- What do you think is meant by British film culture in this context?
- Why wouldn't horror films fit this definition?

Recently the Film Council has put money into several horror films (e.g. *Severance* (Director: Smith, 2006) and *Creep* (Director: Smith, 2004)) but this has also proved controversial.

- Why do you think this use of Film Council money has been controversial?
- Go to the Film Council's website (http://www.ukfilmcouncil.org.uk/infor mation/aboutus/overview/) and make a note of the Council's stated aims. How does the funding of horror films fit these aims?

The following is a list of definitions which make up the Film Council's cultural test for British films. For a film to be defined as British it must score at least 16 points in the test which covers subject matter, cast and crew. The important aspect of this way of defining British film is the weight given to aspects of representing contemporary Britain (e.g. 20 points available for cultural content and contribution).

Cultural test	Points
Cultural content	
Film set in the UK	4
Lead characters British citizens or residents	4
Film based on British subject matter or underlying material	4
Original dialogue recorded mainly in English language	4
Total section A	**16**
Cultural contribution	
Film represents/reflects a diverse British culture, British heritage or British creativity	4
Total section B	**4**
Cultural hubs	
Studio and/or location shooting/visual effects/special effects	2
Music recording/Audio post-production/picture post-production	1
Total section C	**3**
Cultural practitioners	
Director	1
Scriptwriter	1
Producer	1
Composer	1
Lead actors	1
Majority of cast	1
Key staff (lead cinematographer, lead production designer, lead costume designer, lead editor, lead sound designer, lead visual effects supervisor, lead hair and make-up supervisor)	1
Majority of crew	1
Total section D	**8**
TOTAL ALL SECTIONS (pass mark 16)	**31**

Under the cultural test *28 Days Later* scores very highly throughout and certainly represents diverse British culture and creativity.

ACTIVITY

Study the list of key British horror films below.

Key British Horror Films

- *Dead of Night* (Cavalcanti, Deardon, 1945)
- *Quatermass Xperiment* (Guest, 1945)
- *The Curse of Frankenstein* (Fisher, 1957)
- *Dracula* (Fisher, 1958)
- *Peeping Tom* (Powell, 1960)
- *Village of the Damned* (Rilla, 1960)
- *The Innocents* (Clayton, 1961)
- *Repulsion* (Polanski, 1965)
- *The Devil Rides Out* (Fisher, 1968)
- *Witchfinder General* (Reeves, 1968)
- *10 Rillington Place* (Fleisher, 1971)
- *Dr Jekyll and Sister Hyde* (Ward Baker, 1971)
- *Frenzy* (Hitchcock, 1972)
- *The Wicker Man* (Hardy, 1973)
- *Company of Wolves* (Jordan, 1982)
- *Hellraiser* (Barker, 1987)
- *Paperhouse* (Rose, 1988)
- *Wisdom of Crocodiles* (Leong, 1998)
- *The Hole* (Hamm, 2001)
- *The Bunker* (Green, 2001)
- *28 Days Later* (Boyle, 2002)
- *My Little Eye* (Evans, 2002)
- *Dog Soldiers* (Marshall, 2002)
- *Long Time Dead* (Adams, 2002)
- *The Last Horror Movie* (Richards, 2005)
- *Creep* (Smith, 2005)
- *The Descent* (Marshall, 2005)
- *Evil Aliens* (West, 2005)
- *Severance* (Smith, 2006)

How many of these films have you seen?
Which other films would you add to the list?

What is a horror film?

Defining a genre is never straightforward; genres change over time, they are complicated by hybrids, sub-genres, cycles and franchises. This is certainly true of the horror genre which can be categorized in a variety of different ways:

■ **Hybrids**: horror thriller/sci-fi/fantasy/comedy/adventure
■ **Sub-genres**: gothic/slasher/splatter/zombie
■ **Franchises**: sequels, remakes
■ **Cycles**: Dracula, Frankenstein, The Mummy.

The horror genre may also be categorized in terms of institutions (Hammer in the 1960s and 1970s, Universal in the 1930s) and nationality (J Horror, British horror, German Expressionism). That there is a recognizable category 'British horror' suggests that British horror films may be considered as part of a national cinema – dealing with subject matter relevant to British audiences in a distinctive style.

A framework of horror conventions (to be debated and added to):

■ Horror films are set in an irrational, supernatural world. This setting distinguishes the films from other genres (western, gangster) which exist in a believable realistic world.
■ This setting also differentiates the horror film from the thriller which has a rational explanation of events (e.g. if people die in a thriller they stay dead; in a horror film they may well come back to life).
■ Despite taking place in an irrational world the horror film is governed by rigid rules – vampires can only be killed by a stake through the heart, werewolves by a silver bullet.
■ There is little moral certainty in the horror film; the audience may be encouraged to identify with or feel sympathy for the 'monster' and enjoy the deaths of the innocent victims.
■ There are certain conventions which the sub-genres share – the isolated setting, the indestructible monster, the themes of forbidden pleasures – but it is also the case that each sub-genre has its own definable conventions. (See below for a discussion of the conventions of the gothic horror genre.)

ACTIVITY

- How many of the above conventions apply to your selected film?
- Can you add any other conventions to the list?

What is the appeal of the horror genre?

While other genres such as the thriller or gangster film may have scenes which create suspense and even revulsion for the audience, the horror genre is different in that the predominant aim of the film is to frighten the spectator, to make them feel fearful and anxious – not emotions that are usually associated with pleasure. So what is the attraction of the horror genre, and why does the audience enjoy being scared – and disappointed if the film doesn't deliver this effect?

A range of interpretations have been applied to the genre to try and explain its appeal:

- **The play theory**: Audiences enjoy the adrenaline rush, the roller-coaster ride, secure that there is no danger – it's 'only' a film.
- **The psychoanalytic account**: This interpretation argues that horror films allow audiences to gratify repressed desires. In this approach it is argued that horror films allow the audience to express these desires before repressing them again – often with the death of the monster. This idea has been particularly evident in studies of the gothic horror film where the relationship between the female victim and Dracula has been read as an expression of female sexual desire (and the male's fear of it).
- **Fantasies of power**: This reading suggests that we enjoy the power of the monster and are attracted by the monster's violation of social conventions.

PSYCHOANALYSIS: developed by Sigmund Freud, psychoanalysis is the attempt to explain individual human behaviour in terms of the conflict between conscious and unconscious desires. This is done through a long-term process of analysis – or therapy – between a doctor and patient. (This process has also formed the basis for a wide range of films – serious and comic.)

REPRESSION: Freud defines repression as a defence mechanism. It is the way that individuals protect themselves from harmful but attractive desires (often sexual). According to Freud, such desires can never be completely repressed but return, in the form of dreams, for example.

The horror genre: audience and institutions

The explanations cited above to explain the appeal of the horror genre also suggest why it has been such a controversial genre due to the emphasis on immoral, often sexual pleasures and the rejection of conventional society. However, subject matter alone is not usually enough to create such controversy; the anxiety about the horror genre also seems to be to do with who is watching it.

ACTIVITY

Who do you think is the main audience for horror films? How would you go about finding evidence for your views?

1 Use your own experiences:

- Do you watch horror films? If not, why not?
- Is there a particular type you enjoy?
- Do you watch horror films at the cinema or at home? Alone or with friends?
- Has anyone expressed concern about you watching horror films? If so, what were the reasons for this concern?

2 Can you create an audience profile (age, gender, viewing contexts, tastes in other films) from your own experience?
3 What do you think are the limitations of this audience survey?

Other suggestions for creating an audience profile

1 Consider distribution and exhibition:

- Where is the film advertised? (During which TV programmes, in which magazines?)
- Does it have a wide or limited distribution? Perhaps it went straight to DVD? (The international movie database www.imdb.com gives details on how many screens a film was released on.)

2 Read reviews of the film from a variety of different sources with different readerships.

- Which publications give the film more or less prominence?
- Which publications think that their readers would be interested in the film? For what reasons?

Certification – a warning!

It is tempting to define the age of the audience by the certificate of the film and this can give some useful contextual information (e.g. the producers of horror films face a conflict in that the largest cinemagoing audience is young teens but it is difficult to create a really frightening film with a 15 or even a 12 certificate). It is important to remember that a 15 certificate does not mean that the audience comprise everyone over that age (which would be a huge audience). It is also quite likely that 18 certificate films are not only watched by (or even aimed at) people over 18.

Audience and gender

The composition of audiences for films has been less studied than the audience for other types of media. This means that the definition of the audience for horror films has often relied on assumptions about age and gender (e.g the audience is made up of adolescent boys).

■ What does this assumption suggest about society's expectations of gender?
■ Does your own experience support or challenge this view?

In thinking about the audience for horror films it is important to consider the different pleasures that different audience members find in the same genre – or even film. In her book *Men, Women and Chainsaws* (1992), Clover analysed the relationship between the male teen audience and horror sub-genres (slasher, possession films, the rape-revenge movie) but made clear that this was only one section of the audience for horror films which covers a wide demographic:

> ❝ One of the surprises . . . has been the number of what I once thought of as unlikely people – middle-aged, middle class people of both sexes – who have 'come out' to me about their secret appetite for so called exploitation horror and . . . the variety and richness of people's relationships to such texts. ❞

(Clover 1992: 7)

It is interesting to note in this quote that the surprise about the make-up of the audience is not just to do with gender but also class and age.

Censorship: the BBFC

It is useful to consider the development of the horror genre – particularly changes in subject matter – in the context of the history of censorship and classification in Britain. A study of the different areas with which the BBFC was concerned with at different periods – revolutionary politics in the 1920s, juvenile delinquency in the 1950s, sexual violence in the 1970s – can indicate the concerns of dominant groups in the wider society at the time.

The following is an overview of some of the key developments in the history of British censorship. Remember it can be problematic to assume that subject matter was restricted in the 'olden days' with films becoming increasingly more permissive.

> **When cinema first appeared in Britain it was completely unregulated. But from the outset society's moralists were expressing concern about the influence of films. The charge that cinema going led directly to juvenile delinquency was made early and has continued to be made ever since.**

(Richards 1997: 167)

The BBFC (British Board of Film Censorship, later changed to Classification) was a form of self-regulation set up by the film industry (not by the government, as is often assumed) to apply consistent, nationwide standards of censorship. It was – and still is – an advisory body without statutory (legal) powers; local authorities can overrule the BBFC but in practice rarely do.

INFORMATION BOX – SELECTED CHRONOLOGY OF THE BBFC

1912: BBFC set up by the film industry. The main concerns during its early history were films which showed political upheaval (the Russian Revolution took place in 1917).

1917: The aims of the BBFC first made explicit – to ban immoral practices and to maintain the political status quo.

1933: A new advisory certificate – H for Horrific – was introduced alongside the U and A (16+) certificates in response to concerns about Hollywood horror films. In addition, several horror films were either heavily cut or banned completely. *Freaks* (Browning, USA, 1932), the now celebrated film about circus performers, was banned on its release in Britain until 1963.

1937: H certificate became restrictive, admission to adults only. This restriction on the potential audience led to a number of horror comedies which could escape the certificate while exploiting the appeal of the genre.

1942: Increased criticism of the horror film led to the BBFC banning H certificate films. The renewed concern about the genre seems to have been a product of the Second World War – with so much real-life horror, watching horror films for enjoyment perhaps seemed particularly perverse.

1951: X certificate introduced (replaced the H certificate). The new certificate was used by some film producers in advertising as a selling point for their film – to show that it was daring and new – whether in the depiction of horror, violence or sex.

1957: The Hammer production *Night Creatures*, about a plague which leaves only one man alive and terrorized by vampires, had to be abandoned at the script stage when the BBFC said it would ban the film if it was ever made. After this, Hammer worked closely with the BBFC to ensure that their films would gain a certificate.

1960/1970s: Relatively rapid relaxation of censorship rules with the BBFC shifting its position from upholding public morality to licensing films for adults to watch. This period is marked by a number of firsts in British cinema: first swear words, first abortion, first full-frontal female – and male – nudity, first sympathetic depiction of homosexuality. This shift was also evident in the representation of sex and violence, with films such as *A Clockwork Orange* and *Straw Dogs* (both 1971) given certificates.

1984: Video Recordings Act. After the relaxation of censorship and classification in the previous decades a panic about horror films was provoked by new technology – the video – and a particular type of horror film 'the video nasty'. These were predominantly US films although a few British films were affected. For the first time the BBFC was given statutory powers to classify films for home viewing.

2000s The BBFC states that its function is to provide advice rather than to censor or restrict adults' viewing:

> **[The BBFC aims to] give the public information that empowers them to make appropriate viewing decisions for themselves and those in their care. We help to protect vulnerable viewers and society from the effects of viewing potentially harmful or unsuitable content while respecting adult freedom of choice.**

(From the vision statement at http://www.bbfc.co.uk)

The recent sub-genre of horror films – termed splat pack and even torture porn films – such as *Saw* (d. Wan, 2004, US) and *Hostel* (d. Roth, 2005) have been certificated 18 without cuts by the BBFC.

Go to http://www.bbfc.co.uk to find out details of the certification process for individual films.

Case study
HAMMER STUDIOS AND *DRACULA*

Figure 13.3 *Dracula* (1958)

After watching *Dracula* – or another Hammer Horror film from the period – consider the following:

■ Why do you think these films were restricted to adult audiences? Consider themes, scenes of violence, scenes of a sexual nature and representation of gender.
■ Did you find the film frightening? Perhaps it seems – unintentionally – funny. Can you identify what it is in the film which means that today's audiences react differently to audiences of the 1950s?

It was the BBFC which deemed the films 'horrific' and not the audiences; in the USA Hammer horror was seen as family entertainment. Do you think that today's controversial horror films such as *Hostel* will be watched differently by an audience in 50 years' time?

■ Do you know anyone who went to the cinema as a young adult in the late 1950s and early 1960s? Perhaps you could ask them about their memories of the horror films of the period. (Tip: Your teacher probably isn't old enough.)

Horror genre and institutions: Hammer film studios

Hammer film studios, an independent production company, became synonymous with the horror – particularly gothic – genre, developing a style of filmmaking which was successful in the USA as well as in Britain.

Why horror films?

Hammer studios was set up in 1947 with the purchase of a country house in Berkshire which would function as a studio set. To begin with, Hammer films were adaptations of radio shows and American co-productions. The decision to move into horror films could be explained through economic reasons:

■ **Distribution**: To get their films distributed studios had to make a deal with one of the three major cinema chains which dominated British cinema exhibition at the time – Odeon, Gaumont (both owned by Rank) and ABC. Rank had a deal with Ealing Studios and specialized in family-friendly films – rarely showing the new X certificate. In making a deal with Hammer, Odeon would have welcomed the more 'adult' films as a selling point, something different from that offered by the competition.

■ **Competition from television**: The style of Hammer Horror films – use of technicolour and taboo subject matter – differentiated it from the black and white, rather conservative television programmes. Hammer made the first gothic horror films to be shot in colour; this decision was partly for institutional reasons – Universal held the copyright to the Dracula and Frankenstein films and any remakes had to look substantially different to the original black and white films.

■ **Style**: The country house studio was an excellent backdrop for stories set in nineteenth-century Europe but not contemporary Britain.

■ **American finance**: Hammer productions were attractive to the US film studios as an opportunity for co-productions, allowing Hollywood to bypass legislation which limited the amount of money they could take out of the British film industry. Hammer made deals with Warner Brothers and Universal.

■ **Copyright**: Dracula was a commercial success in Britain and the USA, leading to Universal selling the remake rights for all their gothic horror films and therefore enabling the next ten years of gothic film production at Hammer.

In addition to economic factors the social and cultural context of the period is likely to be relevant to the success of the films:

- **Genre**: During the previous decades British film production had been dominated by war films and Ealing comedies. The horror genre provided something different for audiences.
- **Youth audience**: The 1950s may be seen as a period of change, a new generation; the teenager emerged as a niche market with different tastes in popular culture to previous generation's: 'Ten years earlier the films would have been too shocking, ten years later not shocking enough' (Pirie 1973).
- **Classification**: The introduction of the X certificate in Britain and a new ratings system in the USA widened the market for horror films and particularly appealed to a more rebellious youth audience.

Decline of Hammer Horror

In the late 1960s Hammer studios were in a particularly vulnerable position because they were reliant on the horror genre when it was becoming less popular with audiences, and also on American money at a time when American companies were pulling out of the British film industry.

ACTIVITY

Genre theory in practice:

- From your knowledge of genre theory – particularly the relationship between genre, audience and producer – what do you think the producers at Hammer would have tried once the traditional horror film lost its appeal?
- Research the decline of Hammer Horror by going to the following sources (or any others you find relevant):

  http://www.screenonline.org.uk/

  'National Cinemas and Film Movements' in *The Cinema Book* (ed. P. Cook and M. Bernink).

Make notes on the following:

1 List the titles of three horror films Hammer made in the early 1970s. Provide a brief synopsis for each.
2 What attempt has been made to develop the horror genre in these films?

Defining the gothic horror

Dracula is an example of one of the most popular sub-genres of horror – the gothic horror. While we tend to expect gothic horror to be set in the past it is also possible to see the influence of gothic themes and style on horror films with contemporary settings.

Gothic was originally a British, literary genre. Some key novels were:

- *The Castle of Ortranto* (Walpole, 1764)
- *Frankenstein* (Mary Shelley, 1818)
- *Dracula* (Bram Stoker, 1897)

The novels that first developed the genre of gothic horror and the films – which were often adapted from them – share the following aims:

- To provoke the audience into an emotional response rather than an intellectual or moral one. This is part of the reaction against the reason and rationality of normal life.
- To stir up fears, anxieties and desires which are attractive but dangerous and/or taboo. These are feelings which are not usually acknowledged in everyday life, but repressed.

This conflict between subconscious desires and the need to conceal them is represented in a series of doubles in gothic horror:

- Dual worlds (usually symbolic rather than literal) which represent dark and light. This is not necessarily the same as good and evil (although it might be) but rather:

    - *The diurnal world*: light and familiar, the world of convention and institutions
    - *The nocturnal world*: dark and unknown, where the artificial layers of social convention can be stripped away.

- **Setting**: The concept of duality is also apparent in the settings which are often split over two levels (e.g. the house and the cellar, the church and the crypt, the ship and the hold, the castle and the dungeon).
- **Journey**: The characters often undertake a journey between the two worlds. This might be geographical but could be psychological such as in dreams.

■ **The double motif**: Shadows and reflections are used to suggest something unknown about the character. This is also often apparent in the monster which goes through a transformation – the most explicit representation is in the character of Dr Jekyll and Mr Hyde.

ACTIVITY

Constructing a narrative analysis of Dracula

One of the areas of assessment in this unit is the narrative features of your chosen films within the context of genre. To explore this concept you will need to:

■ Produce detailed textual analysis of key sequences.
■ Define how the film conforms to or subverts the conventions of horror.

1 Begin by listing examples which conform to the conventions of gothic horror under the following headings:

   ■ *Setting*
   ■ *Journey*
   ■ *The double*

   Remember: in each of these categories the examples may be literal but also psychological and metaphorical; Dracula makes a physical journey from Transylvania but also a psychological journey from aristocratic gentleman to monster.

2 Select two key sequences which illustrate your examples of narrative conventions. Try to choose scenes which contain examples of more than one convention.

3 Using the chosen sequences write a *mise-en-scène* analysis which refers to the conventions of gothic horror. You will need to consider the way that the setting, props, lighting, colour, costume and so on reinforce the themes of the film.

4 Once you have completed this preparatory work (list of conventions, analysis of chosen sequences) use it to address the following question:

   ■ To what extent is *Dracula* a gothic horror film? Why do you think audiences enjoy this genre?

You will need to refer to specific sequences in your answer (1,000 words).

Case study

Figure 13.4 *The Descent* (2005)

The Descent is the second film selected for this topic area, and the following section suggests a framework for studying the film. The analysis of the film will focus on:

- Film language and film style (micro analysis)
- Narrative and genre (macro analysis)
- Representation of gender

Before continuing with the analysis you need to watch *The Descent*. The first time you watch it you should make a note of the following:

- The names and a brief description of the characters.
- A brief synopsis of the plot.
- Any genre conventions which are initially apparent.

continued

As context for this section read the article 'Fright Club' by Geoffrey Macnab at http://film.guardian.co.uk/features/feature pages/ 0,,152 0651,00.html which outlines the emergence of a new period of British horror films and directors at the beginning of the twenty-first centry.

1 Read the article and make a note of all the new British horror films – and directors – referred to.
2 What are some of the reasons given for the resurgence of British horror films? Organize your points under the headings of audience and producers.
3 How many of the films referred to have you seen – or heard of? Have they been a success? Were they all made and distributed? (You could check on imdb to find out release dates, box-office).
4 This article was written in 2005 – what has happened to British horror films since then?

Analysis of the opening of the film

The opening of *The Descent* is a useful sequence to study because of the way it introduces key characters and plot (narrative), genre conventions and representations which are then developed throughout the film.

Watch the opening of *The Descent* and make notes under the following headings:

- *Film language*
- *Genre*
- *Narrative*

Sample analysis

The film opens with **shots** of the main characters white-water rafting. The soundtrack is **diegetic**, made up of whoops and screams – of excitement rather than fear which the audience might expect at the beginning of a **horror** film. The sequence uses **rapid cuts between a variety of extreme close-up and long shots**. The close-up on the rushing water and the faces of the women emphasize the mood of exhilaration. The first scene also sets up the **narrative tension**; while Sarah and her daughter hug each other, her husband and Juno exchange intense looks. Beth is alone. A close-up on her face suggests that she doesn't know what is happening but that she has guessed – much like the position of the **audience**.

With the sudden tragic accident in the next scene the **genre** would seem to be a thriller or drama centred on the emotional response to an explicable accident. The first indication that this is a horror film comes at the hospital where Sarah is recovering. Instead of the **realistic space** of the river and the road seen previously, there is the first of a series of Sarah's hallucinations or dreams about her dead daughter. As Sarah stands in the hospital corridor, a green light surrounding her, it is not clear if this is a real experience or not. This has a **disorientating effect on the audience** which is further emphasized by the use of a **reverse zoom shot**. Sarah's **costume** – her hospital gown, wild hair and staring eyes – also recall **iconic** moments from other horror films such as *Carrie* (there is another reference to *Carrie* at the end of the film when Sarah's hand thrusts out of the earth). As Sarah runs down the hospital corridor in terror she is enveloped in darkness – **an image which foreshadows her experience in the cave**. The **conflict** between the characters in the film is also further developed for the audience as the camera pulls back to show Juno watching Sarah and then running away.

Many of the elements of this pre-title sequence indicate the structure of the film as a whole, with the shifts between different genres evident in the film language. The mixing of the real world, dreams, hallucinations and the supernatural also continues throughout, culminating in the 'two' endings of the film.

Representations of gender

The Descent is an unusual film because all the main characters are women. In fact there is only one male character of any importance and he only appears in the first few minutes of the film. It is debatable whether the monsters in the film are male – 'that was not a human being' one of the women says when they finally realize they are not alone in the cave. One of the main areas of study of women in films has been the way in which many female characters only seem to exist to be looked at, to provide romantic – and sexual – interest for the male characters (and audience). The role of women in the horror genre has been a controversial area (see information box below) and therefore *The Descent* provides an interesting case study for the changing representation of women in the genre.

continued

Figure 13.5 *The Descent* (2005)

ACTIVITY

Analyse the representation of women by making notes on the following:

- Costume and appearance
- Role in the plot
- Relationships
- Characteristics
- How are they shot in the film – does the camera concentrate on particular aspects of their bodies?
- Choose two sequences which would be useful in illustrating your ideas.
- Look at the information box below. Do the representations in *The Descent* conform to these ideas?

The victim

Do you like scary movies?

> **What's the point? They're all the same, some stupid killer stalking some big-breasted girl who can't act who is always running up the stairs when she should be running out the front door, it's insulting.**

(*Scream, 1996, Wes Craven*)

Another reason for the controversy surrounding the horror genre – particularly for feminist critics – was the representation of women as victims, as damsels in distress. The spectator (assumed to be young and male) was supposedly encouraged to identify with the killer and objectify the woman who was represented in a passive and sexualized way.

More recent work on the genre has suggested another interpretation – the audience (whether male or female) identifies with the hero of the film (the final girl) rather than with the monster.

Characteristics of the final girl

- Boyish attributes apparent from dress, behaviour, even names.
- Strong and independent – the final girl is the first to realize that something is wrong and pursues this belief even when no one else believes her.
- Intelligent and resourceful – to kill the monster the final girl overcomes her lack of physical strength through rational thinking and ingenuity.
- Brave – the final girl sees her friends die but continues to pursue the monster, despite knowing the dangers.
- Serious – unlike other teenagers in the horror genre the final girl isn't interested in superficial pleasures such as drinking and partying.

(Clover 1992)

Some points to note on the representation of gender in *The Descent*

Costume in the film is predominantly the clothing and equipment needed for the extreme activities the women take part in – white-water rafting and caving. The clothing is functional and worn for a purpose rather than to accentuate feminine characteristics. This is also the case with the women's 'everyday' clothes which consist of high-necked heavy sweaters and jeans. The props (such as ropes and pickaxes) also emphasize the physical strength and abilities of the group.

The relationships between the women provide the conflict and dynamic which drives the plot forward; this means that the film defines the women through their relationships with each other rather than to men. Only one of the group fulfils the conventional female role of wife and mother. The dominance of female characters in *The Descent* does not necessarily mean that the representations are positive – part of the conflict within the group is to do with betrayal between characters – and are very far from a feminist idea of the sisterhood. The main conflict is between Sarah (the wife and mother) and Juno, whose desire for adventure and challenge leads them into the 'wrong' cave. The character of Juno raises interesting questions about the representation of gender, particularly the way in which strong women are often signified through masculine characteristics. (A forerunner of the character of Juno may be seen in Sarah Connor in *Terminator 2* and Ripley in *Aliens*.)

The setting of the cave means that the characters are in darkness for most of the film, further removing the opportunity for the women to be objectified by the audience – the need to identify the characters in such a setting also means that their faces in close-up dominate, rather than their bodies.

Suggestions for further work

- While *The Descent* is a horror film it also has elements of other genres – how would you define the film as a hybrid genre? Give examples of sequences which include conventions of more than one genre. (It is also worth noting that the film makes references to many other films – how many can you spot?)
- Compare *The Descent* with *Dog Soldiers*, Neil Marshall's earlier film which centres on a group of male soldiers. Are there similarities in the narrative structure and use of genre conventions? What is the representation of masculinity in the film?

Cherry, B. (2001) 'Refusing to Refuse to Look: Female Viewers of the Horror Genre' in *The Horror Film Reader*, ed. Mark Jancovich, Routledge, London

Clover, C. (1992) *Men, Women and Chainsaws*, BFI, London

Cook, P. and Bernink, M. (eds) (1999) *The Cinema Book*, BFI, London

Cornich, I. (1997) 'Traditions of the British Horror Film' in Murphy, R. (ed.), *The British Cinema Book*, BFI, London

Kuhn, A. (1999) 'Hammer Productions' in Cook, P. and Bernink, M. (eds), *The Cinema Book*, BFI, London

Macnab, G. (2005) 'Fright Club', Monday July 4th 2005, *Guardian*

Pirie, D. (1973) *A Heritage of Horror: The English Gothic Cinema 1946–72*, Gordon Fraser, London

Richards, J. (1997) 'British Film Censorship', in Murphy, R. (ed.), *The British Cinema Book*, BFI, London

14 EWAN MCGREGOR

In this chapter we look at:

- definitions of the star image
- the relationship between stars, audience and industry
- the distinctive characteristics of the Ewan McGregor star image
- how stars create meaning in the film narrative

If you wish to study Julie Christie for your British star study then there is an additional full chapter that can be found in the Resources section of our companion website at http://routledge.tandf.co.uk/textbooks/9780415454339/resources.asp

INFORMATION BOX

This chapter will be directly relevant to your work on FM2: British and American Film – Section B: British Film Topics for the WJEC's AS level in Film Studies.

Problems of defining stars

Not every recognizable actor in a film is a star, not every actor that is promoted by Hollywood or the British film industry becomes a star, and stars are not always the most beautiful or the most talented people in the film. It is these unpredictable elements which make the study of the meaning of stars so interesting.

In Film Studies you will come across different ways of analysing the role of stars. These may be categorized as belonging to either star studies or performance studies.

Star studies examines:

- The role of the star as a form of marketing and publicity in the film industry.
- The way stars are used to differentiate between films – for the audience and industry.

Performance studies analyses:

- The link between the star and the culture which produced them.
- Why some individuals become stars.
- The values the star represents – this may be to do with gender, race, nationality and so on.

When is a film actor a star?

In deciding the criteria for defining a star there needs to be some objective measure beyond whether or not we personally like the actor.

Here are some suggestions for different ways of defining a star:

- **Economic power**: Does the star have the power to 'open' a film? Is the popularity of a star enough that audiences will go to a film just because they are in it (whatever the genre or subject)?
- **Salary**: A few stars – such as Johnny Depp and Tom Hanks – can earn $20 million per film, proving the producer's faith in them as an investment.
- **Profit**: *Forbes* magazine (an economics journal) published a list (2007) which calculated the economic value of stars – what level of return they made on their salary – rather than the box-office return. In this account of economic value Matt Damon was deemed to be the most profitable while there were no British stars on the list. For the full results see: http://www.forbes.com/2007/08/03/celebrities-hollywood-movies-biz-cz_dp_0806starpayback.html.
- **Fame**: How famous does an actor have to be to be a star? Famous across age groups, race and gender? Does an actor have to have global recognition to be defined as a star? Are there different levels of stardom – the A list and the D list?
- **Typecasting**: does a star have to be recognizable across a variety of roles?

- How important are stars to you in choosing which films to watch? What other factors affect your choice?
- Do you have a favourite star (British or American)? What appeals to you about this star – does it have to do with their appearance? The roles they play? How do you express your interest in this star?
- Do you think stars are less important to the film industry now than in the past? If so, can you give any reasons for this?

Stars and the British film industry

In defining stars within the context of the British film industry other problems of definition arise. As a national cinema can the British film industry claim to have global stars, or should we define a British film star as something separate from Hollywood stardom? As with other debates around national cinema, the study of British stars will always refer to Hollywood as a point of comparison.

Background

The star system (a deliberate method for manufacturing and promoting stars) is usually associated with Hollywood, but the British film industry developed its own star system in the 1910s and 1920s as well as copying some of the Hollywood techniques:

- British studios (such as Rank) kept stars under contract so that they could control the parts they played and create a typical role that the star became associated with.
- Rank trained potential young stars in their 'Company of Youth' (or Charm School as it became known).
- An image was carefully built up for the star outside of their films through promotion in magazines, personal appearances and the setting up of fan clubs for each individual star.

Stars were the main factor in audience choice in the 1930s, 1940s and 1950s. The industry press published an annual ranking of the box-office performance of stars, broken down into Hollywood and British actors. Then, as now, British audiences preferred Hollywood to British stars.

The Hollywood dilemma

Since the development of the star system in Britain, stars (as well as directors) have faced a dilemma – whether to remain working in Britain or to go to Hollywood.

What do you think would be the advantages and disadvantages for a British film star working in Hollywood? You could consider types of films and roles available, salary, strength of the industry and so on (it is worth remembering that it isn't just British stars who face this dilemma – or opportunity; Australian, New Zealand and Canadian actors are in a similar situation).

ACTIVITY

Read the following comments made by Ewan McGregor about his career aims and ambitions:

- "I won't buy into the Hollywood thing . . . I want to be in good movies."
- "I would shoot myself through the head before I was in *Independence Day*."
- "If being successful means going to Hollywood, then I will go to Hollywood."

(To read the full articles that these quotes are taken from go to: John Patterson 'Naked Talent' at: http://film.guardian.co.uk/features/featurepages/0,,1050441,00.html and Siobhan Synnot 'The Force is With Him' at http://news.scotsman.com/topics.cfm?tid=515&id=76261 2003)

Ewan McGregor has also entered the debate about the role and function of national cinema, criticizing the workings of the Film Council, the body which distributes Lottery Money to the British film industry:

"UK film makers stuck in a rut", says McGregor

(Gordon Currie, *Sun*, 18 May 2003)

EWAN McGregor has launched a stinging attack on the British film industry for constantly trying to find the next *Four Weddings and a Funeral*. The Scots star said the industry was obsessed with trying to repeat the success of the Hugh Grant film. He said film makers lacked imagination and were in a rut, making one romantic comedy after another.

continued

The *Star Wars* actor launched his tirade while plugging his latest movie, *Young Adam*, during the Cannes Film Festival.

"*Young Adam* is very dark and very edgy. I think it is the kind of film we should be looking to make in Britain," he said.

"It seems that we have become obsessed with romantic comedies, which is all we seem to want to make these days.

"I think it is important that we try to continue to make small and interesting films like *Young Adam*."

■ What connotations and assumptions are evident about British cinema and Hollywood cinema in these quotes?
■ Why isn't the 'Hollywood thing' associated with 'good movies'?
■ What different types of success are available for film stars in Hollywood?
■ What does McGregor find frustrating about British cinema? What types of films would he like to see Britain make?
■ How do these views link to the types of films Ewan McGregor has appeared in?

Ewan McGregor filmography

■ *Number 13* (2008)
■ *Incendiary* (2008)
■ *Jackboots on Whitehall* (2008)
■ *The Tourist* (2007)
■ *Cassandra's Dream* (2007)
■ *Miss Potter* (2007)
■ *Stormbreaker* (2006)
■ *Scenes Of a Sexual Nature* (2006)
■ *Stay* (2005)
■ *The Long Way Round* (TV, as himself) (2005)
■ *The Island* (2005)
■ *Star Wars Episode 3: Revenge of the Sith* (2005)
■ *Valiant* (2005)
■ *Robots* (2005)
■ *Big Fish* (2003)
■ *Young Adam* (2003)
■ *Faster* (2003)
■ *Down With Love* (2003)
■ *Solid Geometry* (TV) (2002)
■ *Star Wars Episode 2: Attack of the Clones* (2002)

- *Black Hawk Down* (2002)
- *Moulin Rouge* (2001)
- *Nora* (2000)
- *Eye Of The Beholder* (1999)
- *Star Wars Episode 1: The Phantom Menace* (1999)
- *Little Voice* (1998)
- *Rogue Trader* (1998)
- *Velvet Goldmine* (1998)
- *A Life Less Ordinary* (1997)
- *The Serpent's Kiss* (1997)
- *Brassed Off* (1996)
- *ER* (TV, one episode) (1996)
- *Emma* (1996)
- *Nightwatch* (1996)
- *Karaoke* (TV mini-series) (1996)
- *Kavanagh QC* (TV, one episode) (1995)
- *The Pillow Book* (1995)
- *Trainspotting* (1995)
- *Blue Juice* (1995)
- *Doggin' Around* (TV) (1994)
- *Shallow Grave* (1994)
- *Scarlet and Black* (TV mini-series) (1993)
- *Being Human* (1993)
- *Lipstick On Your Collar* (TV) (1993)

(**Please note**: you can only use McGregor's British films for the exam; however, the other film and TV work is relevant to our understanding of him as a star.)

ACTIVITY

This activity provides the foundation for your star study and will take several hours to complete, plus time to watch your chosen films.

1   Add any recent films to update the filmography.
2   Begin to categorize the work by grouping titles in terms of:

- Film
- TV
- Nationality: British or Scottish? Hollywood films?

(You don't need to have seen all the films to do this – www.imdb.com will provide details of the nationality of the films.)

continued

INFORMATION BOX – WHAT IS A BRITISH FILM?

Some of the films in the list – *Emma, A Life Less Ordinary* – are difficult to categorize as either British or Hollywood films. You will need to justify your decision through evidence of subject matter, cast, crew, producers and distributors.

3   Which national category has the most films? Has this changed over time? Does this tell us anything about McGregor's career?

4   Now develop two further categories. In how many films does McGregor play a lead role? How often is he a supporting actor?

5   Choose four British films (you will need to watch these) from different periods of his career and make notes on the following:

- approximate budget (high? low?)
- subject
- genre
- plot
- setting; geographical and historical.

6a   Construct a detailed outline of each of the characters McGregor plays (it doesn't matter if some are supporting roles).

To do this you will need to consider the character in terms of nationality, class background, work, relationships (family, friends), appearance and function in the plot.

6b   Can you see any types emerging in the roles McGregor plays? Do you have expectations about how a character played by Ewan McGregor will behave?

Remember: Although the roles may seem very different in terms of class, period, work, type of film and so on, there are still underlying similarities. This may be to do with personality traits and the way in which the audience responds to the character. For example, his roles include idealistic romantics who seem innocent and naive (*Miss Potter, The Rise and Fall of Little Voice, Brassed Off*), causing the audience to feel protective of him.

7   Choose two films from the four which will be your focus films – it's best to choose two in which McGregor plays a major role.

Case study

NORA (PAT MURPHY, 2000)

Figure 14.1 *Nora* (2000)

A British, Italian and German co-production.

A medium budget (in the context of European cinema) film.

One of the production companies on *Nora* is Natural Nylon Entertainment, a British film production company set up by Ewan McGregor, Jude Law, Sadie Frost and Sean Pertwee, which closed in 2003. Ewan McGregor is credited as a co-producer on the film.

Nora is an adaptation of the biography of Nora Barnacle, and the film focuses on her passionate, often difficult relationship with James Joyce, the Irish writer. The film is set in Dublin and Italy during the early part of the twentieth century and could be defined as a costume drama and literary adaptation – a traditional form in British cinema. The film – while only a minor critical and commercial success – did cause some controversy because of

continued

the sexual content. The sexual subject matter of (some of) Ewan McGregor's films and his on-screen nudity has become a noted aspect of his career (*The Pillow Book*, *Velvet Goldmine*, *Young Adam*).

McGregor plays Joyce as a young man before he finds his style – and success – as a writer, and is one of the two lead actors in the film. At the start of the film he is an arrogant but struggling writer who is part of a conventional, religious, upper-class world. His relationship with Nora is a catalyst for his writing career and also causes him to question the Dublin society in which he has grown up. McGregor plays Joyce as an unstable, insecure artist who switches from doubting his abilities to extreme arrogance about his work and himself. The drama of the film revolves around the volatile relationship between Joyce and Nora. Despite being cruel to Nora – often provoked by unfounded jealousy – Joyce is still a sympathetic character due to McGregor's performance which suggests a complex, creative soul rather than a bully.

British film stars and acting traditions

In film – and theatre – acting there are different, often competing styles which actors study and adhere to. In British cinema these may be loosely divided into the tradition of Shakespearean theatre acting and the realist style which emerged in the 'kitchen sink' dramas of the 1950s and 1960s.

THE METHOD: in cinema the most influential style of acting has been the Method. This acting technique demands that the actor identifies very strongly with the motivation and personality of the character in order to create a realist performance. This approach was based on the work of Stanislavski (a Russian actor and theatre director) and was particularly associated with Hollywood stars in the 1950s such as Marlon Brando and James Dean, and in the 1970s with Robert de Niro and Al Pacino.

In British cinema the Method influenced a new style of theatre and film acting associated with social realism. This approach broke with the Shakespearean acting style which had dominated in Britain for so long. The new style was particularly evident in the emphasis on working-class, regional roles and a physical masculinity which had rarely been represented before on screen.

It is difficult to place Ewan McGregor into ether of these categories – although he did train at the Guildhall drama school. One of the defining characteristics of his performances seems to be an instinctive rather an intellectual process; his heroes are stars from the golden age of Hollywood – James Stewart, Henry Fonda, Cary Grant – before the Method was developed. McGregor is quoted as saying, 'The Method, I've never been entirely sure what that means actually.'

Danny Boyle (director of *Shallow Grave* and *Trainspotting*), picks up on this idea, commenting:

> One good thing is that he doesn't waste time intellectualizing the work. He deals with everything very immediately.

(quoted in Brooks 1998: 132)

In his study of Ewan McGregor's career and persona, Xan Brooks argues that this approach:

> Makes McGregor . . . the last of the Great British amateurs; the naive, native genius, with an easy and unhurried air, in a world of stern professionals.

ACTIVITY

Acting and masculinity

Reading through the above quotes there is clearly an opposition set up between acting as an intellectual, cerebral pursuit (represented by the Method) and acting as a physical, instinctive force. The latter is presented here as superior to the former.

It is quite common for male film actors to deny that any intellectual or analytical process affects their performances (e.g. as a drama student McGregor probably did study the Method).

- ■ Why do you think this is?
- ■ You could consider the connotations of acting as a profession as well as society's expectations about gender.

continued

Gender expectations are apparent in the following report in *The Scotsman* (8/09/03):

McGregor: 'My brother does a man's job'

By Craig Brown

ACTOR Ewan McGregor has claimed it is his brother in the armed forces who does "a proper job for a man".

"Colin is a fighter pilot in the RAF and I'm an actor," he says in an interview. "You can't think of two more diverse professions. He took me up in his Tornado once and I've never experienced anything like it. He was doing such a manly thing, a proper job for a man. . . Whereas I wear make-up for a living."

The star image

Phillips (1999) defines the different elements that make up a star as:

- **The real person**: Part of the appeal of stars is that while they are extraordinary they are also ordinary people who are like us. This is one way in which we can distinguish between stars and actors – we have no sense of (or interest in) non-stars as ordinary people existing outside of their film roles.
- **The performer of roles**: The audience becomes most familiar with the star through the roles they play in which they develop certain characteristics. Through this the star can become associated with particular types of roles.
- **The persona**: This is a combination of our ideas about the stars' 'real' life (or what we think we know about it) and the roles they play. It is developed by publicists, fans and through celebrity gossip. It is particularly evident when stars are typecast – when there seems to be a close relationship between the star and the roles they play.
- **An image**: Stars have particular meanings; they represent certain ideas in society often about gender, sexuality and race. A performer can become a star because he or she seems to represent the values of a society at a particular time. In a few cases a star is so famous that he or she becames 'iconized', immediately recognizable through only part of his or her image. (It is quite easy to think of classic stars that are iconized – Marilyn Monroe, Clint Eastwood, Humphrey Bogart – but can you think of more recent stars that would fit into this category?)

Therefore the roles a star plays are only one element which creates their image – what we know of them outside of the films is just as important.

The star moment

Most actors who become stars have what has become known as their 'star moment'. The star moment happens when a film – and their role in it – seems to capture a particular moment in the wider society. Ewan McGregor had a star moment with the release of *Trainspotting* (1995).

Figure 14.2 *Trainspotting* (1995)

Trainspotting is a seminal film partly because it reflected the fears of some sections of society while providing a unique, youthful – and Scottish – voice in British film.

The following are some of the ways in which *Trainspotting* captured contemporary issues:

- Drug-taking was represented as addictive and dangerous – but also enjoyable.
- The marketing of the film drew on 'heroin chic', a fashion movement which was accused of glamorizing the effects of drug addiction.
- The characters – heroes – of *Trainspotting* are an underclass who reject the traditional conventions of working-class life and aspirations.
- *Trainspotting* reveals aspects of city life after years of Thatcherism which had been hidden – a wild, lawless place.

- Tensions evident between social classes in Thatcher's Britain were represented in *Trainspotting* as a conflict between nations, part of the growing campaign for Scottish independence.
- Ewan McGregor, as one of the main – and the most appealing – characters, became the face of *Trainspotting*. This meant that his persona was a product of many of the values of the film – particularly being seen as a Scottish rather than a British star.

ACTIVITY

The 'Real' person and persona

To complete this activity you need to build up a resource of articles, interviews and websites on Ewan McGregor. Archive interviews in *Empire* and *Total Film* are available online as well as on fan websites. He has recently promoted his second bike tour for charity (UNICEF), which has a book tie-in. Unlike other British stars in Hollywood – Hugh Grant, Jude Law – there actually seems to be very little gossip about Ewan McGregor.

1 What do you know about Ewan McGregor's life? How did you acquire this information? How reliable are your sources?
2 Which aspects would you classify as gossip and which are part of his official biography?
3 Can you see any links between his real life and the roles he plays?

ACTIVITY

Star image and narrative meanings

Using your research so far write an analysis of the Ewan McGregor image. You should make notes for the analysis under the following headings:

1 The different elements that make up a star – the real person, performer of roles, persona and image (give examples from specific films to illustrate your points).
2 The 'star moment' of your particular star.
3 With reference to your chosen films analyse:

BRITISH AND AMERICAN FILM (FM2)

- How does Ewan McGregor's image create particular narrative expectations for the audience?
- Does his image challenge stereotypes (consider masculinity and national identity)?

References and Further Reading

Brooks, Xan (1998) *Choose Life: Ewan McGregor and the British Film Revival*, Chameleon, London

Phillips, Patrick (1999) 'Genre, Star and Auteur' in Nelmes, Jill (ed.), *An Introduction to Film Studies*, Routledge, London

15 WORKING TITLE FILMS

In this chapter we will look at:

- the history and development of Working Title Films
- the political and economic context to their development
- common themes and structures in Working Title Films' catalogue
- the co-production format

If you wish to study Ealing Studios as part of British Production then there is an additional full chapter that can be found in the Resources section of our companion website at http://routledge.tandf.co.uk/textbooks/9780415454339/resources.asp

INFORMATION BOX *i*

This chapter will be directly relevant to your work on FM2: British and American Film – Section B: British Film Topics for the WJEC's AS level in Film Studies.

A history of Working Title Films

In 1982, when the British actor and screenwriter Collin Welland collected his Academy Award for the screenplay of *Chariots of Fire* (UK 1981, Enigma/Twentieth Century Fox, Director: Hugh Hudson) he famously announced, 'The British are coming!' The British film industry was in a slump, with homegrown production down to two films a year, and Welland's triumphant announcement quickly proved to be markedly premature.

In November of the same year Channel Four was launched, and along with it came Head of Drama (later retitled Film on Four) David Rose's policy of commissioning (relatively) low-budget films from British independent production companies. It was this policy that created a path for the development of British film, and the creation of a raft of independent production companies, most of which have subsequently disappeared, but one in particular, Working Title Films, has become central to contemporary British cinema.

Working Title Films began life as Big Science Ltd, and co-produced the interesting (if schmaltzy) short film *The Man Who Shot Christmas* (UK, 1984, Big Science Ltd/NFFC/Working Title Films, Director: Diana Patrick). This film brought together co-founders Tim Bevan and Sarah Radclyffe who were working on diverse production projects including a music video with Stephen Frears which led to their first film for Channel Four and the first of many landmark Working Title Films – *My Beautiful Laundrette* (UK 1985, Working Title Films/Channel Four Films/SAF Productions, Director: Stephen Frears).

The critical success of their first feature film gave Bevan and Radclyffe some leverage within the British film industry, though theirs was very much a hand-to-mouth existence with the success of the company riding on the success of each film they produced. They could literally not afford a flop, borrowing, living on credit, and even re-mortgaging property to meet the production costs. It was two years before Working Title released another movie, but, with what was to become the Working Title trademark of breaking the mould, in 1987 they released two films – *Wish You Were Here* (UK 1987, Working Title Films/Channel Four Films/Zenith Entertainment Ltd, Director: David Leland) and *Sammy and Rosie Get Laid* (UK 1987, Working Title Films/Channel Four Films, Director: Stephen Frears).

Case study
MY BEAUTIFUL LAUNDRETTE (1985)

A groundbreaking script by Hanif Kureishi fitted into Channel Four's remit of offering challenging work that would not find a home elsewhere on

continued

terrestrial television. Principally conceived as a television film, it was given a theatrical release as part of Channel Four's commitment to film as film.

The story revolves around the interplay between a right-wing extremist, Johnny (Daniel Day Lewis) and Omar (Gordon Wernecke), the Pakistani son of a journalist and nephew of an archetypal Pakistani UK-based entrepreneur Nasser (Saeed Jaffrey), who are brought together in revamping a run-down laundrette.

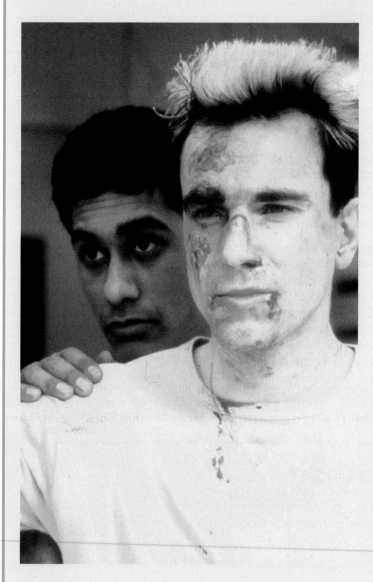

Figure 15.1
*My Beautiful
Laundrette*
(1985)

The film presented audiences with two themes that were present all around them yet largely absent from their screens – homosexuality (particularly among the working class as opposed to the young upper class seen in countless television programmes such as *Brideshead Revisited*), and race. The latter was a defining topic of the 1980s and yet was rarely faced, and challenged received opinions.

Coming after Margaret Thatcher won a second term as British Prime Minister, the film portrays a desolate urban landscape, where decay affects everything from the fabric of the buildings, through attitudes to work, to the physicality of those represented. Reflecting the Thatcherite values of the time, the film is filled with characters that are culturally and morally adrift, from racist thugs through to the immigrant family ruled by the love of money.

Frears offers a critique of the Thatcherite work ethic and the entrepreneur society, showing a white underclass declining under the determination of new immigrant businesses. Yet, even when Johnny decides to 'do some work for a change', the myth of the classless society is revealed in all its ugly clarity.

With interracial homosexuality to the fore it is not surprising that this film caused a considerable stir in a society that was suffering the consequences of political and economic revolution that had as its creed 'there is no such thing as society'.[1]

The success of their first three films (which all dealt with parochial British subjects) alerted the wider film industry to this independent production company, leading first to a Zimbabwean co-production in *A World Apart* (UK/Zim 1988, Working Title/Channel Four/British Screen/AEG/World Apart/Hippo Films, Director: Chris Menges), and significantly their first Anglo-American production *For Queen and Country* (UK/US 1988, Working Title Films/Zenith Entertainment Ltd, Director: Martin Stellman). The success of this film on both sides of the Atlantic gave Working Title a template for co-production that they immediately began to exploit, and one that has been the aspiration for most other British independent production companies.

The success of a raft of subsequent co-productions over the next four years brought both a rising international profile, but also rising expectations that were often difficult to meet through the limitations imposed by being a small British independent production company (albeit one that was consistently punching above its weight). With most of their time spent ensuring capital was in place to complete a film, and less and less spent on crafting productions, Tim Bevan began looking for the corporate backing of a major studio partner. In 1992 Working Title Films joined forces with PolyGram, and saw the departure of Sarah Radclyffe and the arrival of Eric Fellner as co-chairman.

TIM BEVAN (1958–)

Tim Bevan (1958–), the son of English émigrés, returned from New Zealand after working for the National Film Unit, and set up a pop promo production company, Aldabra. Working with director Stephen Frears on a promo in 1984 led to him founding his own feature production company, Working Title Films, along with his then partner Sarah Radclyffe. In 2000 he co-founded a subsidiary – Working Title 2 (WT2). After leading his companies to international success upon international success, and establishing it as Britain's premier production company, he was awarded a CBE (Commander of the British Empire) in 2005 for his services to film. Tim is a governor of the National Film and Television School.

SARAH RADCLYFFE (1950–)

Sarah Radclyffe's (1950–) career has focused on the independent sector since her early engagements as associate producer on film productions such as *The Tempest* (UK, 1979, Boyd's Company, Director: Derek Jarman), and working in television on series such as *The Comic Strip Presents*. . . . In 1984 she founded Working Title Films along with her then partner Tim Bevan and was active in producing films with the company through to 1992. When PolyGram offered support to Working Title Films (making it an independent supported significantly by a studio) Sarah decided to part company in order to continue focusing on the independent sector, going on to produce memorable films such as *The War Zone* (UK 1999, Channel Four Films/Fandango/Mikado Films/Portobello Pictures, Director: Tim Roth); *Ratcatcher* (UK 1999, BBC Films/Canal+/Holy Cow Films/Pathé Pictures International/Les Productions Lazennec/Arts Council of England, Director: Lynne Ramsay), and *Tara Road* (Ire 2005, Sarah Radclyffe/Noel Pearson/Pageturner Productions/Ferndale Films/Surefire Film Productions, Director: Gillies MacKinnon).

Eric Fellner (1959–) began his producing career with the punk biopic *Sid and Nancy* (UK, 1986, Initial Pictures/UK Productions Entity/Zenith Entertainment, Director: Alex Cox) and the punk western *Straight to Hell* (UK 1987, Commies from Mars Productions/Initial Pictures, Director: Alex Cox). In 1992, at the prompting of PolyGram's Michael Kuhn, he joined Working Title Films as co-chairman, taking an executive producer role and an active role as producer on films such as *Captain Corelli's Mandolin* (UK/France/USA 2001, Working Title Films/Canal+/Miramax Films/Studio Canal/Free Range Films/Universal, Director: John Madden) and *Elizabeth: The Golden Age* (UK/France 2007, Working Title Films/Studio Canal, Director: Shekhar Kapur). In 2000 he co-founded a subsidiary – Working Title 2 (WT2) – with Tim Bevan. He is a member of the Board of the British Film Institute and in 2005 was awarded a CBE (Commander of the British Empire) for his services to film.

The financial stability offered by the support from a major studio allowed Working Title Films to move rapidly on to the international stage, and PolyGram being taken over by Seagram and subsumed into its film arm, Universal Pictures, in 1999, further strengthened this. A marked change of direction took place at this point, with the traditionally parochial independent territory being scorned in favour of international prospects. Working Title Films began making films based in the UK but using international stars to aid international acceptance and sales through films such as *Four Weddings and a Funeral* (UK 1994, Working Title Films/Channel Four Films/PolyGram Filmed Entertainment, Director: Mike Newell), films located outside the UK and using international stars such as *French Kiss* (UK/US 1995, Working Title Films/PolyGram Filmed Entertainment/Prufrock Pictures/Twentieth Century Fox, Director: Lawrence Kasdan), and films firmly located in the USA such as *Romeo is Bleeding* (UK/US 1993, Working Title Films/PolyGram Filmed Entertainment, Director: Peter Medak).

The international activity did not prevent Working Title Films from continuing to support British filmmakers and from engaging in what would have been considered traditional 'independent' fare. Films such as *Land and Freedom* (UK/Spain/Germany/Italy 1995, BIM/BBC Films/British Screen/Canal+/Degeto *et al.*, Director: Ken Loach) were developed with the support of Working Title Films, and they continue to promote 'offbeat' work through such films as *Shaun of the Dead* (UK/France 2004, Working Title Films/Studio Canal/WT2 Productions, Director: Edgar Wright).

Figure 15.2 *Land and Freedom* (1995)

ACTIVITY

In small groups research other production companies that were founded or operating at the same time as Working Title Films (such as Palace Pictures, Goldcrest, Handmade Films).

What kind of success did they have?

Where are they now by comparison?

Currently, with a strong slate of high-budget international movies in production or post-production, and planned titles being publicized up to three years ahead, Working Title Films and its subsidiary WT2 is now undoubtedly the most significant player on the UK film industry scene.

Political and economic influences on the development of Working Title Films

Working Title Films was born into the upturn from the worst film recession the UK had ever suffered, where indigenous film production had all but stopped, and the financially significant Hollywood productions were looking to other countries to support production (largely cheaper ones).

Significantly, beyond the film industry, the whole world was in recession, spawning a political shift to the right as Thatcherism and Reaganism took centre stage. Key to both of these political philosophies was the central tenet of entrepreneurship, and it is interesting to note that while Working Title Films is clearly a model of entrepreneurship, it never adopted the ruthless tactics of the financial or retail sectors, instead adapting the traditional 'seat-of-the-pants' approach of the independent filmmaker, and applying its strengths to form a new model (strengths such as willing to find new ways of working, unconventional funding, involving creatives throughout the whole development stage).

The Conservative government had little regard for British film, and one of their early pieces of legislation was to get rid of the Eady Levy (a tax on cinema admissions that supported production of UK-produced films). This had an immediate effect on the industry, sending a fragile film economy into free-fall. This government was also responsible for sanctioning the development of Channel Four, though it seems unlikely they would have foreseen the internal policies that led to David Rose creating Film Four from the Drama Department.

Channel Four, in its early days, was something of a shoestring operation, and it was entrepreneurial in its visionary ways of enabling independent production companies to make films for them. The films were considered low budget (£750,000 or less), though by Hollywood standards of the day they would have been considered no-budget (a Hollywood low-budget film would have worked on a dollar equivalent of £3–6 million). However, in its first two years of operation, Channel Four established a model for international co-production and for pre-sales (selling the film in advance to distributors and television networks in order to finance the production), and this helped lay the groundwork for the way Working Title Films would operate.

The successes of Working Title Films throughout the 1980s meant that as the world economy began to rise out of recession in the 1990s the company was not only in a sound economic position but was also extremely attractive to investors, particularly with its close link to Channel Four and its international associates, and its unique deal securing the support of a major studio (and crucially its distribution network).

With the Labour Party assuming government in 1997, Working Title Films benefited from a catalogue that fitted with the image of 'Cool Britannia' that was heralded in soon after the Prime Minister, Tony Blair, began inviting the industry's glitterati for informal discussions (and photo-opportunities) at Downing Street. The Britain of *Four Weddings and a Funeral* was bankable in the new climate, and with the Chancellor, Gordon Brown, promoting policies of tax incentives for the film industry (particularly for films drawing in international funding), Working Title Films' fortunes mirrored those of the economy, going from strength to strength, strength that has continued into the twenty-first century.

> **If you make one movie at a time the problem is it's boom-bust, stop-go. In the year [2004], you do *Bridget Jones: The Edge of Reason* (2004) you kind of know that film is going to do all right, so you can take a bigger risk at the other end, which was *Shaun of the Dead* (2004). Which turned out all right, thank God, because we also did *Thunderbirds* (2004) which we thought was going to do all right, but didn't work out, and the other two supported it.**

Tim Bevan

> **When we were independents we were very wary about the studios. But what we realized through our experience with PolyGram is that being part of a US studio structure is essential if you want to play the long game in the movie business. Six studios control movie distribution worldwide. The various supply engines, like talent agencies and marketing people, understand the studios and everyone who is playing seriously in the film business will be part of a studio structure.**

(Tim Bevan)[2]

> **We are trying to up the ante a little bit in terms of the scale and diversity of films we make. . . . You have to have films that are going to do $200–$400m in box office revenue, and finding them from here [Britain] is difficult.**

(Eric Fellner)

> **I guess technically not owning the company means we lost control, but the way the film business works is that it's people-driven rather than structure-**

Looking at the above quotes, explore the way Tim Bevan and Eric Fellner have developed Working Title Films and later WT2. Do you feel theirs is a model that could be developed for other production companies?

So what is a Working Title film?

This was once relatively easy to answer, as the films they first made all seemed to address issues of what it is to be British (or, more specifically, English), and particularly what it meant to be an outsider (be it an immigrant in *My Beautiful Laundrette*, or a sexual outsider in *Wish You Were Here* (UK 1987, Working Title Films/Channel Four Films/Zenith Entertainment Ltd, Director: David Leland).

Of course, the general public know them as the re-inventors of a British romantic comedy genre through films such as *Four Weddings and a Funeral*, *Notting Hill* (UK/USA 1999, Working Title Films/Bookshop Productions/Notting Hill Pictures/PolyGram Entertainment Ltd, Director: Roger Michell) and *Love Actually* (UK/USA 2003, Working Title Films/DNA Films/Universal Films, Director: Richard Curtis).

Case study
FOUR WEDDINGS AND A FUNERAL (1994)

Four Weddings and a Funeral was the first of Working Title Film's collaborations with screenwriter Richard Curtis (who had achieved fame with the *Blackadder* television series) and the actor Hugh Grant. Costing approximately $4 million to make, it grossed in excess of $257 million and set the bar for British film production, particularly in its use of soundtrack that spawned a record-breaking number one single for the band Wet Wet Wet.

continued

Figure 15.3 *Four Weddings and a Funeral* (1994)

A romantic comedy that explores the relationships between a disparate group of upper-class friends as they meet to celebrate four weddings, and mourn at the titular funeral, this film has reminiscences in style of the screwball comedies. Richard Curtis was able to bring established contacts to an ensemble cast (such as Rowan Atkinson), enhancing the potential connection with audiences (at least the home audience).

The film was a massive hit in the USA, in part because of the view of Britain it offered that fell in line with the concept of 'heritage Britain' – a land of churches, old pubs and stately homes populated by 'classy' English men and women, with obligatory bumbling fools liberally sprinkled across the social landscape. It helped that not only was one of the stars American (Andie MacDowell), but that there were some minor American characters in the film that carried the flag well.

Such an unexpected success gave Working Title Films considerable international clout and reach, and placed it at the centre of the Hollywood film industry. It also placed considerable pressure on the company to become the romantic-comedy-heritage-film company, a pressure it resisted, but did not altogether reject, realizing that a film like this could help support a number of productions with less potential for such success yet still deserving of being made.

From 2007 Working Title will undoubtedly be reinterpreted as the maker of the British historical epic, as it releases its first sequel *Elizabeth: The Golden Age*. Of course it has been involved in making historically set films since *Wish You Were Here*, and produced its first truly historical costume drama, *Robin Hood* (UK/USA/Canada/Germany 1991, Working Title Films/Twentieth Century Fox/CanWest/WDR Director: John Irvin).

A quick glance at the list of films in its catalogue (see the Internet Movie Database: http://www.imdb.com/company/co0057311/#productionX20company) reveals a list of over 100 films produced since it made its first short in 1984, and probably the only common thread among them is the desire to do something different to what is being produced at the time, and to do it well. It is not by accident that Working Title Films sits at the heart of many spectator's lists of favourites (and often, simultaneously, most hated), and it is the ability to make films for specific audience groups, and to not be pigeon-holed that has enabled the company to ensure that its work remains fresh and successful.

There is, perhaps, an almost indefinable 'British style' about the pacing and structure of Working Title Films (despite or perhaps because of its international nature), and the narratives tend towards the misfit, though not exclusively so. It is easy to categorize them (dismissively) until you look through the catalogue and realize that this is a company categorized only by diversity and the ability to detect changes in the market that enable a reorientation of direction.

Figure 15.4 *Elizabeth: The Golden Age* (2007)

ACTIVITY

Select two or three Working Title Films productions (either in close proximity to each other, or from distinct points across their history) and create a grid of common features, characters, structures and/or characteristics.

Compare your findings with your peers and discuss the possible reasons for your results.

Co-production as a way forward

Co-production has long been a method of sharing risk within the film industry, and when Working Title Films began its life, co-production was merely another revenue stream that often involved pre-sale or pre-distribution deals on world or national rights. Since one of Working Title Films' principal commissioners and partners was Channel Four, and Channel Four pioneered international co-production in the UK, it is no surprise that Working Title Films adopted and extended the model.

The pre-sale of rights (to exhibit theatrically or transmit on television) is a method that enables sellers to bring in much needed income to support production, and for buyers to achieve a potential success at a cut-down price – significantly less than they would pay once the film was completed and was in the marketplace. Initially, Working Title Films explored these deals domestically, but as its success grew it found that the international market opened up to it. There are (of course) risks on both sides, and the biggest risk for a production company is the worry that its film will be a runaway success and the profits will head to whoever it sold the rights to (a bad deal here can see others becoming rich while the production company barely breaks even). Broadcasters usually have the safest option here since they have schedules that need to be filled and they can shunt a film that does not turn out to be as good as expected to a graveyard slot and still make money on it.

In the early days of the Labour administration in the 1990s, international co-production was actively encouraged through tax breaks. The government entered co-production treaties with over 30 countries (including the USA and many EU countries) that allowed many co-produced films to be deemed 'British' and therefore qualify for tax relief (at a level that could see a substantial lessening of the tax burden). Earlier (in 1994) the European Convention on Cinematographic Co-production was introduced, promoting co-productions within the EU, and allowing the USA (or other non-EU countries) up to a 30 per cent stake in a film before it stops being viewed as an EU 'home'-produced film. This was a significant change in approach, as it facilitated Working Title Films' development with Hollywood.

Working Title Films took co-production further by formalizing a relationship with PolyGram (later Universal) in which investment was staged and mirrored against other partners to ensure that the 30 per cent rule did not prevent them from obtaining EU/UK tax advantages. A 30 per cent stake in the budget of a film and the weight of Hollywood support is clearly great seed money and stimulates other companies'/investors' willingness to become involved in a project. It is this advance in the model that radically enhanced both the production processes and the production values in Working Title Films.

Interestingly there is also a 'Cultural Test' that enables producers to determine (for tax purposes) whether their film can be counted as British. This considers not only the sources of investment, but also the cultural expression on screen (how much screen time is given over to Britishness or British characters), and the involvement of British creative talent in the stages of production. A copy of this document may be sourced through the Film Council.

Notes

1 Margaret Thatcher, quoted in an interview for *Woman's Own* magazine 23/9/87 – reprinted on the Margaret Thatcher Foundation website: http://www.margaretthatcher.org/speeches/displaydocument.asp?docid=106689.
2 Tim Bevan, quoted on the Internet Movie Database http://www.imdb.com/name/nm0079677/bio.
3 Eric Fellner, quoted on the Internet Movie Database http://www.imdb.com/name/nm0271479/bio.

References and Further Reading

Chapman, J. (2005) *Past and Present: National Identity and the British Historical Film*, I. B. Tauris, London

Finney, A. (1996) *Developing Feature Films in Europe: A Practical Guide*, Routledge, London

Mather, N. (2006) *Tears of Laughter: Comedy-drama in 1990s British Cinema*, University of Manchester Press, Manchester

Street, S. (2002) *Transatlantic Crossings: British Feature Films in the USA*, Continuum, London

Working Title Films' Staff (2003) *Laundrettes and Lovers: From Storyboard to Billboard: Twenty Years of a British Film Company*, Boxtree, London

Useful Websites

The Film Council: Cultural Test http://www.ukfilmcouncil.org.uk/filmmaking/filmingUK/taxreliefbritfilms/culturaltestfol/

The Film Council: Guide to co-productions http://www.ukfilmcouncil.org.uk/filmmaking/filmingUK/taxreliefbritfilms/co-productionfo/

16 THATCHER'S BRITAIN 1981–1989

> **There are many things to be done to set this nation on the road to recovery, and I do not mean economic recovery alone, but a new independence of spirit and a zest for achievement.**

(Margaret Thatcher, Conservative Party Conference, Brighton, 1980)

This chapter deals with:

- the social, political and intellectual climate of the 1980s in Britain
- possible approaches to British films made during the 1980s

If you wish to study Swinging Britain 1963–1973 rather than Thatcher's Britain 1981–1989 then there is an additional full chapter that can be found in the Resources section of our companion website at http://routledge.tandf.co.uk/textbooks/9780415454339/resources.asp

INFORMATION BOX

This chapter will be directly relevant to your work on FM2: British and American Film – Section B: British Film Topics for the WJEC's AS level in Film Studies.

Films mentioned

As you work your way through this chapter you need to watch at least some of the following films in full and at least short sequences from some of the others:

- *Mona Lisa* (Jordan, 1986)
- *High Hopes* (Leigh, 1988)
- *Letter to Brezhnev* (Bernard, 1985)
- *My Beautiful Laundrette* (Frears, 1985)
- *Chariots of Fire* (Hudson, 1982)
- *A Room With a View* (Ivory, 1985)
- *For Queen and Country* (Stellman, 1988)
- *Resurrected* (Greengrass, 1989)

ACTIVITY

- Ask yourself the questions: Who was Thatcher? What is meant by the term 'Thatcherism'? Compile rough notes of your own ideas as quickly as possible. Perhaps you've heard other people talking about Thatcher: what did their attitude towards her seem to be? Maybe you've heard people using the term 'Thatcherism'. How were they using it and what did they seem to mean by it?
- Sum up in no more than 60 words the way in which you think 'Thatcherism' would be defined.
- If possible, read the definitions that several other people have come up with, and identify any similarities and differences.
- If you are working with a whole class, try to agree on a single collective definition, again limiting it to no more than 60 words.

Thatcher

Margaret Thatcher became leader of the Conservative Party in 1975 and Prime Minister in 1979.[1] Under Tony Blair in 1994 the Labour Party rebranded itself New Labour and has dominated British politics from 1997 until the present. Under Thatcher the Conservative Party didn't rename itself but it did make significant changes to its political outlook, becoming dominated by what was known as the 'New Right'. The common factor between the changes achieved by both Thatcher and Blair within their respective parties might be symbolized by this use of the term 'new'; both Labour under Blair and the Conservatives under Thatcher were keen to re-invent themselves, to cast off their former political clothes and reposition their party in relation to an emerging new capitalist world order based on the global marketplace.

Figure 16.1 Margaret Thatcher

The tacit acknowledgement by both parties was that the world was changing. The old post-war consensus regarding the sacrosanct importance of maintaining full employment and retaining a social 'safety-net' of dependable welfare support for the poorest members of society no longer held. Capitalism was changing, reconstituting itself: it was no longer to be so strongly based around individual nation-states but was taking on a global profile. New communications technology created 'time–space compression' that meant it was increasingly possible to operate businesses as worldwide concerns. In 1988 the journal *Marxism Today* was at the centre of a debate about the nature of the period being lived through.

The discussion was entitled 'New Times' and centred on the idea that there was something distinctively new and different about the 1980s.

For Western economies the old 'Fordist' stage of development was over and we were into post-Fordism, it was suggested. Fordism, named after the early US car manufacturer Henry Ford, was based on the mass production of standardized goods by large, nationally based companies. In this period, stretching roughly between 1920 and 1970, companies employed a predominantly male workforce, used assembly-line production techniques, and favoured hierarchical management structures. The cultural studies theorist Stuart Hall[2] suggested that post-Fordism had very different key characteristics:

- economies were now based on information technology rather than on heavy industry;
- individual companies were now no longer usually overseeing all aspects of production;
- market sectors were becoming increasingly segmented with 'differentiated' products aimed at niche-group consumers;
- the industrial working class was contracting while the number of service sector workers was increasing;
- the workforce now contained more women and there were more part-time jobs;
- major companies were 'multinational' in structure and organization;
- the financial system was increasingly 'globalized';
- the gap between the two-thirds of the population doing well and the one-third not doing so well had increased.

ACTIVITY

- As you study films from the period, ask yourself about the nature of the economy being displayed in each. First of all, is there any focus on economic matters, and second, if there is some element of economic interest, and what are the key features of the economy displayed?
- How is work viewed by characters within the film? Is it seen as an onerous necessity or a source of pleasure, a space within which abilities can be demonstrated or a space within which capabilities are stifled?
- Are there any clear indications of entrepreneurs taking part in Thatcher's 'enterprise culture' that was always emphasizing its support of dynamic, individualistic business people?

'Thatcherism'

Thatcher was very successful in shifting public opinion in Britain towards the right. By echoing popular prejudices in their political statements of intent the Conservatives were able to gain support for their policies. Thatcher it seemed was in tune with key aspects of the popular mind-set held by some sections of the public: the desire to own your own home, the wish to buy lifestyle consumer products, and above all the willingness to blame visible, easily identifiable scapegoats when social and economic problems arose. The 'right to buy' was introduced to enable council tenants to buy their homes at knock-down prices. Credit possibilities were extended by the finance sector in order to enable people to buy more goods on a repayment basis. (The downside to such policies was, however, the loss of social housing stock and increased debt for many people.)

ACTIVITY

- Research the concept of the 'political spectrum'. What does it mean to say a politician or a political party is left-wing or right-wing or occupies the centre of the political spectrum? Where would each of the major political parties in Britain be positioned? Is it generally accepted that any of these parties have shifted their position on the spectrum in recent years, say, since Thatcher came to power?
- If possible, discuss your findings with others, and try to agree your thoughts on these matters, although naturally (as is always liable to be the case with political discussion) there could continue to be some disagreement as to the shifting positions of parties within this spectrum.

The emergence of the New Right in Britain is generally seen as a response to the economic turmoil that began to affect the country from the late 1960s. The winter before Thatcher came to power had been dubbed the 'winter of discontent' with upward of a million public service workers on strike for almost three months. The New Right identified 'enemies' within society that they argued had to be dealt with through strong political leadership if the social fabric of the country was to be maintained. According to this analysis, criminals were responsible for burgeoning levels of crime, scroungers were taking advantage of the welfare system, teachers were failing to exert discipline in schools, and trade unionists were constantly threatening the social order. Academic theorists such as Stuart Hall have suggested that the 'moral panics' resulting from these New Right analyses were crucial in enabling the Conservatives to gain support for their policies based around 'authoritarian populism'. It has also been suggested that the New Right exploited similar popular fears connected to ethnic minorities, implying, for example, that increased crime could be linked to the activities of the African-Caribbean population.

> **MORAL PANIC:** this is a term introduced by Stanley Cohen in *Folk Devils and Moral Panics* (1972) to describe the reaction of society as expressed in the media to some perceived threat to the social norm.

'Thatcherism' existed as something of a contradiction. On the one hand it called for a return to traditional values that had supposedly once formed the bedrock of British society, and on the other its supporters wished to take Britain's economy into a new age of emerging global capitalism; looking to an old (supposed) past while simultaneously looking to a new reconfiguring of the economic future. As an ideology, 'Thatcherism' was in social terms highly conservative, embodying what were seen as 'Victorian' values, believing in individual self-help, effort and aspiration allied to a collective national pride. This was closely linked to a particular version of British history that saw the days of empire as the pinnacle not only of British power but also of individual endeavour. And yet, in economic terms, 'Thatcherism' was liberal, believing in the free market, and allowing market forces to determine the survival of only the fittest commercial enterprises while permitting no nostalgia for formerly successful industries if they were considered to be no longer economically viable. There was within 'Thatcherism' a harking back to a mythical past of former glories alongside a determination to re-invent the British economy in a form that would enable it to prosper under new conditions.

Within the context of changes that were occurring to the global capitalist economy, it is possible that there was no alternative to the advent of 'New Times' for the British economy and resulting changes in British society. Whether it was Thatcher or some other politician at the helm it could be argued actually made little difference; and there is ample evidence to suggest that Thatcher was often pushed by the force of circumstances in a particular direction she had not anticipated. From this perspective, with or without Thatcher, the arrival of information technology, the end of Britain's old manufacturing base, the fragmentation of the workforce, consumer niche-market segmentation, and multinational companies constituted the inevitable landscape of the 'New Times'.

ACTIVITY

1   Working with others if possible, draw up a succinct timeline of political events in Britain during the 1970s and 1980s.

2 Try to find time to compare your timeline with those drawn up by other groups.
3 Question each other as to how you decided which events to include (and exclude). Try to convince others of your reasoning but also be open to the possibility of having your mind changed by contrary perspectives and choices put forward by other people. Some mention might be made of

- rising unemployment figures;
- opposition to the placing of Cruise missiles at Greenham Common and Molesworth;
- the tightening of immigration controls, essentially through the British Nationality Act (1981) and the Immigration Act (1988);
- inner-city riots such as those at St Paul's in Bristol, Toxteth in Liverpool, Handsworth in Birmingham and Brixton in London during the early 1980s;
- Clause 28 of the Local Government Act which prohibited local councils from 'promoting' homosexuality;
- the Falklands/Malvinas war of 1982;
- the Miners' Strike of 1984–1985.

INFORMATION BOX *i*

What may become clear from your research is that the Conservatives were never fully secure in their political dominance. For example, although jingoism on the back of the Falklands war may have helped Thatcher win the 1983 election, her party's share of the vote was still down on 1979. Many of the factors bullet-pointed above led to the mobilization of strongly vocal, well-organized opposition to Thatcherite policies.

Postmodernism

If the economic landscape was changing during the 1980s then so too was the intellectual landscape. Jean-François Lyotard suggested at the end of the 1970s that the key feature of what was termed postmodern culture was a rejection of 'metanarratives'.[3] What he meant by this was that people no longer had any faith that there were 'big answers' to the problems of society, above all and most essentially perhaps that Marxism no longer held an answer; although more all-encompassing was the realization, according to Lyotard, that science could not lead to some perfect knowledge and understanding of the universe out of which ultimate human liberation was possible.

> **METANARRATIVES:** essentially, these are overarching explanations of how things are in the world. The supporters of any metanarrative claim that their 'story' of the world is able to coherently sum up the whole essence of human society and endeavour providing total knowledge and understanding. Metanarratives are sometimes known as grand narratives.

According to other writers, such as Jean Baudrillard and Fredric Jameson, in the postmodern world we now have almost no awareness of history. The sense that historical change is always taking place, and that we are either moving forward on a path of progress or declining towards a state of impending social collapse, seems to have been lost, they say. Instead, they suggest, we live in a 'permanent present', believing the current state of society will continue forever. All that we are surrounded with is in such a state of permanent flux and transformation that we are disorientated and unable to gain any sense of history. Or, according to Baudrillard, we are bombarded with so much contradictory information by the media that it is impossible to form it all into a coherent historical (or political) narrative.

ACTIVITY

To further your thoughts on this you may like to think about the nature of time and space within *Casino Royale* (Campbell, 2006). Here we have a prequel returning us to the original Bond as he becomes 007 and yet the main story clearly takes place within a twenty-first-century world. As we watch, it seems we contain within our 'permanent present' all of the past Bonds we have seen and happily compress a series of past times into present time. Not only that but we do this without any sense of these other images of Bond being locked into a linear concept of past, present and future. Bond exists (and we exist) not within what used to be known as the 'real world' but within a vast network of media-generated images, a hyperreality.

Do you agree or disagree? What seems to you to be right about this argument? What seems to you to be wrong about it?

Figure 16.2 *Casino Royale* (2006)

Such is our sense of disorientation within this postmodern world that we no longer have any sense of a solid, unified self but are more likely to feel ourselves to be fragmented beings, unsure of any single identity for ourselves but much more aware of our existence on several levels and within multiple roles. We no longer live within a single identifiable, clearly delineated space but within a series of intensified dynamic spaces, a hyper-version of space in the old sense. We move within a vast network of images that are not reflections of reality but simulations of reality and that dominate both our public and private experience of the world; we exist within some sort of hyperreality.

ACTIVITY

■ As you study films from the period, ask yourself whether any of these features of postmodernism are displayed. In particular, how is the nature of the 'self' handled? Do characters seem to have a clear sense of an identifiable, solid self? Or do they show features of feeling themselves disorientated, dislocated, split or operating within multiple identities?

continued

Film Studies and the political

The interesting thing for us as students of film is to see how these social, intellectual and ultimately political tensions played out in film from the period. British society is reshaping itself, or is being reshaped by external forces, during this period, and the films of the time are likely to be in some way or other caught up in the changes that are taking place.

On a more practical note the film industry found itself under huge economic pressure in the 1980s. At base, Conservative policies were founded upon a belief in the free market, that if companies and ultimately whole industries were not economically viable they should not be subsidized or bailed out. By the mid-1980s the British film industry was under acute economic pressure, arguably largely because of this attitude. The quota system requiring a minimum percentage of British-made films to be shown in cinemas was first of all reduced and then ended altogether in 1983. The levy which ensured that a certain percentage of box-office takings went back into making British films was abolished in 1985. A financing system which allowed city institutions to offset film investments against tax and therefore encouraged them to put money into British film production was ended. Investment in film in Britain dropped from more than £250 million in 1986 to less than £50 million in 1989.

Those involved in the making of films in Britain, therefore, often found not only that their personal 'liberal', if not left-wing, political beliefs were under attack from Thatcherism but also that their industry was under threat from the same source. As a result it is likely we will find a certain number of films from the period setting out deliberately oppositional political positions to the government of the day. Throughout the media the war in the Falklands was generally presented as a huge patriotic and personal triumph for Thatcher, but in *For Queen and Country* (Stellman, 1988) a black soldier returns from tours of duty in the Falklands and Northern Ireland to the poverty of a south London council estate to find he can no longer claim British citizenship, and in *Resurrected* (Greengrass, 1989) a soldier who suffers amnesia during the advance on Port Stanley in the Falklands is on his return unable to live up to his media status as 'hero' and is brutalized by members of his own regiment.

Case study
MONA LISA (1986)

(Director: Neil Jordan. Screenwriter: Jordan and David Leland. Cinematographer: Roger Pratt. Music: Michael Kamen. Cast: Bob Hoskins (George); Cathy Tyson (Simone); Michael Caine (Mortwell); Robbie Coltrane (Thomas).)

Figure 16.3 *Mona Lisa* (1986)

What are the key elements to George's journey through the film? Would this comprise the plot to the film? Could George be said to be in search of something, or questing after something, and if so what? Is he the hero of the film? And, if so, in what sense(s) would you say he was a typical hero and in what sense(s) an atypical hero? Could George be described as 'an innocent abroad'? What does this term mean? Is George innocent, naive or a fool? What has traditionally been the role and purpose of 'the fool'? If this is George's story, what type of ending does Jordan give him and how could this be seen to be appropriate for the character?

continued

What mysteries attach to the character of Simone and at what points in the narrative do we gain answers to these mysteries? What role does Cathy play in Simone's story? And does this suggest Simone should more correctly be seen as the hero of the story? And, if we were to see Simone as the hero of the piece, what role would this give to George? Does he then become the teller of the story, in some sense a narrator but a narrator with a position and role within the narrative? Could we describe Simone as a femme fatale? Is she dark and deadly? In what way could her use of the gun at the end of her story (framed as it were within George's story) be said to be symbolically appropriate?

What genres would seem to be important for this film? Is it a crime film, or a gangster film? Are there elements of comedy? If so, why are these included; don't they detract from the coherence of the piece? Are there noir-like elements to the film? If so, where would you see these as being and for how long does Jordan maintain that focus? Are there Hollywood-style elements to the film, or would it be more appropriate to see it as a British art-house film? Could you imagine it as a fairy story? If it was to begin, 'Once upon a time there was . . .', how would it continue?

What sort of world is presented to us by the film? You may like to consider why Jordan has chosen to frame the world of Cathy, Anderson and Mortwell within the world of Thomas and George and his daughter. How are the scenes within the 'red-light district' shot? What incidents are attached to this world within the narrative? How do these incidents contrast with those that take place within the framing world of Thomas and George's daughter? How are male–female relationships shown within the dark, noir-like world of prostitution? How is 'the family' represented within this film, not just in terms of direct blood-tie relationships but also wider concepts of 'family-like' relationships? What about Thomas' relationship to George, for example? And don't forget the way in which gangsters traditionally (and Mortwell specifically) use the term 'family'. To what extent would you say this film operates as a vision of 1980s Britain?

How is race represented within the film? Essentially this comes down to your reading of Simone and Anderson. Are they in any way stereotypical black representations? Are either of them more complex than this? Anderson would seem to be a rather flat, one-dimensional character. What is his relationship to Mortwell within the narrative structure, and should this influence your interpretation of Jordan's use of Anderson within the story? Research the roles played by black actors in mainstream British films before 1986. What lead roles do you find before Cathy Tyson's in this film? What roles did Tyson go on to perform?

In what ways does Jordan display his interest in stories in this film, and in what ways does he suggest the construction of narratives might be important for human beings? Would you describe this film as realism or fantasy? Or do you think both are combined in some way within this film? If you see it as combining both, which parts of the narrative would you define as falling into each of these two categories? And, finally, why is the film called *Mona Lisa*? What does 'Mona Lisa' mean? What can you find out about the painting called *Mona Lisa* and the lyrics to the song 'Mona Lisa'?

Case study

HIGH HOPES (1988)

(Director: Mike Leigh. Screenwriter: Mike Leigh. Cinematographer: Roger Pratt. Music: Andrew Dickson. Cast: Philip Davis (Cyril); Ruth Sheen (Shirley); Edna Dore (Mrs Bender); Heather Tobias (Valerie); Philip Jackson (Martin).)

To what extent does this film seem to you to employ stereotypical characters? Which characters would you see as stereotypes and which seem to be fuller, more rounded characters? What is it about the portrayal of these characters that seems to mark them out as either stereotypes or something more than this? Who are we asked to identify with in the film, and what techniques are used to attempt to persuade us to do this?

What is Wayne's role within the narrative? What is Cyril and Shirley's attitude towards him? How are we supposed to see Wayne, and what evidence would you offer for this? Cyril and Shirley seem to laugh at him (for example, when he is on the coach and about to go home). How do you feel about this laughter? Is it holding Wayne up to our ridicule or would you describe it in some other way?

Comedy would seem to be an important element of this film. Which characters would you say we are expected to laugh at and which are we expected to laugh with? How does this sense of our position in relation to characters come about? What techniques are used to position us in this way? Leaving Mrs Bender in the car while he goes to see the character described in the cast list as 'Martin's girlfriend' could potentially operate as a comic moment but how do you feel during this scene? Again, how is this achieved? And, how does this make us feel about Martin (and Valerie)

continued

Figure 16.4 *High Hopes* (1988)

in the scenes that follow? Is this ultimately a tragi-comedy, or is there some other genre label you think would be more fitting?

What vision of 1980s society does this film offer? Where do issues of the economy and consumerism, and attitudes towards work and making money, intrude into the narrative? How would you define each character in relation to these matters? What do you believe the preferred reading of these issues that the filmmakers would like the audience to take away with them would be? How is the audience 'pushed' towards seeing things from this preferred perspective?

What references in the film are there to Marxism, apart from the obvious visit to his grave? How do you see the character of Suzi in this respect? Cyril (and Shirley) would seem to be socialist in their outlook but Cyril in particular seems to treat Suzi's political ideas with disdain. Why is this? What sort of left-wing political position does Suzi seem to represent and how does it differ from Cyril's? How does Shirley's position on these matters compare to Cyril's?

How does our attitude towards Mrs Bender develop and change during the course of the film? Which character's relationship with her seems to most closely resemble our changing attitude? And does this mean we are being persuaded into a particular position of identification by the filmmakers?

Mike Leigh has sometimes faced charges of being misogynistic in his treatment of Valerie. However, in order to be clear about the issue of misogyny we need to look not just at this one character but at all of the other characters in the film, male as well as female. For instance, Cyril is our main character but does not appear to be at all misogynistic.

It is certainly true that Valerie is held up to intense ridicule before being made to suffer in such a way that we can see and feel her pain; and to brutalize a female character in such a way would seem to be misogynistic. And yet, Shirley is handled in an altogether different way: she forms and demonstrates through her actions the moral heart of the film. Cyril may be intense in his political disgust with the world and his desire to changes things (he may be the one most obviously holding on to the Marxist metanarrative). But Shirley sees the injustices of the world just as clearly and yet holds on all the more strongly to her caring sense of humanity. In the film, she is the voice of continuing faith in the worth of human beings and it is she who gently leads Cyril towards the same realization.

So, if Leigh can have such faith in women as he shows in his characterization of Shirley, how can he treat Valerie the way he does? John Hill suggests the problem with defending Leigh against charges of misogyny is that 'Martin's disdain for Valerie is shared by the film'.[4] He is right up to a point. Leigh does work to position his audience in such a way that they have nothing but disdain for Valerie. However, his ultimate objective is not the humiliation of Valerie; rather, that when the depth of her pain is revealed we should be forced to question the ease with which we have adopted such a contemptuous attitude towards her. The scene with Martin's girlfriend is crucial. Without it perhaps our contempt may continue to be for Valerie; with it our contempt shifts to Martin, and we have pity for Valerie and, most importantly, a sense of how we have been too quick to judge.

Do you agree or disagree? Debate and discuss this with others if possible.

(If you have time, watch *Secrets and Lies* (Leigh, 1996) to see how Leigh positions us in the same way in relation to the female character of Monica. Again, the tactic is used in order that we should ultimately be forced to question ourselves and the ways in which we may sometimes be too quick to make value judgements about others.)

Case study
LETTER TO BREZHNEV (1985)

(Director: Chris Bernard. Screenwriter: Frank Clarke. Cinematographer: Bruce McGowan. Music: Alan Gill. Cast: Alexandra Pigg (Elaine); Margi Clarke (Teresa); Peter Frith (Peter); Alfred Molina (Sergei).)

Figure 16.5 *Letter to Brezhnev* (1985)

In what ways might a British audience in 1985 react differently to this film than might a twenty-first-century audience? How would each audience respond to the basic premise of the narrative, namely that a working-class Liverpool girl would send a letter to the Russian President and receive an encouraging reply? Why have the filmmakers chosen to have Elaine fall in love with a Russian? Remember, 'choice' is always our key concern: the filmmakers could have made an entirely different choice that would still see Elaine deciding to get out of Liverpool, leave her family and prepare to undertake a momentous life-changing journey towards something new and unknown. Part of Thatcher's reputation was built upon the strength of her anti-Soviet rhetoric and you may like to research some of her speeches to see if you can find examples of her political stance with regard to both the Soviet Union and communism.

INFORMATION BOX

The Berlin Wall came down in 1989 effectively ending the Cold War during which the world's two superpowers, the United States and the Soviet Union, had opposed each other through propaganda and supporting different sides in conflict zones at every opportunity around the world. During this period, from the end of the Second World War to the end of the 1980s, Europe was effectively divided into two, with Soviet and Eastern Bloc troops ranged against NATO (North Atlantic Treaty Organization) troops in a prolonged stand-off and with nuclear weapons from both sides targeted at major cities on the opposing side.

The counties of the Soviet Union and its satellite states in Eastern Europe believed that communism was the best way to order society, and their economies were based upon strong central control with orders from the government determining the levels of any products that were to be manufactured. The United States and the countries that supported it within Western Europe believed that capitalism was the best way to order society, and their economies were essentially based upon the idea of the free market whereby the level of consumer demand for any product would determine manufacturing levels.

You may like to research more about the details of the Cold War and also try to find out more about the actual ways in which communism was implemented by the Soviet Union and how capitalism operated (and continues to operate) in the Western world.

In what ways are Elaine and Teresa similar and in what ways are they different? You should look carefully at what they do as well as thinking about what they say. Your understanding of film construction will also mean that you inevitably consider the use of clothing and make-up, performance and

continued

movement, and the delivery of lines. The Latin phrase *carpe diem*, meaning 'seize the day', is often used to describe a certain type of poetry that advocates grabbing the moment and living it to the full, but of course this is not an idea that is exclusive to a few poets. In what sense would you say Teresa and Elaine believe in the philosophy of *carpe diem* and would there be a difference between the ways in which each of them interprets this concept? Which scenes would you point to in order to illustrate your thoughts on this?

How would you describe this story? Is it a love story between Elaine and Peter, a Liverpudlian girl and a Russian sailor, or is it something else? In what ways is this film a conventional love story following a classic narrative pattern: a girl and a boy fall in love, there is an obstacle in the way of that love, the obstacle is overcome and the girl and boy are able to be together? In what ways would it seem to you to be different? How do you feel about the ending? Does it work as a resolution? If it does, what does it resolve? What relationship does it focus upon? When is the last moment in the film that we see Peter? Why is this? (Again, remember it is not accidental; a choice has been made.)

Finally, what would be your assessment of the way in which women are represented in the film? There is a strong central focus upon the two women. Could you argue that men (even Peter?) are rather peripheral to their story? The apparently more conventional woman of the two, Elaine, is the one who has the strength to break out and so in that sense seems to be somewhat different, but ultimately it appears that all she wants out of life is to settle down in a 'normal' way.

ACTIVITY

You may have noticed that George in *Mona Lisa* advocates falling in love, getting married and having children as the most vital aspect of human life and that Shirley in *High Hopes* would seem to endorse the same perspective. Is it that, after sexual liberation, feminism and the counter-culture of the 1960s and 1970s, there is some sort of longing for the norms of previous generations (or what others might see as the older comforting myth of romantic love)? Are there differences between the positions of Elaine, George and Shirley, and if so what would these be?

Case study

MY BEAUTIFUL LAUNDRETTE (1985)

(Director: Stephen Frears. Screenwriter: Hanif Kureishi. Cinematographer: Oliver Stapleton. Music: Ludus Tonalis. Cast: Gordon Warnecke (Omar); Daniel Day-Lewis (Johnny); Saeed Jaffrey (Nasser); Derrick Branche (Salim); Roshan Seth (Papa); Rita Wolf (Tania); Shirley Anne Field (Rachel).)

Figure 16.6 *My Beautiful Laundrette* (1985)

continued

How does this film represent the nature of Thatcher's Britain? What direct references to Thatcher can you find in the screenplay? What is the nature of the 1980s British economy displayed here? Which groups seem to be benefiting and which are losing out? Which scenes would you identify as important for understanding the film's position on the British economy? Is there still fundamentally a class struggle at stake here, as Marxism would suggest you always find in a capitalist society? Or are there factors that have complicated the basic Marxist picture? Why does Omar's father say the working class has been such a disappointment to him? Nasser describes himself as 'a professional businessman, not a professional Pakistani'; how important is this idea for the whole film? These two, Nasser and Omar's father (Papa), are essentially presented as political polar opposites, one believing in the entrepreneurial possibilities of the free market and the other believing in the need to control market forces to ensure the poor are protected, but what does the only scene between the two of them demonstrate? See the way in which they embrace, and notice how the filmmakers have carefully withheld this scene involving the meeting of the two apparently antagonistic brothers until towards the end of the film. (You will, of course, notice the ironic cross-cutting to images of Salim being beaten up by the fascist gang that takes place in the midst of this scene.)

See how Omar is very assertive in describing his father as 'socialist' and not 'communist' when he is admitted to the first very carefully proscribed all-male party at Nasser's house. (How do you 'read' the character of Omar? Do we identify with him as the central character whose story we are essentially following? To what extent and in what ways does he continue to remain something of an enigma throughout the film?) How would you describe the range of people present at this party? In what ways is Tania's presence around the edges of this scene important for the film? Why does the camera seem to linger over the white writer's look given towards Omar? Issues involving the representation of the economy, race, gender and sexuality would all seem to be interwoven within a scene such as this. Zaki is also present in this scene. He is a relatively minor character but what importance would he seem to have to the narrative?

Before Omar is admitted to Nasser's inner sanctum he meets the women sitting in an outside room. How are women represented in the film? How is Cherry contrasted with Bilquis in this scene? Consider performance and costume, as well as what is said (or not said). Of course, this will naturally have to be considered in relation to issues of culture. Cherry is characterized as heavily Westernized, but (also notice) extremely materialistic. And all of this will need to be seen carefully in relation to the representation of Tania. Which scenes would you point to as being of key importance to reading her character? One obvious possibility would be the meeting with her father's mistress, Rachel, during the opening of the laundrette. This scene demonstrates the way in which the filmmakers are aware of the complications that are always present in any representation. Tania attacks Rachel very effectively from the position of a strongly independent feminist, but then (through the way in which she looks down when Rachel introduces the ideas of class and generations) recognizes the truth in Rachel's retort. Again, notice how quite subtle elements of film construction – here the way in which the camera draws attention to the performance of eye movement – are critical in reading film.

Overall, does the film present the Asian community in a positive light? And, if it is not an entirely rosy picture that is painted of this community, is the film therefore pandering to ethnic prejudices? (Or is this the same as considering *High Hopes* to be misogynistic on the basis of the portrayal of one female character?) Look at the opening to the film. Why have the filmmakers chosen to begin with this scene? What issues does it immediately raise regarding race? Could this scene be interpreted in line with British nationalist politics, i.e. that 'outsider' ethnic groups are taking over British society? Or would it need to be seen in relation to the rest of the film in order for a fair understanding of the representations at work to be understood?

Obviously you may like to consider the issue of the representation of (homo)sexuality in some detail, particularly perhaps in the context of the politics of the period. Wherever possible try to explore the way in which such things are presented through film construction. For example, watch the scene in which Johnny comes into Nasser's house for the first time. In a very intimate way Omar goes to remove an eyelash from Johnny's face and as he does so the camera frames Tania between the two men watching what is taking place. She has a look of realization upon her face that alerts the audience to the significance of what has just passed between the men. The contradictions within Johnny as a character could form a further very useful study (perhaps this should be seen as an examination of his search for identity). Genghis tells him not to cut himself off from 'his own people' and that 'everybody has to belong'; and Johnny could be seen as on a journey to find out exactly where he 'belongs'. Watch the scene in which Omar's father arrives at the laundrette in the early hours of the morning and see how Daniel Day-Lewis adjusts his performance to become rather childlike and vulnerable (or should that be ashamed) in his presence. Contrast this with his powerfully assertive confidence in the face of Salim that is demonstrated on several occasions. In the end, of course, Johnny has to make a moral choice, a choice that is all the more difficult because the person from an ethnic minority he is forced to defend is precisely the most distasteful Asian character.

continued

Finally, why is the film centred on the idea of a laundrette? It seems a rather strange starting point/central location for a film, but why would it have been chosen? (And, as a minor aside, why do you think the name 'Genghis' has been used for the leader of the fascist gang?)

Heritage films

A film like *My Beautiful Laundrette* may be seen as standing in direct contrast to the popular heritage films from the 1980s. Films such as *A Passage to India* (Lean, 1984), *A Room With a View* (Ivory, 1985) and *Chariots of Fire* (Hudson, 1981) look back to an imagined British past with a sense of nostalgic longing for empire days and supposed British greatness. These films focus on the comfortable lives of privilege led by the English upper classes not with any sense of criticism but with a lavish use of the visual spectacle of landscape, setting and costume that suggests admiration. They seem to offer a sense of stability that is perhaps felt to be lacking in modern contemporary society.

Or is it as simple as that? *Chariots of Fire* seems to evoke traditional British values while celebrating British athletic success in a patriotic way. And yet several of the main characters are clearly 'outsiders': Abrahams is a Lithuanian Jew, Mussabini is of Arab/Italian extraction, and Liddell is from a lowly Scottish background. Does this mean a film like this can be read as something more than a simple celebration of national achievement? Isn't the recognition here more importantly of diversity and the strength of individual personal belief? Doesn't the use of William Blake's 'Jerusalem' within the film further complicate matters and suggest a simple surface reading is in the end inadequate? Although this poem may have been appropriated by the English Establishment as virtually a second national anthem, it was originally a revolutionary poem calling for society to be rebuilt.[5]

ACTIVITY

- If you had to choose a single scene that you believe is crucial to a clear understanding of *Chariots of Fire*, which one would it be?
- Present this scene to others in such a way as to make your argument regarding the meanings to be found within it as clear as possible. You should aim to focus on the ways in which you believe film construction is being used in deliberate ways to create meaning.

Notes

1 Thatcher resigned in November 1990, handing over the leadership of the Conservatives to John Major; and so her period in office spans the whole of our period of interest for this module.

2 Stuart Hall, 'The Meaning of New Times', in Hall and Martin Jacques (eds) *New Times: The Changing Face of Politics in the 1990s*, Lawrence and Wishart, London, 1989.

3 Jean-François Lyotard, *The Postmodern Condition: A Report on Knowledge*, Manchester University Press, Manchester, 1984.

4 John Hill, *British Cinema in the 1980s: Issues and Themes*, Oxford University Press, Oxford, 1999, p. 194.

5 See the ironic use that is made of this same hymn at the heart of *The Loneliness of the Long Distance Runner* (Richardson, 1962).

References and Further Reading

Friedman, L. (ed.) (2006) *Fires Were Started: British Cinema and Thatcherism* (2nd edn), Wallflower, London

Hill, J. (1999) *British Cinema in the 1980s: Issues and Themes*, Oxford University Press, Oxford

Park, J. (1990) *British Cinema: The Lights That Failed*, Batsford, London (chs 7, 8 and 9)

Rockett, E. and Rockett, K. (2003) *Neil Jordan: Exploring Boundaries*, Liffey Press, Dublin

Watson, G. (2004) *The Cinema of Mike Leigh: A Sense of the Real*, Wallflower, London

Useful Websites

www.sensesofcinema.com
www.britishfilm.org.uk

SOCIAL-POLITICAL STUDY

17 Living with crime

This chapter will look at:

- the content and contexts of key films of the British crime genre
- the social and political issues raised by crime films
- the key themes running through films in this genre
- representations of class, race and gender across the crime film

If you wish to pursue an identity study rather than a social-political study then there is an additional full chapter on British Film: Identity Study that can be found in the Resources section of our companion website at http://routledge.tandf.co.uk/textbooks/9780415454339/resources.asp

There are no set texts that define 'Living with Crime', and it is worth considering an approach that encompasses films from different periods (even contemporary periods), and also worth considering an historical context for the crime film. It is important to note that the issues around crime do not merely focus on the criminals themselves, but also on those affected by crime (both direct victims and those that crime touches – families of both victims and criminals, the police and judiciary, those involved in the rehabilitation of criminals, and the wider communities affected by the diversity of crime inflicted upon them in all its many and varied forms). It is also worth noting that swag-bag-carrying criminals are not the only

BRITISH AND AMERICAN FILM (FM2)

people who inflict crime upon communities, and thus it is important to consider crime in its widest context – industrialists, businessmen, politicians and governments can all inflict crimes against a community.

The history of the crime genre

The British crime film is one that evolved very soon after film began to be made in Britain, and of course reflects the societies and the concerns of those societies that produced it. It is no surprise, therefore that the earliest British crime films (including *Footpads* (Paul's Animatograph Works 1895, Director: R.W. Paul) and *Robbery* (Paul's Animatograph Works 1897, Director: R.W. Paul)) grew out of the late Victorian urban industrial landscape where theft and 'muggings' were a daily ordeal for many.

Case study
FOOTPADS

In this earliest example of the British crime film, a gentleman in London (or at least a crude studio set representing London's West End) is violently attacked by street robbers. A policeman comes to his rescue, but is over-powered by the violence of the robbers. In contrast to a moral message (that later became the norm for the crime film) that crime doesn't pay, the criminals in R.W. Paul's film not only succeed, but the police are depicted as impotent in the face of their violent intent.

A number of key features of the crime film are, however, established in this 24-second short, and would be easily recognizable in any contemporary crime film:

■ the 'monied' victim (who is therefore deserving of the attack)
■ the gang of professional criminals who do not blanche at extreme violence to get what they want
■ the 'first on the scene' police officer who becomes a victim of the gang.

It is films such as this that began to set the codes and conventions that modern audiences still recognize today.

Yet urban crime was not the only form of crime presented. Filmmakers such as William Haggar produced films that reflected both rural crimes and the crimes defined by landed gentry. In *Desperate Poaching Affray* (Haggar & Sons 1903, Director: William Haggar) two poachers are chased by gamekeepers, and eventually meet justice at the hands of the police. Similarly, in *Daring Daylight Burglary* (Sheffield Photo Company 1903, Director: Frank Mottershaw) a country burglar is discovered, throws a policeman off a roof, and is then chased across the countryside, over a river, along cliffs, and is apprehended after he tries to escape by railway. Crime was a feature of everyone's life and therefore it became a common form at the start of British filmmaking.

Some key British crime films

- *Footpads* (Paul's Animatograph Works 1895, Director: R.W. Paul)
- *A Burglar for One Night* (Hepworth Manufacturing Company 1911, Director: Bert Haldane)
- *Blackmail* (British International Pictures 1929, Director: Alfred Hitchcock)
- *The Thirty-Nine Steps* (Gaumont British Pictures 1935, Director: Alfred Hitchcock)
- *The Arsenal Stadium Mystery* (G&S Films 1939, Director: Thorald Dickenson)
- *Brighton Rock* (Associated British Picture Corporation 1947, Director: John Boulting)
- *The Blue Lamp* (Ealing Studios 1949, Director: Basil Dearden)
- *Cosh Boy* (Daniel Angel Films 1953, Director: Lewis Gilbert)
- *Yield to the Night* (Associated British Picture Corporation 1956, Director: J. Lee Thompson)
- *The Criminal* (Merton Park Studios 1960, Director: Joseph Losey)
- *The League of Gentlemen* (Allied Film Makers 1960, Director: Basil Dearden)
- *Murder She Said* (George H. Brown Productions/MGM British Studios 1961, Director: George Pollock)
- *Victim* (Parkway Films/Allied Film Makers 1961, Director: Basil Dearden)
- *Robbery* (Oakhurst Productions 1967, Director: Peter Yates)
- *The Italian Job* (Oakhurst Productions 1969, Director: Peter Collinson)
- *Performance* (Goodtimes Enterprises 1970, Director: Donald Cammell/Nicolas Roeg)
- *Get Carter* (MGM British Studios 1971, Director: Mike Hodges)
- *Villain* (Anglo-EMI/Kastner/Ladd/Kantner 1971, Director: Michael Tuchner)
- *Scum* (Berwick Street Productions/Boyd's Company/Kendon Films Ltd 1979, Director: Alan Clarke)
- *The Long Good Friday* (British Lion Films/Calendar Productions/Handmade Films 1980, Director: John Mackenzie)
- *Mona Lisa* (Handmade Films 1986, Director: Neil Jordan)
- *The Krays* (Fugitive Features/Parkfield Entertainment 1990, Director: Peter Medak)
- *Let Him Have It* (British Screen/Canal +/Film Trustees Ltd/Jennie & Co/Pierson/Vermillion/Vivid Ents 1991, Director: Peter Medak)
- *Small Faces* (Billy MacKinnon/BBC Films/Skyline/Glasgow Film Fund 1996, Director: Gillies MacKinnon)
- *Trainspotting* (Channel Four Films/Figment Films/Polygram Filmed Entertainment/Noel Gay Motion Picture Co 1996, Director: Danny Boyle)

- *Face* (BBC Productions/Daigordo Face Productions/British Screen/Distant Horizon 1997, Director: Antonia Bird)
- *The General* (J&M/Merlin Films 1998, Director: John Boorman)
- *Lock Stock and Two Smoking Barrels* (Handmade Films/Polygram Filmed Entertainment/SKA Films/Steve Tisch Co/Summit Entertainment 1998, Director: Guy Ritchie)
- *Sexy Beast* (Film Four/Kanzaman SA/RPC 2000, Director: Jonathan Glazer)
- *Gangster No 1* (British Screen/BSkyB/Film Four/Pagoda Film 2000, Director: Paul McGuigan)
- *Bullet Boy* (BBC Films/UK Film Council/Shine 2004, Director: Saul Dibb)
- *L4yer Cake* (Columbia Pictures Corporation/Marv Films 2004, Director: Matthew Vaughn)
- *London to Brighton* (Steel Mill Productions/Wellington Films/LTB Films 2006, Director: Paul Andrew Williams)
- *Ghosts* (Channel 4/Film4/Head Gear Films/Lafayette Films 2007, Director: Nic Broomfield)

By 1911 (and the industrial economic depression that presaged the First World War), the crime film was presenting a more nuanced picture of crime. In *A Burglar for One Night* (Hepworth Manufacturing Company 1911, Director: Bert Haldane) unemployment as a cause of crime is explored, along with the effects on both criminal and those who love him. By this time the moral message had become a fixed feature of the crime film, and here it is pointedly made that the love and morality of a good woman saves the would-be burglar from his fate.

During the First World War, and indeed for several years after, the British crime film was not prominent, largely due to issues of morale (one could hardly show crime taking place at home when so many families had their young men in France fighting for their country), and later audience sensitivity (post-war there was an increased demand for escapist cinema, and the crime film (often with its semblance of realism) in showing the 'everyday' did not offer the audience the escape it craved).

In the late 1920s Alfred Hitchcock took the crime genre in a new direction through two films, *The Lodger: A Story of the London Fog* (Carlyle Blackwell Productions/Gainsborough Pictures 1927, Director: Alfred Hitchcock) and *Blackmail* (British International Pictures 1929, Director: Alfred Hitchcock). In the former he introduces a character that has come to populate crime films world-wide – the mysterious suspected serial killer, and in the latter he introduces another crime stalwart – the blackmail plot. Both these films are less about the contrivances of plotting to reveal a crime and punishment theme, and more about the intricate strands of the consequences of crime that interweave to provoke a reaction.

Throughout the 1930s the British crime film prospered (particularly as part of the quota-quickie system) and produced a number of formats that became a

repeatable part of the genre, including the investigating policeman or private investigator (sometimes the happy amateur), and famously the cinematic visualization of the Sherlock Holmes mysteries. This growth was temporarily halted in 1939 when war was declared, and again the morale imperative took precedence. However, the crime film soon evolved to encompass new forms of wartime crime, and films such as *Cottage to Let* (Gainsborough Pictures 1941, Director: Anthony Asquith) and *Waterloo Road* (Gainsborough Pictures 1945, Director: Sidney Gilliat) were highlighting the fear of new criminals – the fifth columnist and the blackmarketeer 'spiv' respectively.

In the immediate post-war period attention focused on gangs that had evolved in the chaos of the urban home front (such as *Brighton Rock* (Associated British Picture Corporation 1947, Director: John Boulting), and *Hue and Cry* (Ealing Studios 1947, Director: Charles Crichton)), and as the 1950s became a period when Britain had 'never had it so good' the focus shifted again to look at how youth crime was on the rise. Films such as *Cosh Boy* (Daniel Angel Films 1953, Director: Lewis Gilbert) (and indeed its forebear *Boys in Brown* (Gainsborough Pictures 1949, Director: Montgomery Tully) which looks at the attempts to rehabilitate young men in a borstal institution) became a template for the genre for the next ten years, in part to either emulate or defend against how the genre was evolving in Hollywood.

As the realization took hold that organized crime was a reality in Britain in the 1960s, so the crime film began to focus less on gentleman thieves, blackmailers and common thugs, and more on the work of criminal gangs. Sixties society was rocked by the brutality of what was to become known as the 'Great Train Robbery' and this was replicated (albeit thinly masked) in *Robbery* (Oakhurst Productions 1967, Director: Peter Yates). A similar approach to organized crime marked another departure in presenting the criminal as hero – the comedy *The Italian Job* (Oakhurst Productions 1969, Director: Peter Collinson) saw a gang of British criminals take on a European 'job' to preserve British superiority and honour. The criminal as hero and issues of honour were both confirmed as features of the genre two years later when *Get Carter* (MGM British Studios 1971, Director: Mike Hodges) was released, again establishing new generic elements (the reluctant criminal, the 'professional', and betrayal within the criminal fraternity), and setting a darker tone for the crime film that was to be prominent for the next two decades.

The focus on organized crime continued with *The Long Good Friday* (British Lion Films/Calendar Productions/Handmade Films 1980, Director: John Mackenzie), *Mona Lisa* (Handmade Films 1986, Director: Neil Jordan), and *The Krays* (Fugitive Features/Parkfield Entertainment 1990, Director: Peter Medak), with each adding an individual flavour, be it an IRA perspective, a backdrop of prostitution, or an element of nostalgia. Indeed, the sense that organized crime (at the very least in the form of gangs) dominates the British landscape is confirmed by a smaller scale film of the period, *Small Faces* (Billy MacKinnon/BBC Films/Skyline/Glasgow Film Fund 1996, Director: Gillies MacKinnon), which presents a society dominated by gangs and the need to placate them in urban areas where the law no longer protects.

Case study
COSH BOY (1953)

Figure 17.1 *Cosh Boy* (1953)

Cosh Boy was the first British film to receive an X certificate from the British Board of Film Censors, and it was shocking in its frank depiction of teenage sex, pregnancy, abortion, and, of course, violent robbery and murder. Paralleling the case of Derek Bentley (hanged in 1953 for the murder of a policeman and recently pardoned), the film deals with the progression of a vicious young bully into a hardened robber, and eventually a murderer, set against a backdrop of a bombed-out London (reminiscent of Italian neo-realism).

The sheer brutality of this film in depicting juvenile delinquency is tempered with a rather heavy-handed moral delivery that blames parents for not being strict enough. However, this film remains a film of its time and earnestly attempts to engage with an emerging social problem.

The ordinary 'working-class' criminal came back into focus shortly after this, with films that addressed the victim-criminal and the career-criminal. *Trainspotting* (Channel Four Films/Figment Films/Polygram Filmed Entertainment/Noel Gay Motion Picture Co 1996, Director: Danny Boyle) placed narcotics centre stage and highlighted the crime that drugs inflict on a society, and the resulting criminalization of users, both through society's treatment of them and through their need to commit crime in order to support their habit. Both *Face* (BBC Productions/Daigordo Face Productions/British Screen/Distant Horizon 1997, Director: Antonia Bird) and *The General* (J&M/Merlin Films 1998, Director: John Boorman) offered a story of career-criminals, presenting them as victims of societies that marginalized them because they were poor or unemployable, and continuing the genre convention of betrayal within the criminal fraternity.

The end of the 1990s saw a seismic shift in the genre when *Lock, Stock and Two Smoking Barrels* (Handmade Films/Polygram Filmed Entertainment/SKA Films/Steve Tisch Co/Summit Entertainment 1998, Director: Guy Ritchie) was released and immediately set the tone for countless imitators to follow (sharp-suited 'geezers' with a line of witty dialogue straight out of the Tarantino book of how to make films). A postmodern narrative construction that directly addressed the audience, and used slick computer-enhanced postproduction techniques to present a stylized look at a small corner of the underworld, created a radical new form within the crime genre (one that has often been criticized for form over substance, narrative structuring over content). Guy Ritchie himself revisited the genre on successive occasions to reuse the form and present highly stylized crime dramas (heavy on the black comedy) that would become beloved by both fans (particularly young men) and television comedy sketch shows over the following decade.

While sub-*Lock, Stock* films continued into the new millennium, the early years of the decade saw the revival of the 'problem' film, examining the social problems that lie at the bottom of criminal behaviour. Rejecting the slick stylized narrative and form of Guy Ritchie and his imitators, films such as *Bullet Boy* (BBC Films/UK Film Council/Shine 2004, Director: Saul Dibb) offer a view of the new gangs of the twenty-first century, where race plays a key congregational factor, and gun culture is turning decades of interracial violence inward. Similarly, *London to Brighton* (Steel Mill Productions/Wellington Films/LTB Films 2006, Director: Paul Andrew Williams) offers a grim realism of violence and prostitution, the hidden lowlife behind the façade of modern Britain, as does *Ghosts* (Channel 4/Film4/Head Gear Films/Lafayette Films 2007, Director: Nic Broomfield), revealing the almost endemic nature of crime perpetuated on 'illegal' immigrants, and the real and serious impact of casual crime.

Draw out a timeline of the British crime genre. Highlight on it key films and the type of film being made.

Is there a dominant type across each decade (approximately) of your timeline?

If so, what do you think the reason for this is?

Research what was happening in terms of crime and society around these dominant types of films. Is there a correlation?

Social and political issues of the crime film

Films reflect the society that made them and the audiences that consume them. Therefore, when faced with a perpetuating British genre such as the crime film that has evolved across the history of British film, and still continues to be a prominent British form, it is worth examining both the social and political contexts that produced these films and also the social and political contexts in which they were received.

While early British films were the product of a society that had little faith in law and order to resolve its issues of crime, by the late 1920s and early 1930s the authority figure of the crime-solving police detective had become a common feature of the crime film. It is possible that this was in response to the horrors of poverty, mass unemployment and the Great Depression, where a desire for order and protection from the ravages of crime emerged. It is equally possible that this was a subconscious warning from middle- and upper-class writers, directors and producers that any form of lawbreaking (be it theft or murder, or – implicitly – revolution) would be punished by the lawmakers.

The Second World War changed the face of British society and in turn changed the face of the British criminal. Those who did not enlist (or those not fit enough to be conscripted) into the armed forces saw the 'home front' suffer terrible privations amidst the bombing and the rationing, and saw ordinary, decent folk criminalize themselves through buying food and goods on the black market, through 'looting' bomb-sites, and through using ingenuity to find ways around wartime regulations. Blackmarketeers, 'spivs', thieves and 'fences' prospered, organizing themselves into informal criminal relationships in the absence of any sizeable or effective police force. Similarly, with the absence of a patriarchal figure, and with many women taking work to support the war effort, a generation of young people grew up with a different perspective on authority, one that was happy to challenge or even disregard the norms of the pre-war society.

Case study

BRIGHTON ROCK (1947)

Although set in the interwar years, the behaviour and even dress of the characters in John Boulting's *Brighton Rock* were clearly representing the blackmarketeer – the 'spiv' culture of the war and post-war period. It also offers a preview of the 'razor-gangs' that were to become a feature of the popular press post-war and into the early 1950s, and is clearly reflecting a post-war fear of the breakdown of society.

The central character 'Pinkie' (played by Richard Attenborough) is an amoral gangster who kills a journalist in revenge for the death of his gang leader. A complication ensues and, after being injured in a knife fight, he is forced to marry a young waitress so that she will be prevented from being a witness against his gang and implicitly against him. Believing she is about to betray him, and faced with the superiority of a rival gang, Pinkie decides to kill her by pushing her off of Brighton pier, but, cornered by the police, he falls himself and is drowned.

The film was released in America under the title *Young Scarface*, which in itself locates it in relation to the Hollywood gangster genre, but also reveals how new a form it was for British cinema at this time.

Figure 17.2
*Brighton Rock
(1947)*

Couple these factors to the 'demobilization' of British armed forces at the end of the war, resulting in the return of highly trained (to fight), highly resourceful and psychologically damaged men, and the view that the norms of society were shifting would have felt very real.

This resulted initially in films in which a strong and effective police presence was portrayed (particularly a police presence that was civilized relative to the amoral behaviour of the criminals it faced), with a strong moral message that crime did not pay, and that criminals would face punishment. *The Blue Lamp* (Ealing Studios 1949, Director: Basil Dearden) presented audiences with PC George Dixon (Jack Warner) – a character that would later emerge in the long-running television series *Dixon of Dock Green* – who was facing young criminals whose intended crimes were beyond the traditional values of the older generation of crime gangs. While he is shot and killed by one of the young criminals, they are relentlessly tracked down and eventually captured and disarmed – interestingly (from a twenty-first-century view) by unarmed policemen.

While youth crime was high on the agenda of the 1950s, a number of films from this period reflected on the effects of demobilization on the armed forces. *The Ship That Died of Shame* (Ealing Studios 1955, Director: Basil Dearden) explores the morality of ex-servicemen who drift into crime after engaging in some 'low-level' smuggling to make money in the difficult post-war period. This was later revisited through the comedy *The League of Gentlemen* (Allied Film Makers 1960, Director: Basil Dearden) in which criminal behaviour was justified as taking a reward for loyal wartime service, a reward that was promised but never honoured. Morality is upheld in both of these films with the criminals failing, but in the later film there is clearly a shift of social perspective, as sympathies clearly lie with the criminals and not with the police.

BASIL DEARDEN (1911–1971)   *i*

Born Basil Dear, his career in the entertainment industry began as an ASM at the Fulham Grand Theatre and in 1931 he became the stage manager for Basil Dean. Moving from theatre to film in the mid-1930s with Basil Dean, Basil Dearden (changing his surname to avoid confusion with Basil Dean) joined Ealing Studios as a writer, script editor and assistant director. Staying on after Basil Dean left, he quickly established himself as one of Ealing's leading directors (in partnership with producer Michael Relph), not only working on comedies with stars such as Will Hay, but also making a niche for the social 'issue' film – and hence the crime film.

Surviving the demise of Ealing Studios he co-founded Allied Film Makers along with Michael Relph, Richard Attenborough, Bryan Forbes, Jack Hawkins and Guy Green, and produced a significant number of independent films. He continued to direct until his death in a car accident on the way home from Pinewood Studios in 1971.

The 'swinging sixties' offered a marked social change in attitudes and behaviour, and this change was incorporated into the genre by filmmakers. The sexual freedom and use of narcotics are prominent in films such as *Performance* (Goodtimes Enterprises 1970, Director: Donald Cammell/Nicolas Roeg) and *Get Carter* (MGM British Studios 1971, Director: Mike Hodges) with the latter reflecting a post-1960s disillusionment and a seedy descent into the darker areas of crime, perhaps signposting crime films that would follow a decade and a half later. Significantly, *Get Carter* identifies crime not as 'other' but as something intertwined with 'decent' society from the humble bed and breakfast in which Jack Carter (Michael Caine) stays, to the restaurant being built by respectable businessman Cliff Brumby (Bryan Mosley). In society there was a growing realization that 'decent' society had been hiding its darker side, and that crime was intrinsically linked to business and local politics.

This social realization is made explicit by the first crime film made in the Thatcherite era, *The Long Good Friday* (British Lion Films/Calendar Productions/Handmade Films 1980, Director: John Mackenzie). Set against the backdrop of the regeneration of London's docklands for a forthcoming Olympic Games, John Mackenzie makes explicit links between the approach of gang boss Harold Shand (Bob Hoskins) to the business opportunities presented by the event, and the attitudes and values of the recently elected Conservative government. Brutal, ruthless and corrupt, Harold Shand represents the capitalist entrepreneur that was to dominate the 1980s, and as such indicates the finer distinction between crime lord and businessman. With both councillors and high-ranking police officers on his payroll, Shand appears to be invincible, until he is faced with a betrayal by one of his key lieutenants that results in attacks on his empire by the IRA (a plotline that was too much for the film's original backer Lew Grade at Black Lion Films). *The Long Good Friday* is a strangely prophetic film, not only for its presaging of the docklands development, but also in its parallels with the Thatcherite agenda, and indeed Thatcher herself (gang boss who was betrayed by key lieutenants, and appeared invincible until faced with the IRA).

An element of realism established in *The Long Good Friday* became the marker for crime films throughout the following two decades (with one or two notable exceptions), and as Thatcherite policies began to bite, resulting in significant social upheaval and millions becoming unemployed, the crime film sunk deeper into exploring the underbelly of crime, dealing with the seedier businesses supporting the entrepreneurial façades of crime bosses. Michael Caine's ruthless businessman Dinny Mortwell in *Mona Lisa* (Handmade Films 1986, Director: Neil Jordan) has an air of respectability, mixing with the wealthy and the 'great and good', and surrounded with the trappings of success, and yet once past the superficial he is revealed as little more than a pimp (indeed, a pimp who is trading in young girls). George (Bob Hoskins), a driver working for Mortwell, who has just got out of prison after a long 'stretch', is naively innocent of Mortwell. While he knows the business they are both in, he is an old-fashioned 'villain' who (unlike Mortwell) has not embraced the times and is not a devotee of the 'money at all costs' philosophy that dominated the decade. His 'innocence', or criminal 'decency', allows the audience to realize how seedy and depressingly devoid of humanity this criminal world has become. It is interesting to compare the attitude and values promoted in this film with those promoted in *The Krays* (Fugitive Features/Parkfield Entertainment 1990, Director: Peter Medak), where the Kray twins are depicted as upholding criminal values against a tide of decadence.

A decade later the tide of decadence was depicted with a brutal (if surreal) honesty in *Trainspotting* (Channel Four Films/Figment Films/Polygram Filmed Entertainment/Noel Gay Motion Picture Co 1996, Director: Danny Boyle), where the result of criminals descending into narcotic trafficking is graphically shown in the disintegration of a group of young, feckless, Scottish men. Heroin takes a hold on them and leads them into a criminal underworld where their self-respect, judgement and standards are all compromised. Drug-taking, child neglect, under-age sex, theft, violence and AIDS are all common partners in crime, the products of a drug culture that by the mid-1990s had become the norm.

The world of crime had clearly come a long way since the early days of film, though it is questionable whether it was that crime was different then or whether the choice of what was acceptable to show on screen was more restricted then. Two films that display a marked social separation from this early period are *Bullet Boy* (BBC Films/UK Film Council/Shine 2004, Director: Saul Dibb) and *Ghosts* (Channel 4/Film4/Head Gear Films/Lafayette Films 2007, Director: Nic Broomfield), the former dealing with black-on-black crime and the latter dealing with crimes against illegal immigrants. Both of these reflect a modern sensitivity and offer critiques both of contemporary society and of contemporary political policies that have led to the situations depicted in these films.

ACTIVITY

Select two or three films from the list of key British crime films to analyse. Divide a sheet into two columns headed 'Similarities' and 'Differences'.

Write down what you feel are the key similarities and differences between the films.

Compare your list with others. Do you notice any significant findings? If so, what do you think underpins them?

Key themes in the British crime genre

When watching a body of work across a period of time a number of key themes begin to emerge. Once identified, they can be traced through other films and their development established. Some of the themes that emerge in the crime genre include:

- crime and punishment
- betrayal
- the criminal code

While many films in this genre cry out for the punishment of criminals (indeed, the ending of *Cosh Boy* has the police deliberately delaying their arrival so that the lead character, Roy, can get a beating at the hands of one of his victims), a number have tried to use the genre to highlight problems in the criminal justice system.

While *Good Time Girl* (Gainsborough Pictures/Triton Films 1947, Director: David Macdonald) offered some limited criticism of the treatment of female juvenile offenders (though more would have been present were it not for the actions of the censors), *Yield to the Night* (Associated British Picture Corporation 1956, Director: J. Lee Thompson) offers a much more direct criticism of the need for retribution, and of capital punishment in particular.

Case study
YIELD TO THE NIGHT (1956)

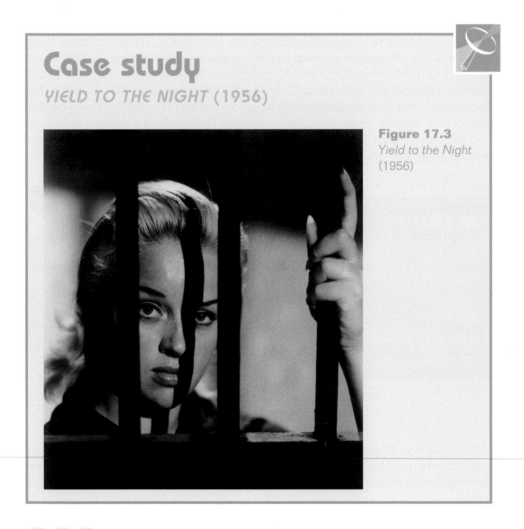

Figure 17.3
Yield to the Night (1956)

Infatuated with Jim Lancaster (Michael Craig) (despite her being married), Mary Hilton (Diana Dors) begins a passionate affair and then falls in love with him. She discovers he has also begun an affair with Lucy Carpenter (Mercia Shaw). She leaves him, and he threatens suicide. He kills himself and, disgusted at Lucy's indifferent reaction to it, she takes his gun.

Mary waits for Lucy outside her flat in broad daylight, and, in a crime of passion, empties the revolver into her to ensure she is dead.

Sentenced to death by hanging, she waits in prison. The Home Secretary refuses to commute the sentence, and she is led away to the gallows.

This film clearly paralleled the case of Ruth Ellis – the last woman to be hanged in Britain – in 1955 and whose case came in the closing chapters of the Abolition Bill (passed immediately prior to this film's release). A strong anti-capital punishment theme is developed not only through the sympathetic portrayal of Mary, but also of the different perspectives to her crime presented by the prison officers who are guarding her after sentencing. Mary's unravelling when finally faced with the unavoidable fact that she is to be executed is a masterpiece of cinema, and a powerful case against capital punishment.

Equally strong anti-capital punishment films continued to be made long after capital punishment was abolished, but often coincided with the debate being reopened in Parliament. Notably *Dance With a Stranger* (First Film Company/National Film Finance Corporation/Film Four International/Goldcrest Films 1984, Director: Mike Newell) dealt directly with the Ruth Ellis execution, and *Let Him Have It* (British Screen/Canal +/Film Trustees Ltd/Jennie & Co/Pierson/Vermillion/Vivid Ents 1991, Director: Peter Medak) looked at the case of Derek Bentley's execution for the murder of a policeman that was subsequently proved to be a horrendous miscarriage of justice.

While in the above examples betrayal takes place in relationships, another key theme in the crime genre is of betrayal within the criminal fraternity, usually with money or women at the root of it. In *The Criminal* (Merton Park Studios 1960, Director: Joseph Losey), an ex-convict who is in the gang that robs a racetrack, is caught and sent back to prison. Unwilling to tell the other gang members where he has hidden the proceeds, they betray him by kidnapping his girlfriend and by having him tortured to reveal the location. From this point onward the concept of 'honour among thieves' is tarnished by betrayal, from the duplicity of the London 'mob' in *Get Carter* (MGM British Studios 1971, Director: Mike Hodges), through the betrayal of gang members in *Face* (BBC Productions/Daigordo Face Productions/British Screen/Distant Horizon 1997, Director: Antonia Bird), through to the brutal revelations of betrayals upon betrayals in *Sexy Beast* (Film Four/Kanzaman SA/RPC 2000, Director: Jonathan Glazer).

Case study

FACE (1997)

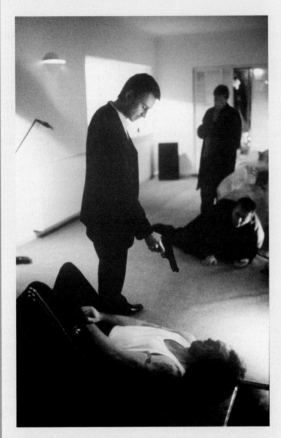

Face – slang in the criminal fraternity for a gangster – follows a group of villains as they undertake a security depot robbery. Betrayal leads to death, and to the proceeds from the robbery ending up in a police station from which the remaining thieves audaciously attempt another robbery. Violent, brassy, and perfectly cast with actors who are believable as armed robbers, this captures the spirit of the times, where desperation overtakes common sense.

The plot revolves around the betrayals, and astute spectators should be able to spot the point when the first betrayal occurs from which all the others multiply. There is little honour among thieves in this film, with everyone out for themselves, and greed being the creed.

Honour among thieves is a small part of the criminal code that 'legitimizes' certain targets and places others off-limits. It is interesting to see how, post-war, this code was slowly eroded (through films such as *The Blue Lamp* and the casual shooting of a police officer, *Cosh Boy* where the robbery victims were largely women, and *Robbery* (Oakhurst Productions 1967, Director: Peter Yates) where 'civilians' were terrorized and brutalized.

However, there were other films that celebrated the code. *The Italian Job* attempts to define British criminals as 'other' to (and better than) their European counterparts, partly through the adherence to the 'code'. Similarly, in *Get Carter*, Jack Carter's motivation throughout is to rectify a breach of the code that meant his 'innocent' brother was killed.

In *The General* (J&M/Merlin Films 1998, Director: John Boorman), the code becomes symbolic of a working-class brotherhood that even the police come to respect (but one, interestingly, that the terrorists do not). The code prevents betrayals, defines who is 'legitimate', restricts activities, and even codifies behaviour towards police.

ACTIVITY

In a film you have watched list the themes that occur.

- Who is the key proponent of the themes?
- What activities do they undertake to demonstrate the themes?
- Are there any instances where one theme comes into conflict or counteracts another?
- How are such instances resolved?

Crime and representation

Historically, with few exceptions, crime in film has categorized criminals either as lower class or as the gentleman thief, and crimes (other than crimes of passion) are largely male preserves that exclude women from playing any significant criminal role. Women may be involved in the detection or punishment of crime (indeed, Margaret Rutherford made a successful career out of playing Miss Marple in a series of British crime films including *Murder She Said* (George H. Brown Productions/MGM British Studios 1961, Director: George Pollock)), but only in recent years (reflecting changes in society) has there been more prominent potential for female criminals.

There are, however, some notable representations that are worthy of closer attention, with sexuality and race being two.

Victim (Parkway Films/Allied Film Makers 1961, Director: Basil Dearden) was a key film in the depiction of what would today be described as a hate crime, with a homosexual falling foul of a blackmailer. Notorious at the time for presenting such issues, and a significant risk for Dirk Bogarde, the first British A-list actor to undertake an openly homosexual role, it allowed the spectator to empathize with the victim as victim, rather than victim as homosexual, and in doing so offered a clear sense that sexuality did not present any distinction in the eyes of the criminal other than a possible opportunity.

It is interesting to contrast this depiction of homosexuality with that portrayed in *Scum* (Berwick Street Productions/Boyd's Company/Kendon Films Ltd 1979, Director: Alan Clarke), where a young borstal inmate is subjected to male rape by a group of other inmates. In a rather salacious approach the warden is seen to observe the rape and yet do nothing other than watch, before shouting at the victim for lying around on the floor of the greenhouse. The warden sees the rape as a 'fitting' punishment and tacitly condones it. There is some irony in the fact that homosexuality is treated sympathetically in a film made at a time when it was still a criminal offence, and yet is presented unsympathetically in a film from a more 'enlightened' era.

Scum also highlights the differing representations of race within the criminal fraternity – though at this time the differences most likely mirror those in wider society at the time. A more significant set of racial representations were put forward in *Sapphire* (Artna Films 1959, Director: Basil Dearden), where investigations into the death of a young black woman revealed the racial tensions and bigotry that lay beneath the surface of 1950s Britain. This is a bold film that deals with the colour bar and prevailing attitudes of the time (only a year after the Notting Hill race riots). While in places offering racial caricatures, Dearden manages to project the subtle differences between white criminals and black criminals, as well as between different races in the general population.

There have been few instances where a non-white race has taken centre stage in the crime genre, and even recently there have been noticeably fewer films concerning crime within ethnic communities, or carried out by non-white protagonists. *Bullet Boy* is, of course an exception that in its strength of narrative and construction, proves that the representations, while interesting, are by no means the most significant feature of this film. *Bullet Boy* has however reclaimed the crime film from the upmarket gangster focus to one where there is a greater sense of realism and of potential to reflect issues that people are encountering. It has re-democratized the crime film, returning it to its roots in a broadly working-class community rather than in an abstract elite.

References and Further Reading

Chibnall, S. and Murphy, R. (eds) (1999) *British Crime Cinema*, Routledge, London

Clay, A. (2003) 'The British Crime Film', PhD thesis, De Montfort University

Hardy, P. (ed.) (1997) *The BFI Companion to Crime*, Continuum, London

Useful Website

ScreenOnline Film Genres – Social Problem Films http://www.screenonline. org.uk/film/id/1074067/index.html

18 WESTERNS

This chapter deals with:

■ the general characteristics and features of westerns
■ possible approaches to two films in the western tradition, one made in 1955 and the other in 1976

If you wish to study film noir, rather than westerns, then there is an additional full chapter on US Film Noir that can be found in the Resources section of our companion website at http://routledge.tandf.co.uk/textbooks/9780415454339/resources.asp

INFORMATION BOX

This chapter will be directly relevant to your work on FM2: British and American Film – Section C: US Film for the WJEC's AS level in Film Studies.

Films mentioned

As you work your way through this chapter you will need to watch at least the first two of these films in full and short sequences from the other two:

- *The Outlaw Josey Wales* (Eastwood, 1976),
- *Bad Day At Black Rock* (Sturges, 1955),
- *Forty Guns* (Fuller, 1957),
- *The Ballad of Little Jo* (Greenwald, 1993)

Further westerns are mentioned throughout the chapter and it would be useful to have access to at least short clips from some of these films.

Westerns and history

The position of the western as a key Hollywood genre reflects the importance of the concept of 'the West' in both the actual history of the United States and in the multifaceted legendary version of that history. When the states of the eastern seaboard had established their independence from Britain following the War of Independence (1775–1782) and began to look for their own new lands to colonize, there was no need to venture overseas; inland, to the west, beyond the Appalachians, there were vast tracts of rugged, open space. By around 1820 most of the land as far as the line of the Mississippi had been occupied and states established. By about 1860 California and Oregon had been established as states on the west coast and there was essentially only the mid-west to fill in on the map in order to create a country that spanned the continent. The key focus for the western is the period that saw the establishment of the mid-west states – around 1860 through to the end of the century. It is this period in the formation of the USA which has been continually assessed and reassessed, mythologized and re-mythologized in the western to the point where it has become a central part of not only how Americans view themselves but also how the rest of the world views America.

It was, predominantly, British, Scandinavian and German immigrants who initially moved west, as more and more immigrants arrived in the east from across the Atlantic. By 1869 the transcontinental railroad was complete and a country that spans four time zones was on the verge of being linked up by networks of mechanization and communication. The people who moved west brought with them their own various European cultures and traditions; but there were also more marginal cultural strands developing out of the African, Asian and Hispanic traditions, to say nothing of an older in-place tradition embodied in a variety of Native American cultures. Irish 'navvies' and Chinese 'coolies' worked on the railways, Mexicans already lived in areas to the South, and from the end of the Civil War, African Americans were nominally freed from slavery and able to move out of and away from the deep South. The history of the period, therefore, involves a huge inland migratory expansion and massive influxes of ethnic groups into a dynamic multicultural mix. Westerns are one of the ways popular culture has interpreted the resulting social complexities (and conflicts) in order to give a coherent sense of 'the American past'. In the process westerns have attempted to establish shared values that are seen as being not only at the heart of this created American past but also equally relevant to the present.

Immigration, of course, does not stop around the end of the nineteenth century; there is a continually evolving society for which the western is attempting to interpret this relatively recent past. The Declaration of Independence famously declared that 'all men are born equal', and partly as a result of this the United States attracted displaced people from all over the world (particularly during the late 1800s and early 1900s). English, Scottish, Welsh, Irish, Italians, Germans, Scandinavians, Poles, Russians and others from Europe flooded into Ellis Island in the late 1800s and early 1900s. Although they were not always made as welcome as the presence of the Statue of Liberty overseeing their entry might have suggested, between 1815 and 1920 more than 35 million immigrants are estimated to have arrived in the United States. The country is seen as a land of opportunity, is often called 'The Land of the Free', and has become known as an ethnic 'melting-pot'.

> **Americans' toleration of diversity has always been easier in principle than in practice. A multiracial and multicultural society built on immigration, both involuntary and voluntary, the United States has nonetheless agonized at various stages about whom it should permit to enter, reside and naturalize.**

(King 2000: 1)

Even as the West is still being won, 'westerns' are being written and the genre is playing its role in shaping people's perspectives. These are entertaining adventure stories written in an easily accessible style, but they are also popular histories mytholigizing the heroic pioneering spirit involved in establishing this recently created country. And when the cinema begins, then the entertainment and the legends are brought to an even wider popular audience.

INFORMATION BOX

If you are a man, the West has also been seen as a place of escape and replenishment where you go to find yourself and true values. In the short story 'Indian Country', written by Dorothy M. Johnson in the 1950s, the central character has a good life in the East but is discontented:

> **He wanted to live among his equals – people who were no better than he and no worse either.**

And so, he journeys into the interior where he is captured by Crow Indians and learns what it is 'to have no status at all'. When, after much hardship, he eventually makes it back to the East, we are told:

> **He did not find it necessary either to apologize or to boast, because he was the equal of any man on earth.**

(There is also a film version of this story – A Man Called Horse (Silverstein, 1970).)

Stylistic features

The iconography of westerns (e.g. certain types of handguns and rifles, horses, saddles, bedrolls, stetsons) are easily recognizable, but it is often the unexpected departures from the norm, such as the use of a whaling harpoon as a weapon in the final shoot-out in Terror in a Texas Town (Lewis, 1958), that are most interesting. Look out for the ways in which the representations used are often highly stereotypical but also how normal expectations can be challenged as in the strong central female character Jessica Drummond (Barbara Stanwyck) in Forty Guns (Fuller, 1957) and how in more recent times the central role in westerns can be taken over more fully by women, as in Thelma and Louise (Scott, 1991) and The Ballad of Little Jo (Greenwald, 1993).

In narrative terms, western-style scenarios may be used in a science fiction film such as Star Wars (Lucas, 1977), or in contemporary dramas set in non-western locations such as On the Waterfront (Kazan, 1954) which takes place in the New Jersey docklands, or in contemporary 'westerns' such as Bad Day at Black Rock or Thelma and Louise.

The western has proved a highly flexible genre able to support notions of patriotism in a politically right-wing sense, as in The Alamo (Wayne, 1960) or to comment on the climate of fear created by the right-wing, as in High Noon (Zinnemann, 1952). It has been able to be used very consciously to give a crystallized version of American history, as in The Man Who Shot Liberty Valance (Ford, 1962) or consciously to try to challenge and potentially rewrite a version of history, as in Brokeback Mountain (Lee, 2005).

Figure 18.1
*Brokeback
Mountain* (2005)

ACTIVITY

■ How should westerns be defined? Should we just be looking at films that deal with a certain period in American history and are set within a certain fairly well-defined mid-west region? Or should we be prepared to consider films, such as *Bad Day At Black Rock*, that are set within later periods but follow recognizable western narrative patterns and integrate recognizable western iconography? Should we consider films such as *Star Wars* that although they may be categorized differently in terms of iconography seem to follow recognizably western narrative trajectories? What role and place within our discussions should be occupied by films such as *Thelma and Louise*, *The Ballad of Little Jo* and *Brokeback Mountain* that in many ways would seem to be westerns but challenge traditional expectations of gender and sexuality within the genre?

■ Watch the openings to a range of films so far mentioned and jot down your initial thoughts on these questions. If possible, discuss your thoughts with others, but only after you've attempted to carefully consider your own position on these issues.

The Civil War as a key reference point

You will often find there are references to the Civil War in westerns. This was a cataclysmic event in American history, dividing the country but also splitting families and friends into one camp or the other. Often, like Ethan Edwards (John Wayne) in *The Searchers* (Ford, 1956), the reference will be to a white man from the South who never formally surrendered. The bullying North in this interpretation has been resisted in their attempt to impose their way of life on others. (The fact that the Southern way of life depended upon enslaving millions of African Americans often seems to be conveniently overlooked.)

The first half of the nineteenth century was a period of economic boom in the USA. In the north-east of the country there was an industrial revolution and in the South an increase in cotton production that emphasized the importance of slavery. In the 1820s the cotton crop doubled and in the 1830s it doubled again in response to increased world consumption. By 1860 cotton represented two-thirds of the total value of US exports. The importation of slaves had been officially abolished in 1808, but the slave population in the South had increased from one million in 1800 to four million by 1860. In 1860 Abraham Lincoln, who the South feared was in favour of the abolition of slavery, became President. By 1861 Southern states had seceded from the Union and formed the Confederate States of America. The North rejected the secession of these states and the Civil War followed.

The North had all the advantages: twice the population (21 million to nine million), 70 per cent of the railways, and more than 90 per cent of the factories. What ensued was a bloody war in which huge numbers were either killed or maimed for life; at the Battle of Gettysberg, for example, more than 50,000 died or were wounded. The South fought a defensive war on its own territory but was eventually broken by General William Sherman's capture of Atlanta in 1864. The following year the South surrendered and shortly afterwards Lincoln was assassinated. It is estimated that 360,000 men from the Union forces died and 260,000 Confederate troops (20 per cent of the white male population in the South).

INFORMATION BOX

Beware of thinking that controversy never attached to 'old' films. While not strictly a western, *The Birth of a Nation* (Griffith, 1915) deals directly with the Civil War, and is often referred to as a classic text in the early development of film language. It was also a highly racist film depicting members of the Ku Klux Klan as heroes and, because of this, cinemas showing it were quite rightly picketed by protesters.

ACTIVITY

- Research the background of John Ford, or any other director of your choice who has been closely linked to the western.
- Prepare a short presentation built around a series of clips from your chosen director's film catalogue that shows what you consider to be key features of this director's use of the genre.
- If possible, present and explain your choice of clips to a group of other students, and allow time for discussion around ways in which your chosen extracts could be considered key features of the genre as a whole, and/or important aspects of this director's particular use of the genre.

Reflecting the period

Classic westerns from the high period of their production, some of which you might like to research for yourself, include:

- *Stagecoach* (Ford, 1939)
- *Duel in the Sun* (Vidor, 1946)
- *Red River* (Hawks, 1948)
- *She Wore a Yellow Ribbon* (Ford, 1949)
- *High Noon* (Zinnemann, 1952)
- *Shane* (Stevens, 1953)
- *The Searchers* (Ford, 1956)

If you have managed to watch any of these films, or clips from these films, you may like to consider whether taken as a whole they seem to you to in any way reflect the nature of the period in which they were made in the United States.

ACTIVITY

- If you have time, watch *Shane*. How does it fit into the picture of the western genre that you're beginning to get? Compile a list of the elements which make it clear to you that this is a western. Compare your list with those arrived at by other people, if possible, and in particular note any ideas they may have that you've missed.

- How is the hero presented? Try to identify particular scenes you believe are critical to an understanding of his character. Analyse the ways in which these scenes are being constructed in order to give the audience a particular understanding of his character.
- Does this film seem to you to in any way reflect the period in which it was made? Is it noticeably different from earlier or later westerns you've seen; and, if so, in what ways?

ACTIVITY

If you haven't got time to watch the whole film, try to at least watch the opening to *High Noon*. Working with others, if possible, find a synopsis of the story and research critical interpretations of the film. Try to find out how critics have suggested the director was deliberately constructing this film as a reflection of American society of the time.

ACTIVITY

- Watch the opening to *High Noon*, or a western of your choice, and make notes on the ways in which this film announces its genre to us.
- You may like to work with others and allocate particular areas such as *mise-en-scène*, cinematography, sound and narrative features to different people to consider. As always try to find plenty of time to discuss your ideas, and ideally have a copy of the film to hand as you are doing this.

More recent examples

As suggested above, in recent decades western-style stories have been used in new ways, perhaps appearing in a science fiction context or using female leads within what has always been a strongly male-focused genre. But there have still been some films that have employed western iconography in what appear on the surface at least to be more traditional ways. These include:

- *Dances With Wolves* (Costner, 1990)
- *Unforgiven* (Eastwood, 1992)

■ *Open Range* (Costner, 2003)
■ *The Proposition* (Hillcoat, 2005)

ACTIVITY

■ If you have time, watch *Unforgiven*. How does it fit into the picture of the western genre that you're beginning to get? Compile a list of the elements which make it clear to you that this is a western.
■ How is the hero presented? Try to identify particular scenes you believe are critical to an understanding of his character. Analyse the ways in which these scenes are being constructed in order to give the audience a particular understanding of his character.
■ Does the film, while still being recognizable as a western, reflect the period in which it was made? Is it noticeably different from any earlier westerns you have seen? If so, in what ways, and does this reflect differences in society? Who are the 'goodies' in this film? Who are the 'baddies'? What role does the sheriff play and how does the audience feel about him?

Approaching westerns

For films in the western mode it is always worth considering:

■ the symbolic role and place of the gun and violence within the narrative;
■ the nature of the locations or settings being used and any potential implications that may attach to this usage;
■ the representation of gender roles, including the often carefully circumscribed role and place of women;
■ the representation of race, in particular the ways in which minority ethnic groups are portrayed (remembering that absence may be as significant as presence);
■ the representation of sexuality (remembering that actors or stars who on the face of it are presented as heterosexual males may be adopted by audiences as gay icons);
■ recurring themes such as revenge, the nature of 'civilization' and the role of heroes, but also the importance of community values;
■ recurring values such as the importance of the family and home, law and order, equality and natural justice.

Case study
THE OUTLAW JOSEY WALES (1976)

(Director: Clint Eastwood. Screenwriters: Forest Carter, Philip Kaufman and Sonia Chernus. Cinematographer: Bruce Surtees. Music: Jerry Fielding. Cast: Clint Eastwood (Josey Wales); Chief Dan George (Lone Watie); Sandra Locke (Laura Lee); Bill McKinney (Terrill); John Vernon (Fletcher).)

Figure 18.2 *The Outlaw Josey Wales* (1976)

In the opening sequence it is quickly established that Josey Wales is a farmer who is working hard to provide for his family. Few words are spoken between husband, son and wife but this only serves to illustrate the tight-knit nature of the family unit. There is a strong sense of a rural idyll but as Josey grapples with the jolting plough this is balanced by a clear presentation of the fact that this is hard work. The long takes, steady camera movements, slow (but purposeful) movements of the actors and the peace and quiet of the surroundings are strongly contrasted with the editing, cinematography, sound and actors' performances in the subsequent

continued

sequence as Josey rushes back with increasing speed towards his homestead and the mayhem created by the 'Redlegs'.

His simple life built around family and the home goes up in flames. The hard-won personal space of home and hearth, such an emblematic focal point in westerns for those who have made it to the West (and a holy grail for those venturing west), is literally and symbolically engulfed in flames. Shortly afterwards the gun, that central emblematic motif of the western, is equally symbolically taken from the ashes and unwrapped by Josey. All that is set up in the western as good (home, family and honest, hard toil) have been destroyed by the brutal intrusion of evil (see the close-up of Terrill's face) into the world. See also how the potential crutch of religion symbolically falls away from beneath Josey in this time of need; to Josey it no longer seems possible that there can be a god. He becomes that traditional western hero, the strong, silent man driven by revenge.

As with many other westerns (e.g. Ford's *The Searchers*) this film is set at the end of the American Civil War (1861–1865), and as with Ethan Edwards in *The Searchers*, so here Josey Wales is the man from the South who doesn't surrender. The violence shown here is the brutality of that particular war, but it is also symbolically the barbarism of all wars. In wars, civilians are murdered, the ideal of the home is destroyed and violent men ('the Redlegs') have an excuse to perpetrate all sorts of merciless acts. The general situation, the potential within man (some men?) for unwarranted violence against innocent family-orientated people, might also be equated to the state of America in the 1970s (and subsequently). One hundred years on from the Civil War, Americans are still killing other Americans, innocent women and children are still being raped and murdered, and all this is still taking place in a country purporting to be based upon Christian values and proclaiming the ideals of family and home. The brutality of one man to another as a theme continues in the film through characters such as the bounty-hunters, the two trappers and the trader.

In contrast with *The Searchers*, the enemies here are not essentially the Native Americans but the European-style 'civilization' of the eastern seaboard. When Josey confronts Ten Bears later in the film notice that with honesty and by pursuing a way of life that does not involve wanton destruction the white man and the Indian can live together ('Governments don't live together – people do,' says Josey/Eastwood. 'It is possible to live together without butchering each other.') And the old Cherokee Indian is given the chance to almost make a speech about Native American history (see what you can find out about the 'Trail of Tears' that he mentions). Notice as well the way he reintroduces this notion of 'civilized': 'They called us the civilized tribes.' The whole film might be said to question the idea of what it is to be civilized, and to examine the way in which those who call themselves civilized are often quite the reverse.

Josey Wales attracts to him the weak and dispossessed of society, and together they journey to a utopian Promised Land where all people can live in peace; but notice, they have to be strong to do this and they have to be prepared to fight back. 'If you lose your head and give up then you neither live nor win, that's just the way it is,' says Josey. Symbolically, Josey is taken back into civilization in the music and dance scene after making peace with Ten Bears. He is able to touch a woman again (i.e. he is prepared not only to show gentleness and love, but also to make himself vulnerable). However, the past doesn't go away, and notice that Josey can't ride away from it, but rather it has to be faced.

ACTIVITY

- Watch the opening sequence up until the point where Josey passes out, noting as many images and sounds as possible.
- Record your impressions, making sure to try to decide what this opening makes you think the film will be about, and justifying your ideas by reference to the images and sounds encountered.
- If possible, discuss your ideas with a group of others. To what extent did you agree with each other's assessments?

ACTIVITY

How is the hero in *The Outlaw Josey Wales* presented? Try to identify particular scenes you believe are critical to an understanding of his character. Analyse the ways in which these scenes are being constructed in order to give the audience a particular understanding of his character. What does the title of the film suggest and in what ways would you say it is appropriate for the film?

ACTIVITY

How would you describe the narrative structure employed in this film? You may like to begin by constructing a flow chart of the events in the film. In addition to noting what happens and when, you should also pay attention to the types of characters who emerge at various points and how they relate to others (in particular to Josey). As always, working with others can enable you to usefully share ideas.

ACTIVITY

- After you have watched the whole film and attempted various approaches to analysis, return to the opening sequence.
- How has your reading of this section of the film changed or developed?
- What images and sounds seem significant now in ways that they did not to begin with?

ACTIVITY

1   Analyse a sequence (no more than ten minutes) of your own choice from this film in terms of its genre and narrative structure.
2   Make notes on your chosen sequence and then if possible discuss your ideas with somebody else, or several others, who are working on the same exercise.
3   Write an analysis (1,000–1,500 words) of the ways in which genre and narrative structure create meaning and generate audience response in your chosen sequence. Give your piece a title in the form of a question:

How do genre and narrative structure create meaning and generate audience response in the *(name or timing of scene)* scene in *The Outlaw Josey Wales*?

Case study
BAD DAY AT BLACK ROCK (1955)

(Director: John Sturges. Screenwriters: Howard Breslin, Don McGuire and Millard Kaufman. Cinematographer: William Mellor. Music: Andre Previn. Cast: Spencer Tracey (John J. Macreedy); Robert Ryan (Reno Smith); Anne Francis (Liz Wirth); Lee Marvin (Hector David); Dean Jagger (Sheriff Tim Horn); Walter Brennan (Doc T. R. Velie); John Ericson (Pete Wirth); Ernest Borgnine (Coley Trimble).)

Figure 18.3 *Bad Day At Black Rock* (1955)

Despite the fact that *Bad Day At Black Rock* is set at the end of the Second World War in 1945, it follows the narrative pattern of a typical western. A stranger arrives in a remote desert town. He is the strong, silent type and, against all the odds following a final shoot-out, he defeats the 'baddies' and restores law and order: these are the conventional elements, or paradigms, to be found in a particular strand of western. *Black Rock* has the stereotypical useless, drunken sheriff who was once a good man but is no longer able to cope and has lost his way in the face of encroaching, bullying evil. The town also has the bumbling town doctor, or 'doc', who is defiant but relatively weak physically and therefore ineffective in the face of evil (somewhat in the mode of 'Doc' Boone in Ford's *Stagecoach*). This is not a town as in *High Noon* where the 'baddies' are about to arrive and are threatening to take over: this is a town in which the 'gorillas', as Macreedy calls them, have already taken over. But just as in *High Noon*, *Terror in a Texas Town* and *Forty Guns*, the townsfolk have clearly been too scared to stand up to the 'baddies'. They have allowed their basic, ordinary, common human decency to be pushed aside by bullies. In *High Noon*, Gary Cooper has to stand alone against the villains. In *The Man Who Shot Liberty Valance*, John Wayne has to kill the embodiment of evil (and threat to democracy), the ironically named Liberty Valance, in order that the gentler 'hero' James Stewart (Ransom Stoddard) is able to restore democratic values in the town. Here, Spencer Tracey as Macreedy has to fulfil the same role before he rides out of town (this time on a train) and allows the community to take over again with a restored sense of self-worth. The difference is that although other westerns are more safely set in the past where they are able to address current issues without appearing to do so, *Bad Day At Black Rock* is set just ten years after the Second World War and deals directly with prejudices (against Japanese Americans, but by extension other ethnic minorities) that were very much still part and parcel of American life.

In genre terms, is this a western? In order to answer this we have to remember that genre is a flexible term. The woman, Liz Wirth, seems to introduce an element of film noir, stereotypically portraying the deceptive beauty of women and their supposed attraction to (and association with) evil. The 'gorillas' however are traditional western 'baddies': Hector wears the usual western stetson and has the cowboy gait, Coley is the stereotypical cowhand with more muscle than brainpower, and their leader, Reno, has the quiet, confident self-assurance of a 'Liberty Valance'. What Reno embodies above all else is prejudice; but the film's analysis is politically astute. What the prejudice is built upon is a willingness to scapegoat anyone who may be seen as an 'outsider' rather than facing up to the real issues.

Thematically, this film may be seen as a thorough examination of prejudice (prejudice against foreigners, but also against the disabled). This is a sensitive subject to be dealing with in post-war America where up to 100,000 Japanese Americans had been interned in barbed-wire camps during the war (and where for much of the country an apartheid-style system is in operation against African Americans). The film is also about the importance of ordinary people speaking out in a town (or a democracy) if you are not to end up with the situation in *Black Rock* described by Macreedy when he says, 'The rule of law has left here and the gorillas have taken over.' You will see how this relates to traditional western concerns regarding the importance of law and order and to ideas of the nature of civilization. You may also be interested to consider how this could be related to the rise of Hitler and the Nazis in Germany in the 1930s where the rule of 'gorillas' was built on using another ethnic group as scapegoats, the Jews.

In narrative terms our two central characters Macreedy and Reno Smith clearly embody notions of good and evil. Macreedy is clearly on a quest/search for the truth and, as is so often the case, that search involves an inner psychological/spiritual process as well as a physical outer process. Macreedy has to find himself again after the war as so many returning Americans (physically and emotionally scarred by the war) had to. Does he become in this sense all Americans searching for renewal after the war? Certainly the film in very contentious terms may be seen to be suggesting that you not only have to deal with fascism abroad but also in your own country.

INFORMATION BOX i

In 1954 the US Supreme Court ruled that the segregation of black and white children in schools was unconstitutional. And around this period the black civil rights movement began to emerge. African Americans in Montgomery, Alabama started to boycott segregated buses as early as 1955.

In 1958 with tension growing over attempts to keep schools in the South segregated, Governor Orval Faubus of Arkansas defied the Supreme Court by closing schools in **Little Rock** and reopening them as private schools.

(If you have the chance to study US musicals an interesting reference to this is made in South Pacific (Logan, 1958). Nellie, a young un-sophisticated small-town American girl from Little Rock, falls in love with Emile, an older and more cultured European, who teaches her about the nature of prejudice.)

ACTIVITY

- How is the hero in *Bad Day At Black Rock* presented? Try to identify particular scenes you believe are critical to an understanding of his character. Analyse the ways in which these scenes are being constructed in order to give the audience a particular understanding of his character.
- Draw a diagram using lines to show Macreedy's relationships with other characters in the film. Macreedy's name should be at the centre of your piece of paper but the lines could be full, dotted, dashed, in waves or in various colours according to your choice. Try to place a short, sharp summation of the relationship alongside each line.
- Add more information to your diagram by showing linkages between other characters. Follow the same approach as above.
- What does the title of the film suggest and in what ways would you say it was appropriate for the film? Whose 'bad day'? Why is it a 'bad day'? Why the name 'Black Rock'?

ACTIVITY

How would you describe the narrative structure employed in this film? You may like to begin by constructing a flow chart of the events in the film. In addition to noting what happens and when, you should also pay attention to the types of characters who emerge at various points and how they relate to others (in particular to Macreedy).

(As always, working with others can enable you to usefully share ideas.)

ACTIVITY

- Working with a group of other people, try to replicate a few scenes of your own choice from *Bad Day At Black Rock* in which the positioning of actors within the framed space seems to you to be interesting in some way. Pay particular attention to the ways in which some characters are orientated towards or away from others, but also to the ways in which characters are orientated towards or away from the camera.

- ■ Experiment with changing the set-ups in order to see if this potentially alters the meanings being conveyed to the audience and, if so, in what ways.
- ■ You may like to film retakes of your chosen scenes with altered set-ups of the actors and then to play these to other people in order to gauge their responses to the changes.

ACTIVITY

- ■ How would you read the one female character in *Bad Day At Black Rock*? Is she the dangerous entrapping femme fatale of film noir whom it is deadly to know, or is she the 'good bad-girl' of film noir (somebody who has been attracted to evil but has been caught up in it without being fully aware of what is taking place and now wants to find a way out), or would you classify her in some other way? What evidence (specific scenes) would you refer to in order to support your ideas?
- ■ What reasons would you put forward for there only being one female character?
- ■ How do you believe female audience members would position themselves in relation to this film? Would they identify with any particular characters?
- ■ If possible, make sure you compare your ideas with those of other people.

ACTIVITY

1 Analyse a sequence (no more than ten minutes) of your own choice from this film in terms of its genre and narrative structure.

continued

2   Make notes on your chosen sequence and then, if possible, discuss your ideas with somebody else, or several others, who are working on the same exercise.

3   Write an analysis (1,000–1,500 words) of the ways in which genre and narrative structure create meaning and generate audience response in your chosen sequence. Give your piece a title in the form of a question:

How do genre and narrative structure create meaning and generate audience response in the *(name or timing of scene)* scene in *Bad Day At Black Rock*?

Similarities and differences

In what ways are *The Outlaw Josey Wales* and *Bad Day At Black Rock* similar and in what ways are they different? To what extent could both Josey Wales and Macreedy be seen to be on a journey? To what extent could they both be seen to be confronted by ever more serious challenges on that journey? Is there anything that happens to Macreedy that is comparable to the initial traumatic attack on Josey's family and home? Is Macreedy setting out for revenge? What are their goals and how similar (or dissimilar) are they? To what extent do they have helpers as heroes and to what extent are they isolated and alone? Are any similarities between them merely superficial, or would you say there are important links between their positions, roles and functions within their respective narratives?

What other similarities in characters or character relationships within the two films would you point to as being interesting in some way? Which character would occupy the same sort of role in *The Outlaw Josey Wales* as Reno in *Bad Day At Black Rock*, for instance, and what would be the similarities and differences between them? Are the 'villains' handled in different ways, or investigated in different ways, in the two films?

If we were to consider the narrative structure what similarities and differences would we note between the two films? How would the resolution phases compare, for example? To what other similarities or differences in narrative structure would you draw attention? Thematically, both films are obviously again, as so often, fundamentally about the struggle between good and evil. What other themes would seem to run across both films? Are there themes that may only be found in one or the other of the films?

Women and the western

One of the areas of representation you have been asked to consider at various points in this chapter has been that of the roles given to women within this genre. In order to help you to reflect further on this, consider the opening to *The Ballad of Little Jo*, up to the point where the central character transforms her appearance into that of a man and rides into town astride a horse. See how western iconography attaching to dress and key objects/props is used to make a statement about not only the place of women in nineteenth-century America but also the roles available to women in westerns throughout the twentieth century. US society has been (and is) male-dominated: Hollywood has been (and is) male-dominated. Here is a western that takes a genre within which women have been continually marginalized and placed in subservient positions, and transforms it by placing a woman centre stage. Or, is the way in which this is achieved only reinforcing male dominance by suggesting that the only way women can achieve a recognized place within this society (and this genre?) is by changing gender?

ACTIVITY

- Watch the opening and ending to Sam Fuller's *Forty Guns*. Compare and contrast the role, place and function of the central female character in the exposition and resolution phases. In doing this you should explore as many facets of film construction as possible – location, costume and props, performance and movement, cinematography, editing, sound.
- Watch the opening and ending to Ridley Scott's *Thelma and Louise*. Compare and contrast the role, place and function of the central female characters in the exposition and resolution phases. In doing this you should explore as many facets of film construction as possible – location, costume and props, performance and movement, cinematography, editing, sound.
- Compare and contrast these two films in terms of their openings and endings.

References and Further Reading

Cameron, I. and Pye, D. (eds) (1996) *The Movie Book of The Western*, Studio Vista, London

King, D. (2000) *Making Americans: Immigration, Race, and the Origins of the Diverse Democracy*, Harvard University Press, Cambridge, MA

GLOSSARY

Agents Not only actors but also directors, screenwriters, producers, cinematographers and others involved in commercial filmmaking have agents. The system under which these people would have been kept on full-time contracts to the studios came to an end during the 1950s, and from this point agents became especially important within the industry as they had the power to continually renegotiate one-off film deals for those on their books.

The role of agents representing top stars is particularly powerful. If as a studio you believe it is the stars who really sell films you will be prepared to pay a large percentage of your budget to secure the services of the star you believe will best embody the image required for your film.

'Blind buying' This means you have to take the films on offer without having a chance to first view them to see if you want them or not.

'Block booking' This means you have to agree to take all of the films produced by a studio in a year including the lesser films in order to get the major productions.

British Isles A geographical definition and includes Great Britain, Ireland, Orkney, Shetlands, Inner and Outer Hebrides, Isle of Wight, Isle of Man, Lundy and the Channel Islands.

British New Wave A movement of well-educated, leftist filmmakers largely from a northern England, working-class background, that used 'realism' to construct stories of working-class lives ('kitchen sink dramas'). Originally working on short films and documentaries as part of their 'free cinema' concept they graduated to feature film production establishing a north of England production base to compete with what they saw as a London-focused and London-centred industry. They included filmmakers Lindsay Anderson, Karel Reisz and Tony Richardson.

Camerawork This clearly and quite simply refers to the work done with the camera in the making of a film. However, the possibilities open to the cinematographer are anything but simple. Fundamentally, the camera can be positioned at any distance from the subject being filmed and at any angle to that subject. It can be turned left or right to follow a subject within a horizontal plane, or tilted up or down to follow the same subject in a vertical plane. It can also be moved at any speed towards, away from or around the subject, and this movement can be as smooth or as shaky as the filmmakers decide. In addition, lenses can be used to give the appearance of movement towards or away from the subject at any speed, or to make the image of the subject either sharper or more indistinct, or even to alter the appearance of the subject in the style of a fairground 'hall of mirrors'.

The only limitation on the fluidity and mobility of the camerawork in any film is the availability of the necessary technology to enable the desired effect to be achieved; and, in general terms, camera and lens technology has developed throughout film history in such a way as to permit increasingly complex camerawork. So, for instance, new lightweight cameras (and sound recording gear) in the 1950s made it easier to take the equipment out on location.

However, what you will find if you get the chance to watch some clips from old silent films is that even from very early in film history cinematographers were devising imaginative ways of getting moving shots with these rather large, heavy wooden cameras. So, yes, available technology must to some extent impose limitations upon what can be achieved, but often it is the creativity with which available technology is used that is of most interest.

Cause and effect This refers to the way in which mainstream films are moved forward by one scene or event having been caused by an earlier one and in turn giving rise to an effect which is seen in a subsequent scene or event. What this means is that everything we see has been motivated by something we have seen earlier and in turn motivates something we see further on in the film.

Chronology The ordering of a series of events in time sequence. This is the simplest way of setting out a story and is important in films such as *Bloody Sunday* (Greengrass, 2002) (see FM2 British Film: Identity Study), involving the shooting of people taking part in a civil rights demonstration in Northern Ireland in 1972, where the development of events in sequence over a set period of time is a vital part of the whole creative enterprise.

Colour This can be used in highly artificial ways for particular expressive purposes as in the make-up employed by the changed Jude in *The Crying Game*, for instance (where it would seem to perhaps suggest the danger of a femme fatale), or it can be employed in an effort to achieve naturalism by re-creating the colours of the real world.

Commercial process A commercial process is one that is focused upon achieving a financial return, in other words, making a profit.

Contrapuntal sound This is a great technique where the sound is not directly related to the image, but when placed together an additional meaning (or depth of meaning) is created. Thus the sound of a boxing match playing on a television in shot becomes more significant when the person watching the match walks into another room and begins beating an elderly person in there. The sound carried across from the television to the room where the beating is taking place is in counterpoint to the image of the abuse, yet serves to make a bigger statement about violence in general. It may be that a mix of contrapuntal sound and the diegetic sound of the beating may heighten this statement further.

Costume and props This refers to items of clothing being worn by characters and objects seen within any given setting. At its simplest, costume clearly acts as a type of uniform, linking a character to a particular group and often to a rank or position within that group. But costume can also 'announce' a character, giving an insight into what this person is supposed to be like; for instance, shy or flamboyant. At their simplest, props work to give an authentic sense of place, but can also be used in more complex ways to suggest important characteristics of particular individuals or even key themes for the whole film.

Cultural identity This can refer to personal identity chosen for yourself or an identity ascribed to you by others. You might choose to describe yourself as 'British Pakistani' showing your identification with what you feel to be an intertwined cultural background, while others might identify you as 'Asian'. However, notice this will in fact only be part of your cultural identity, the racial/national identity part. Your cultural identity will also be formed from your categorization within other cultural spheres such as class, gender and age. So, for example, the key foci of your cultural identity might be young, male, middle-class, Christian, British Pakistani.

Devolution The transfer of power from the British government to individual countries. The Scottish government and the Welsh Assembly legislate on a range of areas which have been devolved from the UK government. These include health, education, asylum and immigration, and the justice system (Scotland only). The Scottish National Party and Plaid Cymru are further campaigning for independence for their nations.

Diegetic sound Diegetic sound is the sound that is heard in the fictional world, the sound that the characters in that world can hear. Most diegetic sound is not recorded 'on location' but is fabricated and 'dubbed' on to the film by sound designers and 'foley artists' (people who generate sound effects such as cutting into a cabbage to make the sound of someone being guillotined).

DVD Digital Versatile Disc, the system that has now almost replaced VHS video. Discs can hold much more information than videotapes (providing the possibility for all sorts of 'extras' to be included alongside the main film) and offer a higher quality image.

Expectations The set of ideas each of us brings with us when we watch any film. These may be expectations to do with story structure, character development, or themes we anticipate will be dealt with; and they will be based upon our previous experience of these things.

Exposition This is the opening to a film, which can often be *in medioreum* ('in the middle of things'). It sets up expectations and possibilities, and introduces key characters, locations and ideas.

Genre This term has at least a double usage here. It can be used to denote different general types of storytelling extending across a range of different media such as fairy-tales, plays and TV soaps; so, simply different types of storytelling. But it can also be used to refer to the classification of films into types such as horror, romantic comedy, thriller or science fiction.

Globalization A perceived economic trend towards the whole world becoming a single market so that major multinational corporations are increasingly able to control trade on a global scale.

Great Britain The collective name for the three countries of England, Scotland and Wales.

'Green-lit' This is a jargon term used within the film industry for obtaining the 'go-ahead' for a film project to move from being a concept to actually starting production.

Hollywood As early as the 1910s the US film industry began to shift its base from the East Coast to what was essentially a place in the Californian desert, a rural area on the edge of Los Angeles. The name 'Hollywood' has, of course, become a term signifying something much more than simply a place in California.

Iconography This simply refers to characteristic features of a genre, the things you expect to see and sounds you expect to hear that taken together collectively tell you the type of film, or genre, you are watching.

As with all other film terms, knowing the name and what it means may be useful but it is not essential; it is recognizing the characteristic features that are signalling to you that this is a specific genre and being able to identify them at work within particular scenes within particular films that are important.

Identity The concept of identity refers to the way that different groups (family, friends, schools, government) in society see us and the way in which we see ourselves. These two views are likely to be different, even conflicting. The factors affecting our identity include gender, race, religion, class, sexuality and nationality which are interlinked and have become more and more complicated. Some people may wish to identify themselves as gay; for others to do so may suggest discrimination or prejudice.

The growth in identity politics such as gay rights and feminism has indicated a move away from political parties to single-issue politics in society.

Ideology A person's or a society's set of beliefs and values, or overall way of looking at the world. The Western world in general is said to be built upon a belief in capitalism, or the idea that what is best for society, or what brings the greatest benefits to a society, is for business to be given free rein to operate without restrictions in an open, competitive market.

Industrial process An industrial process is one that is involved in the manufacture of goods that are being made for sale.

Lighting This refers to the various ways in which the light whether in the studio or on location is controlled and manipulated in order to achieve the 'look' desired for a particular shot or scene.

Marketing This refers to the total package of strategies used to try to promote and sell a film. Large distribution companies in charge of marketing will employ researchers to investigate the market for any particular film and enable them to keep abreast of shifting trends in consumer practices. They will also use focus groups (or members of the public) from the supposed target market to view and comment upon the film at various stages with the idea of altering the script if necessary. Such early showings of the film behind closed doors are known as test screenings.

All of this will occur before those elements more usually associated with marketing, the screening of cinema trailers, the launching of a press campaign and the instigation of a poster campaign, come into play. Although, of course, the planning for each of these strands involving the development of a clear timetable for each stage of the marketing process will be underway even as the film is being shot.

Messages and values Films can be seen in some sense to embody certain messages that they are working to communicate to the audience. They can also be seen to be attempting to advance certain values while questioning others.

La Haine (Kassovitz, 1995) has been attacked as a film that has a message that is anti-police: whether this is true or not would depend upon how we interpreted characters and scenes within the film and how we understood the filmmakers to be using film construction techniques to emphasize and elevate certain perspectives above others.

Metanarratives Essentially, these are overarching explanations of how things are in the world. The supporters of any metanarrative claim that their 'story' of the world is able to coherently sum up the whole essence of human society and endeavour providing total knowledge and understanding. Metanarratives are sometimes known as grand narratives.

'The Method' In cinema the most influential style of acting. This technique demands that the actor identifies very strongly with the motivation and personality of the character in order to create a realist performance. This approach was based on the work of Stanislavski (a Russian actor and theatre director) and was particularly associated with Hollywood stars in the 1950s such as Marlon Brando and James Dean, and in the 1970s with Robert de Niro and Al Pacino. In British cinema the Method influenced a new style of theatre and film acting associated with social realism. This approach broke with the Shakespearean acting style which had dominated in Britain for so long. The new style was particularly evident in the emphasis on working-class, regional roles and a physical masculinity which had rarely been represented before on screen.

Mise-en-scène This is a term that is borrowed from the theatre and really refers to staging, or 'putting on stage'. It sometimes helps to think of the elements that you can see in the staging of a play: a particular location will be suggested on the stage, characters will be dressed in particular ways, particular objects will be carried by characters or will be prominently placed on the stage, and the actors will be directed to move or perform in particular ways. These theatrical elements are the sub-section parts of the cinematic term; and this effectively reminds us of the way in which the theatre is a key element of film's cultural and artistic origins.

Moral panic A term introduced by Stanley Cohen in *Folk Devils and Moral Panics* (1972) to describe the reaction of society as expressed in the media to some perceived threat to the social norm.

Narrative This term is really quite simply used as another term for 'story'. But it can also be seen (perhaps more correctly) as a more technical term relating to attempts to theorize the principles by which stories are structured. Some theorists, for example, have suggested that all stories have 'deep-seated' underpinning common narrative structures.

National cinema Seen by the wartime British government as an essential tool for maintaining morale and promoting 'authorized' messages about Britain to the rest of the world (particularly America, but also to 'the enemy'). All films made in the Second World War period (1939 to 1945) had to be approved by the Ministry of Information, a government department established to oversee the messages and values contained within them and to ensure that they were working in the nation's best interests.

National identity A sense of national identity seems to depend upon some shared stock of images, ideas, norms and values, stories and traditions. Nations might be described as imagined communities or communities that exist in the individual (and the collective?) imagination within the physical borders of a nation-state. This affects the way we see both ourselves and others classified as existing outside the 'in-group'. Yet, national identity does not exist in some singular, uncontested form. Rather it is a site of struggle constantly undergoing a process of reaffirmation or redefinition.

Non-diegetic sound This is the sound that is outside the fictional world, and that characters in the fictional world cannot hear. This would include overlays of soundtrack music and any voiceover narration.

Oligopoly Term used to describe the situation in which a small group of companies exerts powerful almost exclusive control over the business being done within any particular industry.

Paradigm The term used to describe the range of choices available at any given moment of film construction. This covers a huge area, everything from which actor from the paradigm of possible actors should be chosen to play a given role, to which hat (from the paradigm ranging from no hat to top hat to deerstalker) a character should wear at any given point in a film.

It is a useful term for us for one reason only and that is it reminds us that at all times choices are being made in the construction of films and it is our job to try to decide why those choices might have been made.

Parallel editing This refers to moving back and forth between two or more narrative lines of action supposedly occurring at the same time.

Performance and movement This refers to the acting that is taking place but the phrase also helps to define a little more clearly what it is we should be looking for: there is a performance going on and essentially it revolves around movement. These movements can range from the miniscule to the expansive, and can involve the whole body or the smallest parts of the body. Everything is included from slow movements of the eye to sudden running and jumping, and each can be 'read' in some way (or several possible ways).

Pleasure Films clearly give us pleasure in a range of ways, otherwise we would not watch them, and yet studying academic subjects is somehow often seen to be at odds with the idea of pleasure. However, since pleasure is the thing that beyond all else stimulates our initial interest in films we should not dismiss it out of hand. In fact, the idea of exactly how films provide us with pleasure will be a key approach to film for us.

The way in which film gives pleasure is most apparent when we consider not just audiences in general but our own personal response to films and yet it is so often neglected by those of us who wish to study film. Maybe this is because the concept of pleasure does not seem to sit well in relation to the idea of study. Or perhaps this neglect of the pleasure principle is to do with a difficulty in deciding how to study such a seemingly vague notion.

However we view all of this, the concept is clearly important not only in relation to narrative structure but also in relation to the way in which human beings seem to be able to respond to the sheer aesthetic joy of colour, movement, light, shape and size and in particular changing colour, movement, light, shape and size.

The best way to think about the ways in which films create pleasure for an audience is to analyse our own enjoyment of films. Pleasure could be provided by (among other things) an exciting or romantic narrative, the escapism of identifying with characters unlike ourselves or by the visual pleasure provided by the big screen. Film Studies academics have spent a long time trying to explain the different pleasures experienced by film spectators, particularly the enjoyment of aspects of film which do not immediately seem pleasurable such as watching horror films.

Plot Provides the explanation for the way that events unfold in the story; this may be through character motivation, for example.

Poster campaign A marketing strategy involving the use of a prominently displayed series of posters to promote a film. Each poster will be carefully put together to present what is seen to be a desirable image to be associated with the film and will be strategically placed in the press and positioned on hoardings in such a way as to attempt to catch the eye of the film's target audience. The aim will be to present the public with a clearly defined notion of exactly what is special or particular about this film. This is sometimes referred to as the film's 'unique selling point' (USP).

Psychoanalysis Developed by Sigmund Freud, psychoanalysis is the attempt to explain individual human behaviour in terms of the conflict between conscious and unconscious desires. This is done through a long-term process of analysis – or therapy – between a doctor and patient. (This process has also formed the basis for a wide range of films – serious and comic.)

Reading This is a fundamentally important term in our whole approach to Film Studies. 'Reading' immediately suggests a depth of investigation and an intensity of focus that 'watching films' simply does not convey.

Release pattern This is the part of the marketing strategy that determines the number of prints of the film that are to be initially put out to cinemas, which cinemas are to receive the film to begin with, and then how that initial release of the film is to be expanded and built upon.

A film might be given a 'general release' right across the country or it might have a 'select release' to a few cinemas in a few cities where the audience is felt to be right for this particular film. A 'saturation release' would indicate that the effort has been to put the film out immediately to as many cinemas as possible.

A film is usually released first of all within its country of origin before moving out to other countries in a developmental fashion, although it is now possible for a big Hollywood film to have a single global release date.

Whatever pattern is adopted, the key thing to recognize is the way in which market analysts will have worked together to try to decide upon the strategy that will be best suited to maximizing box-office returns on their product.

Repression Repression is the process of being kept down by force (not always physical); it refers to the way that a person's right to freedom of expression whether politically, socially or culturally can be denied.

In psychoanalysis the term 'repression' has a different meaning. Freud defines repression as a defence mechanism. It is the way that individuals protect themselves from harmful but attractive desires (often sexual). According to Freud such desires can never be completely repressed but return, in the form of dreams, for example.

Resolution The final phase of a narrative film that quite simply resolves all the storylines that have been set running. Films may of course leave some matters unresolved.

Satire The use of ridicule, irony or sarcasm to expose vice or stupidity; the lampooning of self-important individuals.

Slasher movie A type of horror film in which the story revolves around psychotic males with plans to murder a group of young people. This sub-genre was at its height in the 1970s and early 1980s with films such as *The Texas Chain Saw Massacre* (Hooper, 1974), *Halloween* (Carpenter, 1978), *Friday the 13th* (Cunningham, 1980) and *Nightmare on Elm Street* (Craven, 1984).

Story The recounting of events of the film in chronological order – although this may not be how they are told in the film.

Swinging Britain This term relates to changes in a whole range of attitudes, behaviours, and moralities where Britain finally shook off the bleak, postwar way of living, where caution, practicality, repression, and obedience were the norms. The term 'swinging' comes from a form of music that was more relaxed and open in its style. The 'swinging sixties' really began in 1963 with the emergence of the Beatles and the Mersey music scene, and its London counterpart. With full employment, young people had a greater disposable income, and music and fashion came to dominate the culture. Confident in peace and prosperity, this 'swinging' approach developed across social boundaries, and an 'anything goes' attitude was popularized.

'The talent' This is a film industry term for the main creative players involved in the production of any particular film. It is often used to refer to the director, the producer, the screenwriter and the lead actors as a group of key personnel, but may include others such as an art director, director of cinematography and musical director.

Technological determinism The assumption that technological progress is inevitable and determines the shape and nature of social change.

Teenpic A film featuring teenagers as the central characters and aimed at teenage audiences. The stories focus on the sorts of problems and difficulties faced by young people of this age.

Television This might perhaps at first seem a strange choice of key term when considering cinema and film. However, TV is clearly in the business of screening staged film dramas and from this perspective is in immediate competition with cinema. On the other hand, as TV has provided a ready-made screen in every home since the 1960s, the potential of a further space in which to show film products also becomes apparent. And when we reach the era of first video and then DVD, these products depend entirely for their success or otherwise upon people having access to screens within as wide a variety of places as possible.

Trailers A short advert for a film put together by the distributors. It will usually comprise extracts from the film in question with an added voice over designed to sell the film. A shorter version of the trailer sometime before the film is due out is known as a 'teaser'.

United Kingdom Refers to Great Britain and Northern Ireland.

Vampire movie A horror sub-genre that owes a lot to Bram Stoker's novel *Dracula* (1897) and tends to feature male characters preying upon female victims, on this occasion by sucking their blood.

Vertical integration The way in which studios in the 1930s and 1940s integrated the whole process from making to screening films under their control.

VHS Video Home System, Matsushita's videotape format which became the home norm for recording after overcoming its commercial rival, Sony's Betamax system, in the 1980s.

Viewing pleasure There is the simple human pleasure of looking, or scopophilia (seen by Freud as one of the infantile sexual drives) and voyeurism, the act of watching others without their knowledge, both of which have been explored in film theory in relation to the act of watching films in a darkened room. But there are also pleasures derived from aspects of the film-viewing experience such as being able to solve mysteries, to follow a causal chain of events, to identify with strong characters, to recognize narrative patterns or genre features seen before, to be surprised or even shocked by images or portrayed events, to be able to experience fear in safety and so on.

Windows A term used to suggest the variety of places that films can now be viewed.

Zombie film A horror sub-genre in which the dead (the zombies) come back to life and attack the living. See *Night of the Living Dead* (Romero, 1968) and *Shaun of the Dead* (Wright, 2004) to compare older and more recent treatments of the genre.

INDEX

171–5; and new technologies 201–2; Old and New Hollywood 160; *see also* 'viewing experience'

cinemas: and audiences 172, 181; early cinemas 172; independent cinemas 169; multiplexes 159, 160, **161**, 172; *see also* attendance figures; exhibition

cinematographers 15; practical video project 101

cinematography 19, 37–54, 74–5; camerawork 45–54; colour and black and white film 37–40; lighting 23–4, 40–5; and practical project 87, 90, 92, 94, 96–7, 101; spectatorship 82

Citizen Kane (Welles, 1941) 64, 115, **116**, 244

city as theme and genre 265

civil rights movement 383

Civil War as reference point in Westerns 373, 378

class: and horror film audience 282; representations in film 272, 306, 310, 315; 'working-class' criminal character 356

Classical Hollywood 64, 141; *see also* Old Hollywood

classification of films: BBFC classifications 184–5; horror genre 282, 284, 285, 288

close-up (CU) shot 46, 48, 97

clothing *see* costume

Clover, C. 282, 295

co-functioning media 157

Cohen, Stanley 332

Cold War 343

Collateral (Mann, 2004) 266

colour: and cinematography 37–40; as new technology 195–6, 197

Columbia 146, 151, 156, 158

comedy genre 260; *see also* romantic comedy genre

commercial process 14; and cinema going experience 172–4; early cinema and demand 172; film as commercial product 118–25, 194; stars as commercial product 206, 215–16

communism 343

competitions as promotion 134

composition 28, 48, 105, 106

computer editing programs 103

concessionary deals 134

conflict 88, 95, 235

Conservative government 319, 328, 331–2, 333, 336, 360

consumption and film 123; and new technologies 193–204; patterns of consumption 175–7; supply and demand 171–91

continuity editing 58–9, 102

contrapuntal sound 91

co-productions in British film 305, 315, 319, 324–5

copyright and Hammer Horror 287

Cosh Boy (Gilbert, 1953) 354, **355**, 362, 365

costume 21, 30–6, 81, 101; dress code and character 33–4; and gender representation 296, 387–8; and genre 256; as symbol 35

Cottage to Let (Asquith, 1941) 354

crab shot 96

crane shot 51, 56

Crawford, Joan 33

creative project 86–107

Creep (Smith, 2004) 276

crime genre in Britain 350–67; historical development 353–4; and representation 365–6; social and political issues 357–61; themes 361–5

crime and punishment as theme 362

The Criminal (Losey, 1960) 363

criminal code as theme 362, 365

criminal as hero 354, 356

critics 155

cross-cutting 62

The Crossing (practical project) 99, 100, 104–6

Cruise, Tom 208

The Crying Game (Jordan, 1992) 33–4, **33**, 36, 38, 51, 79–80, **79**

cult films 186

cultural associations and colour 40

cultural identity 273

cultural test for British films 276–8, **277**, 325

culture and film 165, 250

'cut on action' editing 59

'cut' command 102

cycles in horror genre 279

Damon, Matt 299

Dance with a Stranger (Newell, 1984) 363

Fifty Key British Films

Edited by Sarah Barrow and John White

This book, the latest in the successful Key Guides series, provides a chance to delve into fifty British films considered a true reflection of the times. With case studies from the 1930s heyday of cinema right up to the present day, this chronologically ordered volume includes coverage of:

- The Ladykillers
- The 39 Steps
- A Hard Day's Night
- The Full Monty
- A Clockwork Orange
- The Wicker Man.

In *Fifty Key British Films*, Britain's best known talent, such as Loach, Hitchcock, Powell, Reed and Kubrick are scrutinised for their outstanding ability to articulate the issues of the time from key standpoints. This is essential reading for anyone interested in film and the increasing relevance of the British film industry on the international scene.

ISBN13: 978–0–415–43329–7

Available at all good bookshops
For ordering and further information please visit
www.routledge.com

AS Media Studies: The Essential Introduction for AQA

Third edition

Philip Rayner and Peter Wall

AS Media Studies: The Essential Introduction for AQA is fully revised for the 2008 specification with full colour throughout, over 100 images, new case studies and examples. The authors introduce students step by step to the skills of reading media texts, and address key concepts such as genre, representation, media institutions and media audiences as well as taking students through the tasks expected of them to pass the AQA AS Media Studies exam. The book is supplemented with a companion website at www.asmediastudies.co.uk featuring additional activities and resources, further new case studies, clear instructions on producing different media, quizzes and tests.

Areas covered include:

- an introduction to studying the media
- the key concepts across print, broadcast and e-media
- media institutions
- audiences and the media
- case studies such as *Heroes*, *Nuts*, and the *Daily Mail*
- guided textual analysis of real media on the website and within the book
- research and how to do it
- a production guide and how to respond to a brief

AS Media Studies: The Essential Introduction for AQA clearly guides students through the course and gives them the tips they need to become proficient media producers as well as media analysts.

ISBN13: 978–0–415–32965–1 (hbk)
ISBN13: 978–0–415–32966–8 (pbk)

Available at all good bookshops
For ordering and further information please visit:
www.routledge.com